T3-BUW-209

— A Maverick Publication —

From the IRON CURTAIN to the GOLDEN GATE

by

Erwin Schmidt

Printed in the United States of America.

Cover Illustration by Claudia Huetter

Maverick Publications
Drawer 5007 • Bend, OR 97708

Dedicated to: Lu, my loyal companion of 36 years.

To the millions of refugees who have escaped from communist oppression.

To my friends and neighbors of the Golden State of California who have made me feel at home again.

Prologue

In August of 1960 a long and often difficult journey came to an end in San Francisco. A journey that started behind the Iron Curtain in 1946 and ended in the beautiful city by the Golden Gate.

For almost thirty years now, California has given me the home I had been searching for. It has become the safe haven, the quiet refuge after the turbulent storms of my early years.

Time has been generous and has softened the harsh memories of those years, until a few years ago, when the mailman delivered a harmless little envelope.

In a letter from Communist East Germany, my little niece proudly announced that she had joined the "Young Pioneers."

My first reaction was shock. Had nobody ever told her that her uncle had risked his life to escape from Communism? How could she do this to me? During all these years I had thought of her as a cute little girl, and suddenly I pictured her as a wide-eyed fanatic, shouting communist slogans and waving the red flag with the hammer and sickle. In my imagination I could just see her marching down the main street of my old home town, screaming, "down with Yankee Imperialism."

Suddenly, with the memory of my old hometown emerged a vision of a young boy, proudly wearing the uniform of the Hitler Youth, and carrying the flag with the swastika. I shuddered as I recognized the striking similarity. Just a different flag, a different hero. Her's was Lenin, mine had been Adolf Hitler.

There are certain stages in everybody's existence which become the milestones on the road through life. I had reached my first milestone when I attended school for the first time in 1934. Four years later, in 1938, I had arrived at the magic age of ten, old enough to join the Hitler Youth Organization. Although membership at age ten was mandatory, nobody had to drag me in by force. Just like any American boy eager to join the Boy Scouts, I wanted to belong. I wanted to march down main street in my shiny new uniform with all the other boys, and participate in sports and other outdoor activities. The political intent behind all this was never clear to me. At this age I would have followed any banner, or any party, whatever the name.

My father did not seem to share my enthusiasm. At home he always made derogatory remarks about the Nazi bullies, but then what did he know? In his late forties he was probably too old to understand.

It was downright embarrassing for me to go into town with him, because he stubbornly refused to respond to the now customary "Heil Hitler" salute by just answering with a clear and simple "Good Day" or "Good Morning."

This of course caused a lot of raised eyebrows from the true believers. I tried to make up for father's lack of etiquette by raising my right arm and responding with the Nazi salute.

By 1939 Hitler had silenced most of his critics and skeptics. He was riding a wave of popularity. His Army had annexed Austria and had marched into Czechoslovakia. Encouraged by his success, Hitler invaded Poland.

According to official German press releases the Poles had started the conflict. Since the government was our only source of information, we had no way of knowing the real story. We had no idea that a long, bloody war had just started. A war that would cost the lives of millions and would change ours forever, and while my parents were praying for peace and an end to hostilities, I was busy collecting scrap iron and other materials for the war effort. My secret hope was that the war would last long enough to give me a chance to fight for the Fatherland.

Summer 1944—Facing Reality

Hitler's war machine had come to a halt on all fronts. Allied troops had landed at Normandy. The German Army was in retreat in the East, but the Nazis did not call it retreat. They called it a strategic correction of the front lines.

I was now sixteen years old, and was beginning to have my doubts about our illustrious leader. When my draft notice arrived, I received it with mixed emotions. There was never any doubt that I was going to serve, but it was more a sense of obligation than a believe in the cause any more. I was also aware of the emotional strain on my parents. My brother, who had been drafted in 1943, was now reported missing on the western front. Three of my cousins had already been killed on the battlefields, now it was my time to go.

The Navy and Airforce had started drafting sixteen year old boys to serve in fire fighting and anti aircraft units. I had hoped to be assigned to the anti aircraft artillery, but the Navy wanted me to report for duty as a fire fighter in the former Polish port city of Gdynia. The port city, called Gotenhafen by the Germans, was an important Naval base for the Baltic fleet.

The probing fingers of the big searchlights crisscrossed the night sky, and the pungent smell of artificial fog filled the air, as our train pulled into the station shortly after midnight. The sound of the anti-aircraft guns echoed from the hills around the city as we jumped off the train and scrambled for the nearest shelter. Before we could find it in the dark, the sirens sounded the end of the alarm. No bombs had fallen this time.

The region was relatively calm, in spite of the reception

we had received. The big battles were fought on the western front, and the eastern front was still far away.

Summer turned into fall as we spent our time in basic training. With the exception of a few minor probing attacks, enemy activity was mostly limited to reconnaissance flights. It was the calm before the storm.

By the end of 1944 the situation began to change rapidly. The Russians had broken through on all fronts and were advancing fast in our direction. Soon I was getting more action than I had bargained for.

Prelude to the Bitter End

Our first big test came on December 18, when enemy bombers staged one of their heaviest attacks. Wave after wave came in, despite heavy anti aircraft fire. The sky was ablaze, and the ground was shaking from the impact of the heavy bombs. Their targets were the big, heavy cruisers, which the Navy had concentrated in Gdynia.

The "Schleswig Holstein" took a direct hit, setting her ablaze. Her crew, unable to control the raging fire, was forced to abandon and blow up the badly damaged ship. Another big ship, which was tied up at the shipyard, was also hit. This time our unit was called into action.

Black smoke poured from the big ship as we approached the scene of destruction. We discovered early that fire was not the only enemy to fight. The bitter cold turned our hoses into giant icicles, stretching across the deck still littered with the mutilated bodies of the fallen sailors. I was sick to my stomach, as I stared into the face of war as it really was. There was no music playing and no flag waving, only death and destruction all around.

It was a difficult fire to get under control. Smoke was everywhere, and our movement and visibility was restricted by our gas mask and respirator. Every time we thought we had it under control, it would flare up again.

When we returned to our barracks after three days of misery, we mourned the loss of two of our comrades. They had run out of oxygen deep inside the ship before they could find their way back topside.

There was little sleep from now on. If we did not fight any fires, we had to dig anti-tank trenches in the surrounding forest. Our only tools were pick and shovel, and the ground was frozen at least a foot deep.

The city was filled with women, children and older men, all fleeing from the advancing Russians. The Navy began urgent preparations to evacuate them by sea. It was the only escape left.

The Russians had broken through in the south and had reached the river Oder. We were trapped. As our circle became smaller and smaller, more retreating army troops poured into the city. The big guns of the heavy cruisers tried to stem the tide in the north east, as the Navy rounded up anything afloat for the evacuation of wounded soldiers and civilians.

One day I received the welcome news that I was assigned to the "Wilhelm Gustloff," a big passenger liner which had been used by the Navy as a troop ship. It was scheduled to sail westward with about 5,000 people. When my orders were revoked at the last minute I was deeply disappointed. How could I know that it had probably saved my life? The "Wilhelm Gustloff" had barely passed the Hela Peninsula when she was hit by a torpedo, fired from a submarine. Only about 500 people were rescued from the icy waters.

It was a reminder that even a place on a ship was not a ticket to freedom without risk. It was however at least a chance to get out. Otherwise the outlook for the future was depressing. Even if I survived the final assault on the city, my best prospect would then be a Russian POW camp. Hardly much of a choice.

My spirits got a lift, when I learned that my orders had only been changed to another ship. This one, also a former passenger liner named the "Potsdam," was ready to sail at the end of February. This time the Navy took no chances. A major convoy had been assembled and a few destroyers and other smaller vessels supplied added protection. After two days at sea we reached the German island of Rügen where our bigger ships dropped anchor off the town of Sassnitz.

Now the difficult task of unloading our human cargo began. Because of our size, we could not enter the port and therefore had to transfer our passengers into all kinds of smaller boats. It was not an easy job, considering that we carried only wounded soldiers, old people, women and children. Most of them had never been on a ship before. Now, anybody able to walk was expected to climb down a steep, constantly moving gangplank. A few people panicked and fell between the boat and the ship, some got rescued quickly, others disappeared under the icy waters of the Baltic. To make matters worse, our activity got interrupted by enemy aircraft, causing even more terror and panic among our passengers.

Our transfer to the "Potsdam" had only been intended to get us out of Gdynia before it fell to the Russians. Now a PT boat flotilla, stationed in Sassnitz, became a temporary home.

Before the Navy could take any further advantage of my services, Allied bombers solved the problem. In one night they caused heavy damage to the port facilities and sunk one of the bigger ships outside.

Allied planes now dominated the skies and attacked at will. The German Luftwaffe was not to be seen anywhere. I was now convinced that the war was lost. The image of my hero Adolf Hitler had faded. I was now beginning to understand the tragedy he had led Germany into, even though I could not comprehend the magnitude of it.

Again I received marching orders. This time I was ordered to report to an anti-aircraft unit in Kiel. I knew the war could not last much longer. The Russians were pushing toward Berlin, while Allied troops advanced from the west.

The port city of Kiel marked the end of my career in the Navy. I was officially released, but instantly ordered to report to a newly forming infantry division in the northern province of Schleswig Holstein. Given the chance, I would have used the opportunity to depart for home, but the Navy had apparently anticipated this possibility. All of us were loaded onto trucks and delivered straight to the camp of the new unit.

We were the remnants of an Air Force without planes, and a Navy without ships. The last hope of the Third Reich. Almost every man of our company had experienced the war first hand, and was well aware of the futility to keep on fighting. With the war now raging inside Germany, we were all concerned about our loved ones at home. There was no longer any sense of purpose. Everybody was just waiting for this war to end, and nobody was willing to lay down his life for Adolf Hitler any longer.

After a short training with infantry and anti-tank

weapons they started moving us out, one company at a time. Our objective was the embattled city of Berlin.

Travel by any means was now a hazardous venture. Roads and rail lines were under almost constant surveillance by enemy aircraft, and barely an hour had passed when our train was attacked near the city of Neumünster. When the smoke cleared, it was discovered that five guys from our outfit had taken advantage of the ensuing chaos and disappeared.

I had made similar plans with two buddies from my hometown, but we considered it more prudent to wait until we got closer to home. With every mile closer we reduced the risk of getting caught.

Military police and patrols from the SS were roaming the countryside in search of deserters. Every soldier found separated from his unit, and without proper travel documentation was considered a deserter. He was shot or hanged on the spot without trial. Especially the SS was trying to stem the tide of desertions, and many a poor soldier could be seen hanging from a tree with a sign around his neck. The sign would read, "I am a deserter."

Our opportunity came during the night, when our train was slowing down near a town only fifteen miles from home. Enemy aircraft was causing a disturbance, which could not have come at a more opportune moment. We were as close to home as we would ever get.

Nobody paid any attention as the three of us jumped off the train and disappeared into the dark night. About fifteen miles was all that remained between us and the safety of home.

We had heard rumors that the war had reached our region, and the sound of gunfire in the distance seemed to confirm this. As we approached our hometown, a gray and misty day was beginning to dawn. We had taken a narrow country road, and had not encountered any patrols up to this moment.

Suddenly we came upon a roadblock, and in the dim light of the beginning day we spotted the shadowy figures of two men. It was too late to run, so we walked slowly toward the shadows on the road. To our great relief they turned out to be two old men belonging to the Home Guard, called "the

Volkssturm." As I came closer I recognized one of them as and old man from our neighborhood.

He did not seem to know me, but under the circumstances I thought it better not to identify myself. There was no need to let everybody know that I was back in town.

Old Mister Hansen was in his late sixties, and he looked almost comical with his rifle, which was about as old as he was. It was a study in contrast which demonstrated the hopelessness of the situation. On one side two old men who should have been enjoying their retirement, and on the other side three young kids who should still be in school.

The two old men took their job very serious. "They shoot at anything that moves," one of them said, pointing to the other side of the river Elbe.

We knew what he meant. The next mile would be visible from the enemy side, and the daylight would not be in our favor. We took their advice and continued with extreme caution. Without incident we reached the neighborhood where my two friends were at home. We shook hands and promised to keep in touch.

A short time later I arrived at our neighborhood. The street looked deserted as I approached our house. The artillery on the other side of the river had started firing again and I could hear the explosions of the incoming rounds down at main street. When I found our gate locked, I climbed over the fence.

I had barely touched the ground, when my mother opened the side door leading to our patio. A garbage bag she was carrying fell to the ground. She stood there as if she had seen a ghost, unable to say anything. The agony and sorrow of the last years was deeply etched in her face. She looked very old to me. Her entire body was trembling, and so was her voice when she finally spoke.

"My boy," she said almost in a whisper, "is it really you?"

Her tears started flowing as we stood in the doorway, embracing while the deadly sound of artillery shells roared overhead. One of her sons had returned home.

End of April 1945—The Final Days

The artillery fire had increased steadily after dark. We could hear the discharge, followed by the howling sound of the incoming shells. For the last few days the cellar had become our home.

At times during the day we would venture outside in search of food, but most of the time we were forced to seek shelter from the deadly shelling. My father was not at home. He was on duty with the volunteer fire fighters. I had returned home only a few days ago, a deserter from Hitler's army. Now my only concern was to stay out of sight and survive the last few hours of World War II. Allied troops were poised on the other side of the river Elbe, ready to cross for the final assault. Our home was located on a little side street. Only two buildings separated us from main street, which was the target of the artillery.

I was extremely tired from all the excitement of the last few days. The last thing I heard was the impact of a shell hitting the street in front of our house, causing the ground to shake.

Even though I fell quickly into a deep sleep, subconsciously I was aware throughout the night of the explosion of more shells and the sound of machine gun fire, followed by the rumbling noise of heavy equipment.

When I woke up, I saw my mother standing at the foot of the stairs, shaking in terror.

"They are here," she said.

"Who is here?" I asked, still half asleep.

"I don't know who they are, but they are not Germans," she replied.

"Be careful," she pleaded when I started climbing the stairs for a better look.

I could hardly believe my eyes. The entire street looked like an armed camp. There were tanks, troop carriers and trucks everywhere. No doubt our town had fallen. The guns were silent and as far as I was concerned, World War II had ended.

All of a sudden it dawned on me that I still had my uniform upstairs in my bedroom. I had to get rid of these things and do it fast. I had no desire to spend the next few months in a POW Camp. Running upstairs I collected all the incriminating equipment, dashing back down to our backyard I started digging a big hole in the ground. Twenty minutes later the evidence had disappeared.

The advance troops turned out to be British and Canadian, but a week later American troops moved in. It was May 7th, 1945. Germany had officially capitulated.

With the American occupation came new problems. We had to vacate our house when a company of army troops decided to set up quarters in our street. With two other families, we moved into a neighbor's house where we barely had enough room to sleep on the floor. However, sleeping was only a minor problem. The biggest problem was our food supply. With the capitulation of Germany all communications as well as distribution of supplies had ceased to exist. Now we discovered the benefit of our American occupation. Their field kitchen was stationed right in front of our house, and there were always some leftovers. Their ordinary rations were for us sheer luxury. We had not eaten this well in a long time. Even discarded coffee grounds became a treasured possession, because we had not tasted real coffee in years.

Although the troops had orders not to fraternize with the German population, the soldiers did not take it too seriously. Even Private Joe from Texas discovered that my mother was not really that much different from his mother back home.

Barely two months after the cessation of hostilities our life very slowly returned to some kind of normalcy. At city hall the Nazis were replaced by civilians who did not have any connections with the old regime. People returned to their places of work, if they were still there. Our stomachs were still growling from the lack of food, but everybody was glad that the violence had stopped. Now there was hope of a new start and a better tomorrow. Even my father, who never cared very much for politics, was optimistic.

"It can't get any worse," he said.

Hope changed to despair however, when it was revealed that a deal had been made, determining borders for the zones of occupation. According to those plans our town would be under Russian control.

The news hit like a bombshell. We were horrified by the thought of the Communists moving in, but there was nothing we could do about it. Within twenty-four hours the Americans withdrew, and the Russians moved in as our population looked on in a state of shock. Only four miles separated us from the western border. A few people left in a hurry, but most of us had no place to go.

The New Dictators

The Russians wasted no time. Old time Communists were installed in leading positions, qualified or not. One day my boyhood friend Bruno came storming into our house.

"They have started rounding up all the younger men," he said. "Let's go and hide."

"Where are we going to hide?" I asked.

"At my grandparents house," he replied.

His grandparents owned a house on the outskirts of town with a large garden adjoining the forest. At the far end of the garden was a little shed, which could very well serve as a shelter for us. The local woods started right behind the fence, offering an excellent escape route in case of trouble. My mother was instructed to visit Bruno's grandparents the following day, to discuss the matter of supplying us with food. Then, grabbing an old blanket, we ran out of the house. On our way we picked up another friend, who was not yet aware of the trouble.

Our escape was well timed. That same night they came to our house searching for me. Two Russians, accompanied by a local Communist who supplied all the information and directions. My parents told them that I had gone to the near-by villages in search of food, and they did not know when I would return.

For three weeks we remained in seclusion, while our parents took turns supplying us with food. All the time they had to be careful not to be followed by a local Communist. Several times the Russians returned to our house to see if I had returned. Once in the middle of the night, they even found their way to Bruno's grandparents. Grandpa made a lot of noise and talked loudly before opening the gate, so that we had plenty of time to escape into the woods.

Most of the young men who had been picked up returned home after spending three weeks in a re-education camp. A few were held back, because they apparently had a learning problem. The three of us returned safely from our hideout, but stayed out of sight as much as possible.

Bruno went back to work in his fathers barber shop. His dad had been taken away by the Russians barely a week after their arrival. He had been a member of the Nazi Party. At that time the family did not even know if he was dead or alive.

One day a former classmate came to visit. He was the only one of my class who had joined the Communists Party, mainly because his father was an official of the party.

"Would you like to join the Party?" he wanted to know.

That was a tough question.

I could not very well tell him that my opinion of the Communist Party was very low, and that I thought they were no better than the Nazis we had just gotten rid of. What was I going to say without risking my neck? I was convinced this fellow would not hesitate to turn me in.

"We are not a very political family," I said lamely. "I have never thought of joining any party."

"This is different," he responded. "We have to take sides now for a new order."

"Let me think about it," I said.

After giving me a lecture on the virtue of the Communist Party and our liberators, the glorious Red Army, he departed.

"Don't wait too long," he admonished me.

The only reason I had not yet tried to escape to the West, was that I was absolutely convinced that this was not the final solution. The rumor that the Americans would return would not die. Every day we heard the story that they would be coming back tomorrow. We all repeated it, because that was what we wanted to believe. It was a case of wishful thinking. I vividly remember the day when word spread like wildfire that the Americans were marching in again. People were running into the street to welcome them back. Here the feeling was not "Yankee go home, but Yankee come back."

Joy turned to despair when people realized the truth. The returning Americans were Russians. Russian POW's, returning home from camps liberated by American troops. The Americans had given them a set of American army uniforms, and were probably never aware of the cruel joke perpetrated on us. Many people were crying openly, when they realized their mistake.

The Russians had started mobilizing people to work on projects important to the Soviet Union. They dismantled whole factories, entire rail lines, and re-started industries which could produce goods needed in Russia. I had gone back to work in a department store where I had worked before, but it was not to be for long. The state now controlled everything, and soon we discovered that we had nothing to sell. Also, the owners were informed that the store was taken over and belonged now to the "people."

One day I found a postcard in the mail, instructing me to report for work at the local shipyard. I did not pay much attention to the instructions, because I was already working and therefore this directive should not concern me. I should have known better. Barely two hours after I had gone to work the next morning, I was picked up by police and taken directly to the shipyard.

"The next time will not be so easy," they warned me.

At the shipyard I found myself in the company of many people with no experience whatsoever in shipbuilding. With most of the male population still in POW camps or killed during the war, we were either too young or too old. There were men over sixty five who had worked their whole life in offices and unaccustomed to physical labor. Many among us had been shopkeepers, owning their own shoe store or butcher shop. All of their stores had been confiscated and belonged now to the "people." The former owners had elected not to work as employee in their own store.

The attitude among us was defiant. We had not applied for these jobs and saw no future in them. We could not openly refuse to work, but the quality of what we produced was questionable at best. In order not to be accused of sabotage, we acted just plain stupid and clumsy. The few active Communists among the crew laughed at us and said it was about time the bureaucrats got their hands dirty. There was no financial benefit in working anyway. Since money did not really buy anything, the only reward would be a coupon for a pair of work pants. If anybody achieved above his quota, his picture would be posted on the bulletin board as a hero of labor. I was just biding my time, waiting for the day this would all change again.

It was not only the business community that was suffering under the new regime. Every facet of life was now affected. Villages were turned into collectives. Farmers were told that their land now belonged to the "people." The former owners considered themselves lucky if they were allowed to remain in their own homes. The decision about what to plant and how much was now handed down from a central committee. Production quotas were established with no consideration given to the fertility of the soil. At harvest time those quotas of grain or potatoes had to be delivered. Any shortage was considered an act of sabotage. The farmer was under a constant threat to produce. Many of them, after delivering their quota, had nothing left for their own consumption or for the planting of next years crop. The worst part was that nobody had made any plans for storage and distribution. Tons of precious food were rotting while the population was going hungry. Our whole life, our whole thinking revolved around food. People would descend upon the harvested fields in search of a few leftover heads of grain. Every single grain became a precious possession, but with so many people scouring the fields inch by inch, it became an exercise in futility.

One day I found a better way to supplement our meager resources. In our neighborhood I had discovered a large barn, containing tons of barley. With the help of two friends and under the cover of darkness we broke into the barn one night, helping ourselves to the priceless commodity. Each one of us got away with about 200 pounds before the night was over. It was no easy task getting it home, because the Russian patrols were still out in force. We could carry hardly more than fifty pounds at a time and had to make several trips. Before dawn we had it all safely stashed away in the attics of our homes. During the following months we ground it by hand, and it helped us greatly to get over the worst food shortage we had ever experienced.

Summer had turned to winter, and I was beginning to give up hope for a change. There was no indication that the Russians had any intention of giving up territory. The town was plastered with signs and banners, proclaiming the familiar slogans of the Communist Party. There were pictures of Stalin, Lenin and Marx everywhere, and streets and parks were renamed in honor of them. A certain segment of the population began to join the Communists in the expectation of some benefits or a better job. People started to withdraw, because they did not trust their own friends and neighbors any longer. My former classmate warned me that a joke I had told had reached party headquarters. "You've got one foot on the train to Siberia," was the way he put it.

I had made fun of the fact that the party was taking over all private property and turning it over to the "people."

"I am going to figure out how much of it is mine," I had said. "Then I am going to sell my share and move to the West."

The Communists were not laughing. Neither was I, as I became more and more desperate. I hated to get up in the morning and go to a job I did not want. The only good news we received in many months came just in time for Christmas. My brother, who had been missing on the western front, was alive and well in a British POW camp. It was the only thing to brighten our family holidays.

The Church had never been in fashion under Hitler, but had always been tolerated. Now under Communism the Church was more like a missionary outpost in a pagan land. Any kind of religion was discouraged by the Party and it was a miracle that services were still allowed. Christmas did not exist on the Communist calendar.

On this special day, Christmas, 1945, the churches were filled to capacity, probably for this very reason. This was our way of demonstrating our feelings, the closest we ever came to a public demonstration.

Thanks to the stolen grain in our attic, my mother had managed to grace our table with a few traditional goodies. The brown cookies were made with homemade molasses, in another cookie oatmeal substituted for coconut. It was not much, but these holiday delicacies added to the best of all gifts that Christmas—the knowledge that my brother was alive and well.

As the year 1946 dawned on a gray wintry morning, I was certain that this would be my last year under Communism. This system had nothing to offer but despair, hunger, and chaos. Worst of all was the constant threat of being picked up by the secret police and dispatched to a Siberian labor camp.

The Iron Curtain—July 1946

We sat around the kitchen table in silence. Finally my father lifted his head and looked at me. "You know," he said, "we survived the Kaiser and World War I, we survived Hitler and World War II, and we will survive the Russians and Communism, just give it time."

"Times are different now," I replied. "I am not going to sit around here and wait for the Americans to return."

We had this same discussion over and over again. I felt sorry for my parents who had spent a lifetime, hoping from one regime to the next, that things would improve. I knew that West Germany was also in ruins. That life was just as hard over there, but at least there was a new beginning and new hope. My mind was made up. I was not going to trade one dictatorship for another. Tonight I was going to cross the border, no matter what price I had to pay.

Two friends who thought like I did were going to meet me after dark behind the wall of the cemetery. We had been planning our escape for many weeks, always careful not to let anybody know of our intentions. Only our parents knew about it. Naturally my parents did not approve, but they also knew that my future under this regime was in question. I had been warned already by my former classmate to keep my mouth shut, and that my attitude was not appreciated. I had the ominous feeling that a one way ticket to Siberia had been reserved in my name. It was time to act before it was too late. My parents knew me well enough to know that I was not going to conform, and, in the long run would be in more danger by staying. The biggest danger I was facing now was crossing the heavily guarded border, and that thought was on everyone's mind as we sat around the kitchen table.

There was that painful silence again. Everyone with his own thought's. Finally it was time to say good-bye, and I must admit it was only after many years that I began to realize how my parents must have felt at this moment. Their only other son still a POW in England, but at least alive, and their youngest son about to leave home for good, facing danger at the border and an unknown future in the West.

All of a sudden I was in a hurry. I wanted to break the somber mood before we all started to cry. Entering the bedroom, I put on my jacket and grabbed my backpack containing my meager belongings. On this trip I could take only my basic clothing necessities. We had to be able to move fast and there was no room for anything else. I would be happy if I just got myself across this border in one piece.

We said good-bye, and mother turned quickly to hide her tears. My father pressed my hand as if he wanted to hold onto me forever. I turned, opened the door and after looking in all directions disappeared into the dark night.

It was now completely dark outside; not a soul walked the streets except for an occasional Russian patrol passing by. The curfew had been lifted some time ago, but there was nothing going on at night anyway and people just did not venture out after dark. The town seemed deserted. It had rained during the day and the sky was still under a heavy cloud cover, but this could work to our advantage. We had known the area around the border since our childhood days.

As I approached our meeting-place behind the cemetery, I felt confident that by tomorrow I would be in the West.

My two friends had already reached the cemetery without incident. Without delay we started moving toward the border, which was about four miles away. We talked very little. Our thoughts were still at home with our families, whom we had just left behind.

As we got close to the border we took a short rest. From now on we had to move in total silence. We could run into a Russian border patrol at any moment. Fred, who knew the area better than anybody, took the lead. He was followed by Karl, while I took up the rear. The ground was still wet and soft, and the only sound we could hear was the wind stirring the pine trees.

The forest stretched almost all the way to the border. Only the last 500 yards would present the biggest challenge as the terrain would be more open. There would be no trees to give us shelter, only flat marshland, covered only in parts by swamp grass. No one knew for sure what the border looked like on this night, because none of us had seen the border region since the Russians had taken over.

As long as we moved through the forest we felt safe among the trees. The time was close to midnight, and we knew that we would reach the open fields in about fifteen minutes.

We moved on in total silence, our steps more and more cautious. About one mile to the left was the main highway, and we could hear a truck moving in the direction of what was supposed to be the Russian headquarters just half a mile ahead. The time had come to proceed with extreme caution. Over at the headquarters we could hear a barking dog, a terrifying sound to our ears. We were now getting closer and closer to the border. The next thirty minutes could decide our fate. Was it going to be freedom in the West, or was it going to be jail in the East?

Fred had stopped, and we moved up to have a short conference. We could only whisper because nobody would dare to talk out loud at this stage.

"The end of the forest is only about 100 yards away," he said. But we could not see anything, except the dark shadows of the nearest trees.

"Let's move on, no talking and watch your step, the next 300 yards are going to be crucial." With this Fred turned and started moving again. Karl and I followed in the same order.

We had barely moved fifty yards, when the silence was broken with a sharp "Stoi!"

That command came out of the dark shadows in front of us.

Total frustration is probably the best way to describe my feeling at this moment. We had felt so confident, and now we had apparently run straight into a Russian border patrol.

Since I made up the tail end of our group, I thought maybe they had not seen me in this total darkness. I dropped behind some bushes right were I had stopped, but one of the Russians must have heard the noise.

In broken German he said, "Come out, there are more."

My heart was pounding, but I did not move. I saw a short flash of a flashlight and my hopes began to fade. One of the

Russians was cursing, and I realized he was cursing the flashlight that apparently wouldn't work any more.

Should this be my lucky break? The flashlight did not work and they did not have a dog, because if they did I would have found out by now.

The next thing I heard was steps coming closer to my hiding place.

"Come out," the voice said again in broken German.

Again I did not move, but I thought they must have heard my heart beating. A few more steps, and now I could see a Russian soldier standing right in front of my hideout. He was so close, I could have reached out and touch his boots. I could also see his submachine gun, and it was pointed right at me. It was time to quit, and very slowly I got up. The last thing I wanted to do at this moment was to scare this guy, because he had his finger on the trigger.

He moved in behind me and I could feel the weapon in my back. Saying something in Russian he pushed me forward with such force that I almost fell to the ground.

We joined my two partners, who were also held at gun point only a few steps away. As far as I could make out there were four Russians and only three of us. Resistance was hopeless. Besides, they had the guns, we did not.

The guy in charge barked out some orders and our captors again started sticking their guns into our backs, pushing us forward. Fifteen minutes later our group marched into the headquarters of the border patrol, a former country estate of a German industrialist.

Large pictures of Stalin, Lenin and slogans in Russian hung everywhere. A mean looking sergeant got up from behind his desk. We could feel that he did not appreciate the disturbance at this early hour of the morning.

The man in charge of our group made his report to him and the look in his face said it all.

"What kind of trash did you bring in here?"

Again he issued some orders and the guards started pushing us down a hallway, down some stairs into the basement and into a room about twelve by twelve feet in size. Besides bright lights, there was no furniture in this room.

The mean looking sergeant had followed us down the

stairs and under his watchful eye they began taking apart our belongings. The clothing was thrown into a corner and valuables like watches and rings disappeared into their pockets. After being certain they had not missed anything of value, they marched out, leaving us alone in our misery.

Fred spoke first, and "ssshit" was all he said. That's what we all wanted to say. The darkness and our knowledge of the territory, all that had been in our favor, and yet we had to run straight into a patrol. Call it bad luck.

Since we didn't know if someone was listening we kept quiet, everybody with his own thoughts, and everybody was worried.

I checked out the door but it was solid as I had expected.

We just sat down on the floor and waited for the things to come. With our watches stolen, there was no way of telling what time it was.

After several hours the door to our jail opened and two guards came in, that is only one came in while the other remained at the door with his submachine gun pointed at us. First he wanted to find out if there was anything left to steal. When he found out that he was too late and there was nothing left to be taken, he started cursing everybody in sight. I stood closest to the door, so he grabbed me and pushed me outside. After locking the door again, the two marched me up the stairs, down the hallway and pushed me into a larger room. In the middle of this room was a large table with a chair in front of it.

I was pushed into the chair and looked right into two bright lights, pointed straight at me. The guards took up positions at the door while I waited for someone to come marching in.

To my surprise a voice in fairly fluent German came out from the darkness behind the lights. I had to listen to a long sermon about the crime I had committed and was told that the Red Army would not tolerate this. Then he started asking me questions about my name, age, home town and family.

How does one explain his presence at the border, in the middle of the night and with extra clothing in his backpack?

During our waiting hours down in the basement I had plenty of time to come up with some kind of a story that would have a chance to be believed. Since I had been living under Russian rule for almost a year now, I also knew that most Russians believe in their own propaganda. That's what my story was based on.

First I told this guy how sorry I was to get involved in this mess. If I had known what kind of a crime I was committing I would not dream about doing it. I also brought up my father, a working man who had been exploited by Hitler and the Kaiser before him, until finally liberated by the victorious Red Army. Our family was happy to live under the protection of the Red Army. There was only the problem with my brother. He had the misfortune to end up in a British POW camp. Although recently released from the camp, he was now living in Hamburg West Germany, living there under miserable conditions, unable to find work and desperate to come home.

"That's what the clothing in my backpack is all about," I said.

"All he has is his old army uniform."

Not a sound came from behind the bright lights while I was delivering my sad tale. Since I could not see his face, I had no clue as to the effect of my story.

The man behind the light spoke again.

"You are a fool," he said. "You could have gotten killed."

I agreed with him.

"Why doesn't he just come to the border and we'll let him in?" he asked.

"You don't understand," I replied, "the propaganda over there is appalling. The capitalists tell everybody that the Russians shoot anybody that comes even close to the border."

I had the feeling this made sense to him. Maybe this explained why there was no traffic into East Germany. He tried again to trick me with some questions, but I stuck to my story. It was the best I had and I was going to sell this one. The man behind the bright lights asked me several more questions and I had no problem with an answer. In fact I was pretty calm now and felt comfortable with my story. I almost believed it myself.

After awhile he said something to the guards at the door, and I was taken down to the basement again, this time to another little bare room. The door was shut behind me and for the first time I was all alone and in complete darkness.

Later I was taken up again for interrogation. This time I was grilled by another German speaking officer. He told me that I was in deep trouble, that his partner did not believe a word I had told him, and that my situation was serious unless I started telling the truth. He also told me my companions had contradicted my testimony.

Again I stuck to my story mainly because it was the only one I had and in my opinion the only one believable. This was repeated one more time, and again I held onto my story. There was no sign of my companions.

It must have been twenty-four hours since my last meal and my stomach was growling, but nobody made any attempt to feed me. After I was returned to my cell I laid down on the floor and must have fallen asleep. There was no way of telling if it was day or night outside, when I heard the guards coming for me again. I was hungry and I was dead tired by now, and I wasn't sure if I would rather have a good meal or a nice bed to sleep in.

Again I was picked up, this time to be taken outside. It was so nice to see daylight again and the air was fresh like early morning.

The guards marched me across the yard to a big barn on the other side. The building was of solid brick. I was pushed into a very small room inside this barn, a room not bigger than twelve by six foot wide with a little window about twenty by twenty inches. The room must have been used as a chicken pen, because the walls were covered with dry chicken manure and the smell was still there. To my biggest surprise I found my two companions here, as well as four other people. Even our belongings, or whatever was left of it was here. It was great to see my friends again, but I was careful not to make any big speeches. I didn't know the other four people and in these surroundings I did not trust anybody, even other Germans.

The place was crowded with seven people, barely enough room to sit on the filthy floor. Our conversation turned to our experiences at the interrogations, with everybody being careful not to brag about the stories he had told. All seven of us had been captured the same night.

Hours passed, who could tell. We could see a guard posted at the outside of our barn. Once in a while there was shouting out there, and at times we could hear shots being fired not too far away. About early afternoon the guards came in and led all of us outside. One of them, a German speaking corporal, told us to take our belongings. The mean looking sergeant, I had named him Ivan the Terrible, came out of the main building and started cursing and kicking dust. I suspected he was giving his farewell speech.

The German speaking corporal took the lead with another soldier, his submachine gun ready. The tail end of the convoy was made up by two more soldiers with submachine guns, and after Ivan the Terrible had admonished the troops we marched out of the compound onto the highway.

There was no traffic on the highway, because the border was completely closed. I kept my eyes open for any chance to escape, but those Russians were too scared to let us out of sight, even for a second. Having seen Ivan the Terrible in action I could understand why.

After a little over an hour we reached the outskirts of my home town. It was embarrassing to be herded down main street of my home town like a bunch of criminals under heavy guard. Within the next five minutes we came across the first familiar faces and I was certain it would not take long for my parents to get the word.

Our group marched down main street, at one point only half a block from our house. I looked over, but could not see my mother. My father, I was sure, was still at work.

People on the street hurried past us as if we had a contagious disease, but they were just afraid to talk to us. The guards kept their eyes on us and on everybody that came even close. I suspected that we would be taken to the headquarters of the secret police, but to my surprise we marched right through town and continued down the highway. Finally we ended up in a little village about three miles east of my home town.

Again we got locked up in a farmhouse which seemed to be some kind of a command post for Russian troops. This time the room was a little bigger than the last one at the border, but still no furniture, just bare walls.

Outside was a lot of hectic activity, and I had the feeling a lot of drinking was going on. This was bad news for us. I had seen a lot of drunken Russians, and I knew they were unpredictable under those conditions. They could be sentimental and extremely brutal at the same time, and it did not take very long to get our first taste of the new masters.

Three soldiers walked in, and we could smell the vodka. One of them held up his arm, pointed at his wrist and screamed "Uhr, Uhr," the German word for watch.

None of us wanted to be the first one to tell him that we had already donated everything at our first stop. Finally Fred held up his arm, showing his bare wrist and said "nix Uhr, nix Uhr."

Before he could get his arm down or even in front of his face, a fist hit him with such brutal force that blood started streaming from his nose. A sergeant entered just in time to prevent more serious harm. He was on his way to pick up one of our group and the interrogations started again.

One by one we were brought before a German speaking officer and again we told our stories. Before I was taken back to our jail I asked for some water and was surprised to get it, but still no food. The interrogating officer hinted that a good meal might be waiting if I started telling the truth, but I knew that if I changed my story at this time I would be in even more trouble.

We spent another night as guests of the Russian army, wondering what tomorrow would bring.

The next morning one of the other four captives was taken out for interrogation and after about twenty minutes we could hear a lot of commotion and a lot of shooting coming from the other side of the fields. There were soldiers running in all directions. Four guards came in and pointed their weapons at us.

What had happened?

One of our men had escaped, or had he? We never saw him again and I hope he did make it. The only problem for us now was that our captors were mad as hell. We got pushed around like cattle and we all knew one wrong move could be our last one. Apparently our time table had been set, because we got pushed outside, lined up again and marched off in the direction we came from the day before. This time we landed in my home town, in the basement of the headquarters of the secret police. This house had been the property of a veterinarian, who fled to the West as soon as the Russian Army moved in.

Here the tactic changed. I had no doubt that our new interrogators were professionals. To my surprise I was taken before a high ranking officer who spoke fluent German without any accent. He was acting as the good guy who was concerned about my well being. Soon I found out that he was a deserter from the German army during the battle for Stalingrad. I also knew this guy had to be a fanatic Communist in order to be where he was. I was determined to play his game. He was my best chance if he believed my story.

"You know we have something in common," I said.

"I also defected from the German army."

I could tell he was interested. Without interrupting he listened to my story. I told him how I had defected during the final days of the war, on my way to fight the Russian army and to save the city of Berlin. For once I did not even have to tell a lie. I felt my interrogator liked my story. If I could convince him of the truth, it would greatly improve my situation.

All of a sudden it got sticky again.

"Are you a member of the Communist party or the Communist Youth Group?" he wanted to know.

"I have been considering it," I said, "but so far I have not joined."

There was no use in lying about this point, because it was easy for him to check it out.

"What about your father?" he asked, "is he a Party member?"

"No," I had to answer again, "but he is a working man and he was never a Nazi either."

It was too bad I could not even produce an uncle or some close relative who was a member of the Communist Party. I knew I couldn't score any points along the party line, but I was hoping he was buying at least the rest of my story.

It must have been almost an hour when he called the guard and had me taken down to the basement again, this time into a single cell. When the door shut behind me I found myself in total darkness again.

A short time later, thirty minutes at the most, the door opened and again I was led upstairs to a different room. This time it was the bad guy, a real bully.

It was too bad, he said, that the border guards had wasted their time with trash like us. They should have wasted us right on the spot.

I got the feeling he didn't like me at all, but I was smart enough to keep my mouth shut. His plan was to get me scared, and I must admit I was not exactly encouraged by his tirade. When he was finished, I discovered he was not the only one present in the room. While he was the only one I could see, there were two more people in the room, hiding behind the bright lights.

All of a sudden I thought, "This must be it, this is the board of directors or whatever one might call it in these circles." These people probably held my fate in their hands.

I felt like a criminal before the parole board, trying to make a good impression. My voice was kind of shaky, when I tried to answer all questions that were thrown at me faster and faster. I was a Nazi, I was a war criminal, they accused me of every crime that had been committed since 1933. Since I was only eighteen years old at this time they could not possibly believe it themselves I thought. After painting me a picture of the hard life in a Siberian labor camp, where I could pay for the crimes I had committed against the Soviet Union, I was again taken back to my dark cell. There I spent my last night as it turned out.

Early the next morning I was released, but not before I listened to a sermon by the former German deserter. I agreed to never try to cross the border again, I agreed to work hard for the glorious Soviet Union and for a new Communist Germany. I would have agreed to anything. All I wanted to do is get out of there and eat and sleep. Twenty minutes later I was home to the relief of my mother, who was worried sick.

Food was still very scarce in 1946 and still on coupons. People would get up at four in the morning to go to a store and stand in line for hours. Mother had saved a few grams of butter, and also a little piece of meat for the day I would come home. Since we owned our own little garden, at least we had potatoes and vegetables. After a good meal I went to bed and slept for almost twenty-four hours.

Mom and Dad tried very hard to convince me to give it up, but I was more determined than ever to try it again. This time I couldn't afford to fail.

The following day Fred was released, but he had no information on Karl. After dark he came over to our house to find out what my intentions were. His parents had told him that I had been released a day earlier.

We had a long talk that night and we both decided to try it again. There was no time to waste. The Party and the police would start pestering us again about not going to work as ordered.

This time we decided to make our move during daylight hours, and we decided to do it in a narrow strip of land between the highway and the river Elbe. This narrow stretch of land was covered with trees and shrubs right up to the border. We had a chance to take a good look at this area during our march from the border station, which led us down the highway. We felt the terrain offered good protection, and if we could spot the border guards first we should be able to get around them.

That was our plan, and two days later we were on our way again.

We moved with caution, but there was no problem until we reached an area about a mile from the border. All of a sudden the forest became crowded. Within about thirty minutes we were able to avoid three Russian patrols of two men each. They always had a fairly loud conversation going so we had no problem in spotting them first and avoiding them. Our advance had slowed down considerably, but there was no use rushing it. This time we wanted to play it safe.

By mid afternoon we had moved up to about 300 yards from the actual border. We kept right on top of the riverbank, which allowed us to overlook the approximately 50 yard wide strip between the river and the top of the bank. At the same time we could see everything going on between us and the highway.

The whole area was crisscrossed by trenches and foxholes, leftovers from World War II. This was the place where the British Army had come across the Elbe during the last days of April 1945.

Another fifty yards, and we could almost smell freedom.

Suddenly there was trouble ahead.

I had spotted them first. Two border guards at about hundred yards, but coming straight at us. Closer and closer they came. I could hear dry branches cracking under their boots. They did not talk to each other. Absolute silence, only steps coming closer and closer.

We had both taken cover in one section of those trenches. I was flat on my belly, face down, my heart beating, ready to explode.

Still those steps were coming closer. Then there was silence. No steps, not a word, but I knew they stood right on top of us. I could almost feel their eyes on my back, but still I did not dare to move.

"What if they shoot us in this hole," I thought. "If they throw a little dirt over us, nobody will ever find us."

It was almost a relief when I heard a voice in broken German say, "Hey you, come out."

I could have cried at this moment. We came so close and yet so far, and I knew I was in deeper trouble than ever before.

Within twenty minutes we reached the same place again that we had just left a few days ago. The first person we had to run into, turned out to be "Ivan The Terrible."

He walked across the yard as our little group approached. He was all smiles and seemed to be cracking jokes with our guards. All of a sudden he recognized me as a recent customer of his establishment. His mongolian eyes turned to a narrow slit, and before I could protect my face he was all over me, cursing and hitting me at the same time. My left eye was swelling and my lip was bleeding, and the trouble was I couldn't even defend myself. The guy was like a madman. When he finally let up, he ordered the guards to take us over to the big barn building and lock us up in the already familiar chicken pen. Again the place was crowded with five people in such a small room.

All I could think of was escape. I was hurting all over, but wasted no time in inspecting my surroundings. It was then, that I made a useful discovery. The building, even though of solid brick, was very old. The mortar joints were old and brittle, and when I tried a key that I had left in my pocket, I was able to scrape out the mortar and loosen a brick. My companions looked at me in disbelief. "What are you up to?" one of them asked. "Wait till it gets dark," I said. "I'll be out of here and if somebody wants to join me that's fine." I was hoping that somebody would join me, but nobody seemed to be interested. Everybody was scared, even my buddy Fred was not willing to risk it. I was scared too, but I was also desperate, so desperate that I had to try it. I did not want to face Ivan again.

The wall I was working on was an inside wall. Even if I should make it out of this room, I would still be inside the barn with a guard posted at the main door. I kept working on my wall during the last hours of daylight. It was less risky because of all the commotion outside. Some of the guards off duty were playing soccer in the yard, and we could see our guard watching the game with interest. By the time it was dark, I had enough bricks loosened to create a hole big enough to crawl through. Now it was just time to wait.

Fortunately nobody ever came to pick us up for interrogation. Fred and I had a long talk. At first he didn't think I was serious about escaping, but when he realized I was, he almost apologized for not joining me. He thought it couldn't be done.

We spent the next few hours with small talk, just to get my mind of what was ahead of me. Then it was time to watch the guard.

The outside was peaceful now with the exception of a patrol coming or going once in a while. As far as I could see through our little window, our guard was leaning against the wall of our building not far from the main barn door. He did not move at all, and I decided it was time to go. Very careful I started to remove the bricks I had loosened, and then, with the help of Fred I was on my way. With both arms stretched out over my head and Fred pushing, I had no difficulty clearing the first hurdle. That was the easy one.

The big test was still to come.

My companions wished me good luck, but everybody was very quiet, knowing there was a guard outside. It was a strange feeling to stand outside of our little jail, but the worst was still ahead, I still had to get out of this building.

Only a few steps separated me from the corner where I could see right through the big, wide open barn door. The bright outdoor light was illuminating the whole inside in front of me.

Step by step I approached the big opening. Where was the guard?

I had moved over to the left side, knowing the guard was always posted on the right side. Without making a sound I reached the door. As I looked around the corner very careful, I could see the guard still leaning against the building in the same position. It looked as if he was taking a little nap. His submachine gun was hanging around his neck across his chest.

I could not afford to stumble through the dark barn, looking for another way out. I had to try it. Taking a deep breath I stepped outside. Step by step I moved to the left, away from the guard and at the same time keeping my eyes on him. About five more steps separated me from the corner of the building, when out of the main building walked another soldier. It was probably the time to change the guards.

I will never know if he had spotted me or not, but I could not take that chance. I was too visible standing against the wall under fairly bright lights. So I followed my first impulse and started running. I was certain that I would make it to the corner before he had his gun ready.

It took a while before he had figured out what was going on. This gave me the head start I needed and I took good advantage of it. I ran straight down into the swampy grassland, knowing that there was only about 200 yards between me and freedom. By the time the alarm sounded I had crossed a little creek and found myself in the midst of five foot high swamp grass. Behind me I could hear orders screamed and guards running in all directions. A car was racing down the highway to the last checkpoint.

A fog began to spread over the landscape like a gift from heaven. I could use all the help I could get at this moment.

At first I felt protected by the high swamp grass, but I soon realized its danger. It was noisy as I made my way through it, and it didn't take very long before the first bullets whistled over my head. The Russians stuck to the high ground on the highway and the terrain behind me, content with firing their weapons at whatever moved. There was no place to take cover from the bullets.

The fog was getting heavier by the minute, giving the whole landscape an eerie feeling. Behind me I could now hear the sound of dogs barking, but I was more worried about the bullets.

After a while it was quiet, only an occasional burst of gunfire broke the silence. I didn't dare to move and I was hoping that no animal in my vicinity would move and draw their attention. An hour must have passed, maybe two, when I finally decided it was time to start moving again. With extreme caution and in slow motion I moved forward. The high ground around me remained silent. I thought I must have reached no-mans land by now, but if the Russians spotted me they would not hesitate to enter.

A little dam interrupted the otherwise flat terrain. The top of the dam felt hard and firm under my feet, like a walkway. Down on the other side I came upon another creek, this one wider and deeper. As I was still debating with myself if I should try to cross or follow the dam to the highway, I heard voices coming from there. To my despair the voices turned out to be Russian.

Very careful, without any noise, I slid down into the creek, just holding onto some shrub at the edge. Two dark figures came out of the fog, passing right on top of me not more than twenty feet away and disappearing again. I knew the dam could not be very long, so I waited patiently for their return.

The water was cold, but after a short while the voices came back. By now I had decided to use them as a guide. As soon as I felt safe to do so, I climbed out of my cold and wet hideout and followed the voices. I could now recognize the dark treetops on the highway sticking out of the fog.

My guess was right. The voices turned to the left, and

after a few minutes I heard some more voices, then a motor starting and a vehicle slowly driving east.

I had taken my shoes off, because they made so much noise with all that water. Walking like a bowlegged cowboy, I reached the highway and turned to the right. Slowly I moved from tree to tree, and after about fifty yards there was a light in the dark. The light was like a beacon on a stormy ocean. There was no holding back now. I started running as fast as I could.

When I got to the barrack at the British checkpoint there was nobody outside. A soldier jumped from behind a desk, when I pressed my face against the window. After he recovered from his shock, he opened the door and stared at me.

"Where the bloody hell did you come from," he asked.

I didn't have to answer that question. He knew where I came from. He awakened the sergeant in charge and soon there was a group of soldiers all around me. Everybody seemed very concerned, because I must have really looked pitiful.

"Was it you they were shooting at all night?" they wanted to know. Within minutes they came up with some dry clothing, but even with a blanket over my shoulder I was shaking like a leaf. After some hot tea and a few sandwiches I laid down on an empty bunk bed. It was 3:30 in the morning. Although I was dead tired, I could not sleep. Again and again I had to look at the soldiers to make sure they were not Russians. The English language never sounded better to me than at this moment. At noon I was awakened and introduced to a captain of Army Intelligence. He asked me to follow him to headquarters to answer a few questions.

I said good-bye to the British soldiers and thanked them for their hospitality and first aid. As I stepped out of the barrack, and before getting into the car, I paused for a moment and looked down the highway. There, at only a few hundred yards was the Russian check point.

What a feeling. I was free, really free. I had made it to the West.

The captain drove me to a villa on the outskirts of the

little town. This was headquarters for the district. He explained that he would like to have some information from me, but there was no hurry. I was shown to a room, and after a nice meal it was bedtime again.

When I woke up it was early in the morning. After a hearty breakfast I was introduced to three more intelligence officers, then we sat down for questioning.

What a difference a few miles can make. Here I realized for the first time the tension between the former allies. They British wanted to know everything of what was going on over there. What kind of troops, what uniforms, where located, how many? There were detailed maps, and I was glad to help and give them any kind of information I could. Afterwards the captain gave me a letter, addressed to the British commander of a refugee camp near the city of Luebeck. One hour later, with transportation provided by the British Army, I was delivered to the camp.

There were several thousand people in this camp, refugee's from all over Europe. All trying to find a new home and a new life somewhere. Many people from the eastern countries, who could not go home. Some waiting for visas to the United States or Canada and most of them just trying to find a home and get a new start somewhere in West Germany.

I could not even think of going to the United States or any other foreign country, because I had no sponsor, no relative in any of these countries, and as a German citizen I was not considered a victim of nazism.

The British officer in charge of our section turned out to be very helpful in analyzing my situation. He told me about the German Labor Service, whose members were former German soldiers under the command of German officers. These units were attached to British Army units and under orders from their commanding officer.

It all sounded very good to me, for the simple reason that I had no place to go, and here I had food, clothing and shelter all in one.

With his help I was assigned, and reported to one of the best units available. This unit consisted of only one company and was stationed in the city of Hamburg, the place that had been my goal anyway. My first lucky break.

Hamburg-West Germany
August 1946

The Germany of 1946 was in shambles. It's big cities reduced to piles of rubble, it's economy none existent. Trading was done on the black market, because the German currency was worthless. People of the upper classes traded in their furs and diamonds for some butter, eggs, and potatoes. The farmer was suddenly the richest and most respected man in the land, and survival was a full time job for the average citizen. The country was divided into four zones of occupation, each one governed by a military government.

I found myself now in the northern part of Germany, which was under the control of the British Army. And while life was hard everywhere in the Germany of 1946, there was a feeling of a new beginning in the western zones.

The people of Eastern Germany were paying the highest price for Hitler's madness. Not only suffering under a brutal occupation by the Russian Army, but also under a local German Communist administration installed by the Russians. This was the Germany of 1946.

Once I arrived in Hamburg and reported to my new unit, I was fitted with a new uniform and assigned to a barrack and a work detail. Our uniforms were British Army uniforms except the color was brown. The company was attached to a unit of British Royal Engineers, stationed also in Hamburg and responsible for operating a large army depot which served the troops of the British sector. Every morning trucks delivered us to the depot, where we spent the day loading and unloading supplies. At five in the afternoon the trucks would pick us up for the return to camp.

My new unit was under the command of lieutenant Dietrich, a real genius when it came to organizing things. In civilian life he had been a promoter of theatrical and musical events. The man knew absolutely everybody in German show business. He had been able to locate and transfer talented people into his unit. One of them, a former stage designer for the Berlin opera, created a masterpiece on the little stage of our mess hall. Our very own band played "Sentimental journey" and other favorite tunes when we invited the local girls for dancing. No local boys allowed, in order to keep competition to a minimum. We staged variety shows in our camp that would have been impossible to get under one roof in any German theater. All this free of charge, because everybody owed our boss a favor, or tried to get closer to him.

I was really beginning to appreciate the new home I had found, and the relative security of having a place to sleep as well as a regular meal.

Life on the outside was grim, especially in the big cities where people could not supplement their meager food supplies with produce from their own little home gardens. A pound of butter sold for hundreds of marks on the black market. One single cigarette sold for eight marks, and smokers would pick cigarette butts out of the gutter, if they could find one.

By October of 1946 our British commander requested a group of twelve English speaking men for guard duty at the depot. The break-ins in and around the depot got so bad that patrols had to go out every night to try to stop it. Since I spoke the language adequately, I was qualified to join. Our group went on guard from six PM to six o'clock in the morning. Every patrol consisted of two Germans and two British soldiers. The British soldiers had the gun, we carried a nightstick.

There was however no violence. The people that climbed on the trains and over the fences were harmless civilians, just trying to survive. Among them ten and twelve year old children. We all felt sorry for them and many times did we look the other way. Only when we came across the pro's who did things at a bigger scale, did we clamp down. To stop it was impossible. It was all around us, it was a way of life, and pretty soon we would all get caught up in it.

As we got to know each other the relationship between us

and the British soldiers of the guard became closer. In time they all found out about the value of goods on the black market, and they started out by selling their cigarettes and rations and trading it for goods like cameras, etc. Since most of our British soldiers had a language problem, we became the matchmakers, the wheelers and dealers. Soon it was like a drug problem. Once they got the taste of it they wanted more, and it didn't take long before we started stealing the things we were supposed to protect. The split was always a fair fifty-fifty, because we handled the goods and we could not afford to get the British mad at us. It got so sophisticated that we had deliveries made by trucks of our own unit. Since we had access to all buildings, we had no problems in finding and issuing legitimate transport papers, in case they got stopped by military police.

Christmas 1946 came and our lieutenant made good use of his connections. Considering the bleak reality and the hardship of life all around us, it was a very festive occasion. Stars from the Hamburg opera were our guest's, singing with us our favorite old Christmas songs, and also bringing us arias and duets from popular operas. Every one of us, and every one of our guest found a little gift on tastefully decorated tables. It was really a night to remember. Our British unit had made a very generous contribution, and major Reed, our commanding officer and his staff came to present it. A member of our unit had worked for months on a beautiful oak cabinet for the major, which was then presented to him.

The major felt very much at home at our camp. He never missed any of our special theatrical events and even stopped by once in a while for dancing. On this Christmas night of 1946 the major and his staff were so impressed by the performances of our guest, that they stayed with us all night until the party finally came to an end.

New years eve was only a week later, and our band played music for dancing. As midnight approached, many of us got a little sentimental. We were all thinking of home, and of loved ones we could not be with for one reason or another. As the last seconds of 1946 ticked away, I couldn't help but feel grateful that I was among friends and especially that I was free. All these years of war and destruction could not be made up overnight, but I was hopeful for the future, hopeful for 1947.

In a recent letter from home, my mother had sent greetings from an old friend and neighbor of ours. She had included the current address of his nephew in Hamburg.

His nephew Peter had spent the war years with him, when the bombings in Hamburg had reached it's peak. We had attended school together and had become close friends.

Mother had added, "Why don't you visit Peter and his parents, they will be pleased to see you."

I had thought about Peter many times, wondering whether he had survived the war. We had lost contact in 1944, when he was drafted by the Air Force, while I had gone to the Navy.

Enjoying a day off, and anxious to see my old pal again, I decided to pay him a visit that same day. The days were short, and it was already late afternoon, when I got on the subway. As soon as I left the station, I was faced by a landscape of total destruction. Although there were a lot of bombed out buildings in Hamburg, this part of the city was almost totally destroyed.

After wandering through this desolate area for a long time, I was ready to give up.

"Mother must have made a mistake, when she wrote down the address," I thought. How could anybody live in these piles of rubble? Meanwhile it was getting dark, giving the area even more the appearance of a ghost town. Only the streets had been cleared of debris, otherwise there was no sign of life.

A lonely shadow emerged from the ruins of what must have been a big apartment building. By this time I had lost all sense of direction.

When the shadow came closer, I recognized an elderly man.

"Pardon me sir," I said. "I am looking for the Wagner-strasse."

"You found it," he replied.

"Would you know the Schroeder family?" I asked.

To my surprise he answered, "Sure, they live next door."

For the first time that night I had to laugh.

"What do you call next door in this pile of rubble," I asked the old man.

He grabbed me by the hand and walked about fifty yards down the street. In the dark I could recognize a walkway, leading to the top of the pile of bricks.

"Follow this trail across the top," the man said. "From the other side you will see a light."

The man was right. As I reached the top of the ruin, I could see several lights on the other side. One of them turned out to be the Schroeders.

I was amazed, what they had made out of their basement. With a few pieces of furniture, salvaged from their bombed out apartment, they had managed to create a cozy little room. The city of Hamburg was full of people like the Schroeders. People who had been able to make the best of a bad situation.

Peter was at home, alive and well and could not believe that I had escaped and was now living in his home town. There was so much to talk about, so much had happened in those two years we had not seen each other.

After we had told our stories about how we had survived the war, we also told his parents another story. Our favorite story about our visit to Hamburg in 1943.

Peter's father had managed the dining room at police headquarters in downtown Hamburg. We had been on our way to summer camp, and had been forced to stay in Hamburg before catching our next train.

It was only natural that we had used the opportunity to visit his parents, who lived in a small apartment at the headquarters building, only a few blocks walking distance from the station.

We were just in time for supper, and Peter's mom had made a special effort to put a few extra goodies on the table. His Father was busy at his job, but had found a few minutes to greet his son.

We had barely sat down, when the air raid sirens went off. Peter's mother was a volunteer at the first aid station, and had to leave in a hurry.

"Run to the bunker at central station," she told us before storming out of the apartment.

There we sat with all the good food in front of us, and nobody wanted to be the first one to run to the bunker. No one wanted to admit he was scared. We tried to be cool, before cool was even fashionable.

We still sat there when the anti aircraft guns behind the building opened fire, and the first bombs started falling. Now there was no holding. We raced out of the building into the deserted streets. Bombs were exploding all around us, and the sound of shrapnel could be heard when it hit the ground. It was a miracle neither one of us got hurt.

In record time we reached the bunker, where we found the doors tightly closed. Our frantic knocking was noticed and someone opened the heavy doors. The door was hardly shut behind us, when a bomb hit the side of the bunker. The sound of the explosion reverberated through the massive structure. The ground shook and the lights flickered, but no damage was reported.

Twenty minutes later the sirens sounded again. This time to indicate the end of the alarm.

No harm had come to Peter's parents and their apartment, we were happy to find when we returned.

"We could have stayed here," said Peter. He tried to sound brave, but I knew he was just as scared as I was.

That we had not gone to the bunker immediately after the alarm, was not mentioned to his parents until today. Now we could laugh about it.

It was way past midnight, when Peter led me across the rubble to one of the more populated main streets. We promised to stay in touch.

One day in February I had the misfortune of being in the wrong place at the wrong time. I had taken a streetcar down to St. Pauli where the black market was at it's best. It was like an outdoor market, but the police was always keeping an eye on the situation. Every once in a while they would bring in the paddy wagon and pick up everybody suspected of trading.

While I was talking to a dealer, trying to get some price information, the cops blocked off the area and started loading us into the wagons. Since I did not have any goods on me I was released two hours later.

My lucky stars must have been out of position, because that same night while on guard duty I had another misfortune.

With my British partner I was on our usual round. We had instructions to keep the fires burning inside the office barracks. It was bitter cold outside.

When I entered major Reed's office I noticed a beautiful bottle on his desk.

''Cherry Liquor,'' the label said.

''That would do some good in this cold, and a little sip would hardly be missed,'' I thought.

My partner who had followed me could barely wait for his turn. I told him since I saw the bottle first, I should also have the honor of the first sip. He agreed and never had to regret his decision.

As I took a good sip, a bitter taste came to my mouth.

''Damn it,'' that was no cherry liquor.

I grabbed a wastepaper basket, spit it out and faster than a bullet ran into the restroom. There in the mirror I saw a man with ruby red lips, red teeth, and a bright red tongue.

Meanwhile my partner was having a good time congratulating himself for letting me have the first drink. It took me all night to get my lips and teeth clean enough, so that I could show my face in public again. What I had actually swallowed was red ink, and I had the funny feeling the major had set a trap for somebody.

Lesson number one, never judge a bottle by its label.

Only two weeks after this little episode I was in trouble again. This time I had company.

The officer of the guard at the British main unit always came to inspect the guards at the depot. Over a period of several months we had noticed that he never came past midnight. If he wasn't there by midnight, he would not come at all. That had always been a pretty good rule, until tonight.

The trouble was that we had concluded it was too cold out there to run around and freeze our butts off. Our two British partners didn't even bother to get up and get dressed, while my German partner and I sat in the British guardroom passing the time by playing cards. It was one o'clock in the morning, when somebody rattled the iron main gate like a madman. When I looked out the window, I recognized the staff car and our sergeant major rattling at the gate.

I awakened the corporal in charge, as well as our two partners and told them what was going on. There was no time to waste, the sergeant major was getting impatient. We could not run outside now, because he would be able to see us.

Our two partners grabbed their uniforms and in their underwear ran down into the restrooms, located in the basement. We followed. Meanwhile the corporal went outside to open the gate. We heard voices upstairs, then doors shutting and again silence. Someone came down to tell us the sergeant major and the corporal had gone outside to inspect the guards.

Once outside, two of us went to the left, two men to the right. As it turned out, the other two crossed his path first.

The sergeant major suspecting foul play, confronted them as if he knew all about it. Our two partners fell for the trap and admitted the whole thing.

Five minutes later, with our partners in his entourage, he crossed our trail.

Patiently he listened to our report, while our companions were unable to give us a sign that all was lost. All of a sudden his voice thundered through the cold night. "You dirty bastards," he screamed. "I'll get you for this."

The resulting three days in the guardhouse was more a formality than punishment, at least in our German unit. The cell was a small room at the end of our barrack, with bars across the window and no heater. In those three days we spent only a total of thirty minutes in there, the rest in the relative comfort of our own room. When the British officer arrived at the camp for inspection, there was always enough time for our guard on duty to alert us, and put us where we were supposed to be. Our British partners did not fare as well as we did, but that was regular army.

Spring arrived, and soon it was summer of 1947. The bitter cold of winter was replaced by a heat wave, and the fire pond in the center of our camp came in handy as a swimming pool. There were rumors that the Labor Service

Groups would be dissolved, and by September these rumors became fact. The camp of Munsterlager became our last stop.

It was a sad moment, when our unit was lined up for the last time. I had made many friends during my year in Hamburg. Most of us had one thing in common. We had no place to call home. I was among the few lucky ones that could at least account for the whereabouts of my family. Many among us did not know if their family was still alive. They were lost somewhere in the East, trying to flee from the advancing Russian armies, while the men had to serve in the German armed forces. But many among us knew their loved ones had perished during air raids of the big cities, and that there would never be anybody to go home to.

We were officially released from the service. Everyone of us was now alone with the decision of what to do with his life.

My closest friend Lutz and I decided to go west to check out the Rhineland. We traveled by train to the city of Duisburg and stayed a total of two days. It was cool and wet most of the time, and ruins everywhere. We got so disillusioned that we got on the next train back to Hamburg. This was more like home to us, although we realized for the first time how hard it was to be on our own. Gone was the comfort of our barrack and the certainty of our daily meals. Now we never knew where the next meal would be coming from and if there would even be a next meal. With winter approaching we had no place to stay. Many people were still living in the basement of their bombed out homes. Every square inch of livable space was used.

Plans for the Future

Ever since I was a little boy, water has had a magic attraction for me. The books I read were mostly about the Navy, ships, the oceans and foreign lands. At age fourteen, I became a member of the Marine Hitler Youth and learned all about seamanship there was to learn. Now I was determined to get into the Merchant Marine and let it be my springboard to the outside world. There was just one little problem. There was no Merchant Marine in Germany, not counting a few small, rusty old ships which not even the victorious Allies wanted. So it was a matter of getting the next best job available, a job on the water that could be used later as a stepping stone for the Merchant Marine.

In a small town on the river Elbe, thirty miles from Hamburg, we found that kind of a job. My friend Lutz and I hired on with a salvage and tugboat company. This company had contracted with the government to salvage the destroyed bridge over the river Elbe at Lauenburg. It was hard work, dangerous and dirty, but we had a meal to eat and most of all a place to sleep on one of the barges. Our divers cut the tangled and twisted members of the bridge under water, or place explosives to be detonated. We worked in support of the divers or on the barges, lifting out the pieces of the bridge.

Icy winds swept across the river. It was almost winter again, and our hands were sore and frozen stiff. But as long as the river did not freeze, work on the bridge continued. Christmas 1947 was a far cry from the festive holiday we had experienced a year ago in Hamburg. Lutz and I spent the day alone on the barge, the rest of the crew had gone home.

Trouble With the Russians Again

In the spring we moved up river and dropped anchor on the East German side about ten miles above my home town. Here the river Elbe formed the border. One side was East Germany, the other side was West.

I had mixed feelings about seeing the Russians again. However, I now carried a West German passport in my pocket, and besides, I needed the job. I had no other place to go.

Our status was unique. Since we held West German identification cards and food coupons, we had to purchase our supplies on the Western side. Because we performed a job benefiting the Eastern side, we were allowed to go ashore and visit the village behind the dike. The border guards treated us with suspicion, but were apparently under orders to leave us alone.

After a month on this job we had our first run-in with the Russians. In our little dinghy, Lutz and I were on our way to the Western side. The sun was already low on the horizon. Our little boat was loaded with several sacks of coal, which served as a trade for additional food supplies with the local farmers. As we approached the Western shore, we heard shots being fired on the other side. At first we didn't think anything of it, but suddenly we both saw the water splashing up around us. One shot ripped a hole through our boat right at the waterline. By this time we had reached the shore, jumped out and pulled up the boat with our valuable cargo.

They stopped firing, probably realizing we were on West German soil. Taking cover behind some willows, we observed the Russians watch us through binoculars from the opposite dike.

The farmhouse was only about 200 yards from our position, but nobody had noticed our precarious situation. That was because a dike stretched all along the river on both sides, and all buildings were located behind the dike.

We didn't dare to go back to the boat until it was totally dark. Under the cover of darkness we made our way to the farmhouse and got help.

Our transaction completed, and after a free dinner, the farmer helped us to fix our boat as good as we could. Luckily it was very dark as we made our way back to our ship, rowing as silent as we could, and with the ship's position lights as our guide.

The next morning we protested to the Russian officer in charge, while he accused us of smuggling people across the border. He was convinced we had people in the boat and didn't believe our story about the sacks of coal.

Several days later one of our crew members, while on his way back from the village, was approached by two men. They claimed to be fugitives from a town about fifty miles from there, and offered him money to take them across the river. The guy was smart enough not to take the bait. He was convinced the East German police was checking us out.

"Their accent was definitely saxon," he said, "and they sure looked like police to me."

A week later we did take a family to freedom on the other side. It was a husband and wife and their little son, relatives of one of the farmers. They had been hiding out for over a week with the farmer's family, and the farmer had been reluctant to ask us after he heard about our troubles. Several of the farmers behind the dike had owned boats, but not anymore. The Russians had confiscated and destroyed every boat in the vicinity of the border. That's why they kept a wary eye on us. In our possession was the only boat for miles around, and they couldn't take it away from us.

Being so close to home was a great temptation for me, and on one of the following weekends I was on my way to see the family again. They could not visit me, because nobody was allowed even close to the border. People living in the border region carried special passes.

For me it was relatively easy. All I had to do was go to the village, which I was allowed to do. Very casually I stopped at the farm, owned by our friend whose relatives we had recently taken across the river. He owed me a favor, and with his help I made it out of the village without running into the Russians. During the time we had spent at this location I had noticed that the patrols kept mostly to the top of the dike. From there they had the best overall view. Once I got away from the immediate border area I had no trouble, and after a three hour march I reached home. I did not dare to use any public transportation, because I was too close to the border and the police watched train and bus stations day and night.

It was a surprise when I showed up at home and mom and dad were very happy to see me. The food supply was still critical, but mom always had some special treat for a special day, and this was one of those special occasions.

On Sunday morning my friend Bruno stopped by to see my parents and get the latest report on how I was doing in the West. He could not believe his eyes, when he saw me in person. We talked for a long time about the other side of the border. He wanted to know all about the Western zone. His family had still no word about his father. The barbershop was now confiscated and Bruno's clientele consisted only of the Russian Army.

Before he left he said, "Should you ever have any problem with the Russians, get a message to me. I have some connections."

Little did I know at that time how soon I had to take advantage of those connections.

On Sunday afternoon I was on my march back. I was careful not to be recognized in the streets because word spreads fast in a small town, and the East German police had a pretty good spy network in operation by this time.

Without incident I got as far as a little village only three miles from our village, and here the story of my life repeated itself.

Rounding a corner, I found myself confronted by three Russians, a corporal and two soldiers. I decided to play it cool and continue on my way, but my first reaction was to run, and they must have noticed that slight hesitation. They must also have known everybody in the village and recognized me as an outsider.

I tried to talk my way out of it, but to no avail. The man in charge of this post was a sergeant, and with him my story fell on deaf ears. He was not impressed by my story about the important work I was performing for the Russians. What he wanted to know was what I was doing in his village. A little later I found myself on my way back to where I had just come from.

I was the only prisoner, accompanied by the two soldiers who had captured me. Riding a bike, the two were constantly pushing me forward until we reached the next town. Here I was locked up for the night. Early the next morning our trio continued on our trip back to my home town.

Thank God I didn't run into any familiar faces from the past, but the building was still the same. Fortunately the guard leading me down to my cell in the basement understood a little German. Wasting no time, I asked him if he knew Bruno the barber. At first he didn't want to talk, until I mentioned the magic word, "Vodka."

A Russian will do almost anything for a bottle of vodka, and when I told him that Bruno would have a bottle for him, he was ready. All he had to do was tell Bruno where I was, nothing else.

As I found out he went to see Bruno as soon as he was off duty, and he must have received his reward, because I did not hear any complaints.

Two hours later I was taken upstairs before a young lieutenant, and this was probably the first time a Russian had treated me like a person. I was cautious, wondering what he was up to, but apparently he just wanted to look me over.

After a casual conversation of about ten minutes he suddenly asked, "Do you know Bruno the barber?"

"Sure," I said, "he is a good friend of mine."

He told me that Bruno had come to see him on my behalf. "If you are a friend of Bruno, you can't be all bad," he said laughing.

Before I realized what was happening he said "I will let you go this time."

I recovered from my surprise in time to ask him for a slip of paper, to make sure I made it safely back to my destination this time.

I was glad I did. Again I was stopped as I approached the

village, but my piece of paper with a big stamp on it held up under close scrutiny. They let me go.

When I finally got back on board, I had to listen to a sermon by the skipper. He was mad I had not told him of my travel plans, but I knew he would have tried to talk me out of it.

I did not care if he was mad or not. I was damn glad to be back, and without Bruno's help I would probably still be sitting in some dark basement waiting for the next interrogation.

I never had a chance to pay him back for what he had done for me. Bruno himself escaped from East Germany a year later and lives today in the West.

Our job was finished in early June of 1948, and a new contract called for another job on the eastern side farther up river. As for myself, I had enough. I could not stand watching the border patrols day after day. I wanted to keep more distance between us, and quitting my job was the only way out. Since Lutz felt exactly as I did, he also handed in his resignation.

"We got hired as a pair, we might as well quit as a pair," he said.

Back to Hamburg we went. We felt like soldiers returning from the front lines, and I swore to myself that in the future I would keep a respectable distance from the border and the Russians.

Otherwise not much had changed in Hamburg. The black market was still flourishing, but now there was talk about a reform of the German currency. When we arrived in Hamburg we found a cheap hotel room in a back alley of the Reeperbahn. It was not the Ritz or the Palace hotel, but it was a roof over our head, a place to sleep.

The first night out, we returned to our favorite dance hall, and it felt good to be on familiar turf again. This was a different world. People wanted to forget the misery of the outside world for a few hours.

The following night we ran into good old Albert, our buddy from the Labor Service. At 55 years of age he had been one of the oldest in our group. He had once owned his very own nightclub at the famous Reeperbahn, and lost it all in one night of bombings. His family had perished that same night, while Albert was fighting the Russians at the eastern front. Despite it all, Albert was always in good humor and had a good word for everyone.

At first I had not recognized him, because Albert was a bouncer in a nightclub, and he looked more like a general from Napoleon's army. In a way it was sad to see the former owner of a nightclub as a bouncer, but this was survival. I was sure Albert would make it again one of these days. He was just that kind of a guy. He was so glad to see his old buddies again, and got us a good seat in the house, plus a couple of free drinks.

During the day I was still pursuing the chance to get into the Merchant Marine, but so far without any luck. My good friend and companion Lutz had given up. The water was not his favorite element. His only relative, an uncle, lived in a small town not far from Hamburg. When he visited him one day, his uncle invited him to stay with his family, and Lutz accepted.

After another night at the Reeperbahn our trails went in different directions. Lutz moved to his uncle, while I found a job in salvage operations a few days later. It was not what I wanted, but it was in Hamburg-Wilhelmsburg. Cleaning up a bombed out oil refinery was our assignment.

Again it was dirty work and very dangerous. A lot of unexploded bombs were still under the rubble, and before my first week was over we had lost two men in a bomb blast.

The company provided living quarters on an old mine sweeper, so at least I could stay in Hamburg. On Saturday nights we would go dancing, or on Sunday we would watch a soccer game at the Volkspark stadium. It was a welcome break from the hard work during the week. As far as the Merchant Marine was concerned, I kept my eyes open and in early October I got my first break.

Sure, it was nothing to brag about, no fancy passenger liner going to the south seas, but it was my first step. Since there were thousands of unemployed sailors on shore, I knew that if I wanted to get in, I had to accept a ship that nobody wanted.

That ship was the S.S. "Comet," probably the oldest salvage tugboat of the Bugsier Company. The only thing that stood between me and a job on the "Comet" was an official seaman's book, and that required proof of past experience.

I wasn't worried so much about the experience, but in Germany papers and certificates are very important. However, I had done my homework, and my story went something like this.

In 1944-45, I had sailed out of a port that now belonged to Poland. That could not be verified. I had sailed on a ship that I was sure was sunk in the Baltic in February of 1945.

The officials took my word for it, and suddenly I was the proud owner of a German seaman's book, issued by the British Military Government, and allowing me to visit foreign ports. The most important piece of paper was mine.

S.S. "Comet," A Humble Beginning

On the following day I reported to the "Comet," stationed in Brunsbuettel at the entrance to the canal that connects the Baltic with the North Sea. During the day we supported salvage operations that were going on right in front of the gates to the canal. The unpleasant part was that we were on call twenty four hours a day. Our territory was the upper part of the river Elbe, a very treacherous stretch of water. Any time a ship was in trouble in our sector, we had to go out and stand by for help, no matter what kind of weather. At this time of the year the weather was always bad, and besides, ships seldom run into trouble in good weather.

Our first big job came along in November. Storm warnings were flying, and at times the wind was reaching hurricane force. A big Norwegian freighter had run aground and was in danger of breaking up. We received a call at dawn and got under steam immediately. Another tug from our company, stationed at Cuxhaven, was already on the scene. We had to fight our way against the tide and against the storm, some times more under water than above. Progress was slow, but the storm had reached its peak and seemed to subside. When we approached the troubled ship, there was not much we could do, except stand by and hold our own bow against the swell. Trying to get a line across now would have been hopeless.

It took three days and three nights to get the big freighter released. We had to wait for a high tide, until we finally succeeded. The freighter had been stuck on a sandbank, and there was no apparent leak. She went up to Hamburg under her own power, while we returned to our stations. Everybody was dead tired, but with the satisfaction of a successful job and glad it was finally over.

Now the daily routine with the salvage operations started again, but ready to go at any time when the call came.

Tugboats are the vultures of the sea. The competition between the big tugboat companies is fierce, but the rewards can also be big. Once a ship is in trouble, it becomes a race to be the first one on the scene.

Life on board was like a little family. We all got along fine, even with the captain. However, lately there was a little tension between the crew and the old man. The reason was cockroaches. Our crew was greatly outnumbered by those little critters, and frankly, we got a little tired of them. The ship had to be fumigated from top to bottom, from stem to stern. A spray can would not do the job any more. Our captain kept promising, but could never find the time to have it done. A strategy meeting was held, and it was decided to help things along. Part of our plan was the captain's wife. Since we were always on call, she came visiting almost every weekend. Everybody had noticed by now that the old lady was very much in charge, as far as the captain's family was concerned. In other words, she was The Boss, and that was the foundation of our brilliant plan. We all ate our meals together in the big cabin. The scene was set.

On the following Sunday we were all sitting down for dinner. The first course was a vegetable-beef soup. Everyone seemed to be in a good mood, waiting for things to come. We were holding our breath in anticipation of the big scene. All eyes were on the old lady, when she started stirring her soup with suspicion, trying to sort out something on her plate. Her old man watched in horror as she placed a giant cockroach neatly on the rim of her plate.

"Would you tell me what this," she starts asking him, but before she can finish her sentence she jumps up and storms out of the cabin. The captain, with an accusing look at the straight faces around the table, drops his spoon and follows. Had he turned around at this moment and seen that big smile on our faces, he would have known who was behind this conspiracy.

She left Sunday night for home, telling all of us that she would not set foot on this tub until it was properly sanitized. We all agreed with her that this was no place for a lady.

The captain went ashore early Monday morning to take care of some urgent business, as he put it. For the rest of the day we didn't see very much of him. On Tuesday morning at the breakfast table he informed us, that thanks to his long time and tireless efforts the company had authorized him to fumigate the ship. The next trip up to Hamburg should take care of the problem once and for all. His old lady was not mentioned at the table.

Meanwhile it was early December and the days were getting shorter. All of us were looking forward to a night out on the Reeperbahn in Hamburg. On the following Friday we received orders to tow a big barge, loaded with scrap metal from the salvage operation, up to Hamburg.

Even with a fully loaded barge the trip takes only a few hours. In spite of the cold and humid weather the mood on board was festive. We didn't talk about anything except plans for the weekend in Hamburg. The closer we came to Hamburg, the wilder our plans.

But. . .mother nature had other plans for us. Fog began to settle over the river, very light at first, almost unnoticed. The captain was the first one to get restless. He talked to the engine room and asked if they could get us a little more steam.

"We have given you all we got," came the answer.

"I don't like this at all," said the captain and stared nervously at the shoreline, which now almost disappeared in the fog. It was more and more as if some magic force was pulling a milky curtain across our bow. There was no more talk about our wild plans for a night out. Our festive mood had given way to a much more subdued one. We had reached the outskirts of Hamburg at the town of Blankenese, and what all of us were afraid of finally happened. Within minutes the fog became so heavy that visibility was probably no more than twenty feet. Since the captains home was in Hamburg, he wanted to get there as bad as we did, but the responsibility was too great. Very reluctantly he gave the order to turn starboard. He wanted to get out of the main shipping channel.

I had just handed over the helm to the bosun, and the captain ordered me to the forward section to take up the lookout position. We knew that a number of burned out wreck's had been set aground in this section. We had seen them many times while passing. The engine was turning slow as we moved into the spooky grey world around us. We had no radar, only the compass on the bridge told us in which direction we were going.

I was straining my eyes until they hurt. Several times I began to see things that didn't exist. Then it happened. This time there was no doubt. Out of nowhere appeared the big dark shadow of a ship.

"Turn starboard, turn starboard," I screamed, and the helmsman reacted instantly.

Not a second to soon, because we just barely scraped along the big black hull of a burned out wreck. We went side by side, not more than two feet of water between us. At first I stood there like someone that had just seen a ghost. Then I felt that I was getting a little too close to the action, and started running. I had almost reached the stern section of the tug, when disaster struck again. I couldn't believe my eyes, when a second big shadow came barreling right down on us. This one was moving.

There was just enough time for me to hang onto something, when the impact occurred. A big bang and the rattle of scrap iron was all I heard. We had just been hit by our own barge. We had changed course so fast, that the barge behind us never had a chance to change direction. She hit the last ten feet of our stern, and pushed us against the wreck on the other side.

The "Comet" had sprung a leak, but it appeared as if our pumps could handle it. As soon as we assessed the damage we dropped anchor. It was hopeless to stumble around blindfold in these ghostly surroundings.

The captain was cursing heaven and earth, but there was no one to blame. Since we had already proceeded at slow speed, the damage was kept to a minimum. A little more speed, and the "Comet" might have found its resting place next to all the other wrecks. But, who knows, maybe a little more speed would have gotten us out of the trap we caught ourselves in.

The engine room kept the pump going all night, the deck hands turned to regular watches and the rest of the crew bedded down for the night. Anyone who would have been foolish enough to mention the word Party and Reeperbahn again, would have run the risk of great bodily harm.

Everybody was up early to take a peek outside, but the fog was still hanging in there. Only the sound of a foghorn, or the bell of a ship at anchor broke the silence. Ship traffic on the Elbe had come to a halt. At around two P.M. the fog lifted enough for us to get underway. For the first time we could inspect our surroundings, and we were glad we had dropped anchor. There were two more wrecks within less than half a mile from us.

Without incident we reached our destination where we dropped our barge. There was no major damage to the barge, but the "Comet" had to check into a local shipyard for repairs.

At least part of our weekend was saved, and five of us decided to let off some steam at the Reeperbahn. Our destination was the "Zillertal," a bavarian type dance hall with a real ump pa pa band in lederhosen. Most of us had been there many times and it was always fun.

West Germany had recently had the long expected reform of the currency. Every citizen had received 40 Marks of the new money. So all of a sudden money was valuable again, indeed very valuable. The sailors who had thrown money around in the past, were now hanging onto every mark. So why would any sailor spend ten marks for a bottle of booze in a nightclub, when he could buy the same for 3 marks in the duty free zone of the port.

When we entered the Zillertal, we carried a good supply of booze hidden under our coats. We paid the entry fee of two Marks, and each one of us ordered a beer. That's all we intended to spend. It was custom in Germany that people could bring their own drink, by paying a so called cork fee. However, that fee was posted at the Zillertal at the stately sum of five Marks, a rip-off as far as we were concerned.

Another person that was concerned was our waiter. He could not understand how a person could buy a beer two hours ago and get more and more intoxicated without ordering another drink.

At first we had our supplies hidden under the table, but as the night progressed we got bolder and more careless. Finally the bottle was right in the middle of our table.

The waiter, who had been circling our table, stopped by to inform us of the house rules.

We laughed and ignored him completely. In less than five minutes his boss made his appearance, but his pleas fell on deaf ears. With a few drinks under our belt we felt on top of the world. When he started mentioning the police, our spokesman got up from his chair.

Our spokesman was Hans, a sailor about the size of a professional wrestler. Hans was normally a pussycat, but for this occasion he put on his meanest face possible and threatened to demolish the whole place unless they stopped pestering us. The boss, fearful of bigger trouble and possible bodily harm, finally convinced Hans to sit down again and promised likewise not to cause any trouble. He kept his word and we kept ours.

We left at two in the morning, and to add insult to injury, our spokesman Hans asked the waiter to please call a taxi for us. The occasion called for a grand exit, but before leaving we made friends again with our waiter by giving a very generous tip for all his troubles. We didn't want him to suffer from a loss of income on account of a few stingy sailors.

The following week all of us had to take a few days off to allow time for fumigation and other repair work. I used this time to follow my dream of getting on a real ship, one that was sailing to foreign ports. Chances were still very slim, but I was willing to take almost anything that became available. My chance came in the form of a 900 ton steamer called "Ludwig." It was small and it was old, but it was a ship, and it was scheduled to sail for Antwerp-Belgium.

S.S. "Ludwig," Trip to Nowhere

After spending the Christmas holidays with friends in Hamburg, I reported to the S.S. "Ludwig" on December 27, 1948. Next to a big Panamanian freighter the "Ludwig" looked like a little bathtub, but I was not discouraged. For me it was a step forward, a seagoing ship.

The German Merchant Navy of 1948 did not possess any vessel over 2,500 tons. All the bigger ships which had survived the war, had been taken over by the victorious Allies as war reparation.

Our captain was about sixty years old, and had seen better days and better ships in his life, but he wanted a job as bad as I did. We had to make the most out of what we had, and I was soon to find out what that meant.

On December 30th we cast off, and as we steamed down the river Elbe we had reports of storm warnings for the entire North Sea. Those warnings got worse by the hour, and as we passed the last point at Cuxhaven, the signals went up for a wind force of ten to twelve. Several ships, including bigger ones had dropped anchor to wait for the passing of the storm. The pilot ship, normally stationed outside near the lightship "Elbe I," had been pulled in. It just wasn't possible anymore to drop off a pilot. Since our ship was too small and therefore not obligated to carry a pilot, we didn't have to worry about getting rid of him.

The captain made no attempt to drop anchor or even slow down. Like a destroyer going into battle he steamed proudly past the line of big ships at anchor, straight into the turbulent North Sea. I was wondering what the crews of these ships were thinking, when they watched us sailing past. It didn't take very long, and I was wondering what our captain was thinking about, when he decided to continue on his course.

We reached a point about three miles from "Elbe I." The

wind was howling without interruption, and finally our captain was forced to slow down, like it or not. For about an hour we held our position without progress. The weather reports gave no hope for improving conditions. With only about one hour of daylight left, the captain realized he was wasting fuel. Reluctantly he gave the order to turn around and seek shelter in the port of Cuxhaven. Because of our small size we could safely attempt to enter the port and tie up at the pier.

The captain was in a bad mood, but the crew was happy. Even though we continued our sea watches during the night, at least we found some rest during off hours. As the last day of 1948 dawned, the storms fury was undiminished, the captains mood was not improving, and the crew was hoping it would last a little longer.

By mid afternoon our New Years eve party had begun, and by nightfall our party was in an advanced state, with everyone making the best out of the situation. The captain was out on deck every five minutes, looking at the sky, and looking at the signal tower to see if the storm warnings had been taken down.

Our party more or less ended by default. I remember we all toasted to a happy New Year at midnight, but afterwards we just dropped in our bunks one by one.

A few blurred rays of light proclaimed the first day of 1949. The sky had cleared a little, but there was still a strong north west wind blowing. Most of us were seeing the new day through a haze, which had nothing to do with the weather. Our captain was pacing the deck of the bridge like a caged tiger. None of the bigger ships made any preparation to lift anchor, but this did not deter our fearless leader. By noon his patience was running out and he ordered the crew to get ready to sail.

There was a lot of mumbling and grumbling, but thirty minutes later we cast off. Again we steamed past the big ships still at anchor. The wind had slowed down a little, but the "Ludwig" was rolling in heavy seas. We were sailing in ballast, which means with no cargo, and this made our little vessel even more unstable.

Progress was slow. By nightfall we had reached the open North Sea, somewhere northeast of the island of Norderney. It appeared as if with darkness the storm was picking up speed again. At eleven o'clock I took my turn at the helm again. Most of the time I couldn't see anything but water in front of me. The waves of the North Sea are shorter than the waves of the Atlantic, and we barely lifted our bow out of the water when the next one came crushing down on us. It was a scary sight as our little tub got slapped around like a toy. A warm meal was out of the question that day. Our cook tried desperately to have at least some hot coffee for the crew, but even that turned out to be quite a chore.

My one hour turn at the helm was almost over, when suddenly a big wave came rolling in. Our bow went down, the stern came up with the whole ship shaking violently. I was afraid our bow wouldn't come up again. All I could see in front of me was water.

The captain, who had been leaning against the compass was getting nervous and ordered the engine to slow down even more. After about three minutes the chief engineer came storming up to the bridge. He was mad as hell.

"What are you idiots trying to do, kill us all?" he screamed.

I could not see his face on the darkened bridge, but I could almost see his eyes sparkle. Never before had I seen this normally quiet man so furious, and never before had I heard anybody talk like this to the captain.

What apparently happened was that we had lifted our stern so far out of the water that the propeller was running dry. We were lucky we had not lost our propeller completely, but it looked as if we had sustained some damage to our shaft.

For the next 24 hours it was only a matter of holding our position as good as we could, with the engine at slow speed. All of us were still suffering from the after effects of our New Years party, and half of the crew was seasick. Because the forward section of our ship was under water most of the time, it was impossible for us to get to our cabin. I got soaked while trying to make it from the bridge down to the lower deck. Since I had no chance of getting to the cabin for a change of clothing, I had to find some other way of drying what I was wearing.

If one is looking for a warm spot on a ship, there is no

better place than the engine room. I laid down on the metal grating above the engine room, where the hot air rises. This may have been a good idea for drying my clothes, but it did not exactly improve my feeling of well being. We had been rolling around for over 24 hours now. Even though I was feeling the effects of the last party, I did not get seasick, until now that is. Only a person who has been seasick can understand the feeling. The agony of constant motion. I would have paid any price if somebody could put a stop to this rolling and up and down motion. It feels as if your stomach rises and falls with the ship. I must have thrown up a hundred times until there was nothing left in my stomach. I considered going out there to get some fresh air, even at the risk of being washed overboard. Who cares? Life was not worth living any more.

We made it back to Cuxhaven, and was I glad to see land again. Under normal conditions I would have been very disappointed that we did not make it to Antwerp, but this time I was so glad to set foot on firm land again, no matter where. Once in Cuxhaven it was determined that the damage was more severe than first thought. We received instructions to return to Hamburg for repairs.

I still wonder what the captain was trying to prove by going out in that kind of weather. This was not a trans-atlantic race, and he was risking his ship and his crew. For what? The ship owners must have asked him that same question, because once we got to Hamburg he was called to the main office. When he returned, his face was grim and the news was bad. The company had decided to lay off the whole crew.

I hated the idea of being on the street again, but in a way I was glad I didn't have to go out to sea again on this little tub. This was probably the shortest job I ever held in my life. Nine days. The entry in my newly acquired seaman's book read's under destination: For the trip to: "At sea and back." Not a very glorious beginning of my career as a world travelling sailor.

Before I started looking for a new ship again, I wanted to spend a weekend with my old friends in Lauenburg. Since nobody had a phone, I was unable to call in advance and find out if anyone would be home. As it turned out, two of my best friends happened to be out of town, but I was not ready to give up on my weekend plans.

My next stop was our old hang-out, the local dance hall where I found a lot of familiar faces.

The dance ended at two in the morning, and I ended it by taking one of my old girl friends home. Unfortunately she was still living with her family and there was no way I could stay with her. She was concerned about me standing there in this bitter cold night, but I assured her not to worry. I was simply going to spend the remaining hours in the warm comfort of the railroad stations waiting room.

It was however not as simple as I had anticipated. When I got down to the station I found to my horror the station was closed and completely in the dark. What now? With the temperature below freezing and snow on the ground, a park bench was out of the question.

On the tracks behind the station I could see the dark silhouette of a parked train with passenger cars. I jumped over a hedge and went over to the parked train. This time I was lucky, the cars were open. I took off my warm coat, laid down on one of the benches, covered myself with the coat and was asleep in a matter of minutes.

I found out later that I could not have slept for more than an hour, when I was awakened by bright lights and a tremendous jolt. It took a while to figure out where I was and by that time the train had started moving into the now well lighted station.

Thinking the train was ready to leave, I grabbed my coat, ran to the exit and jumped off the moving train. I landed only about ten yards from a uniformed guard of the railroad police. Even though I had committed no crime, my reaction was to run and that of course made me look suspicious. The guard blew the whistle. With the coat draped over my arm I rushed past surprised looking passengers, while I was now chased by at least three guards. After jumping the hedge again I dashed down the empty street and disappeared into the dark night. I didn't dare to go back, and maybe sit in the warm comfort of the now open waiting room. I just wandered through the cold night and waited for the first restaurant to open at eight in the morning.

For my return to Hamburg I took the bus, because I did not want to be seen at the railroad station. I guess there was still some of that old German respect for authority left in me.

S.S. "Carl Rehder," First Step to the World

The following day in Hamburg it was back to the seaman's hall again, waiting for the phone to ring, and the magic announcement that a ship was in need of a crew. For me that ship turned out to be another old steam ship the S.S. "Carl Rehder." At 1,200 tons it was still a small ship, even though it was bigger than the "Ludwig" and not quite as antique.

It was January 12th, 1949, when I signed on. A very cold and blistery day with temperatures below freezing. On my way to report to my new ship, I came past several big foreign vessels. It was like a child looking at displays of beautiful toy's at Christmas time. I could almost smell the fragrance of tropical flowers and feel the warm sand of far away beaches. How I envied those sailors on these beautiful ship's. If only I could sail on one of these big ships I would be in heaven.

After a while I had reached my destination. Here was reality for me. How small she looked against all those giants I had just passed. The "Carl Rehder" was loaded and ready to sail. Destination Gent-Belgium.

This was my first trip to a foreign country, and what an experience it was. The stores were loaded with all kinds of goods, many of them I had not seen for years. Especially tropical fruits like bananas, coconuts and oranges were still not available in German stores. There was coffee, real coffee that could be sold in Germany for a good price.

We received only a specified amount of foreign currency, so we had to shop for items that brought the biggest return back home.

Most of our crew had been in these countries like Holland, Belgium, France and England before. For me it was my first trip and I experienced for the first time the anti German hatred in these countries. I had read about it in German newspapers, but to experience it first hand was something new for me.

It started already when the longshoremen came on board to unload our cargo. Most of them would not even talk to us, and the ones that talked did it only to tell us what the Germans had done in their country during the war.

I could understand their anger, and I felt deeply ashamed of what my countrymen had done to them and their families, but I did not feel guilty. I was five years old when Hitler came to power, so I had evidently never voted for him. I had never killed anybody in my life and had never been in this country before. The only crime I had committed was that I was born in Germany. Here I was facing people I had never seen in my life and they were spitting at me because I spoke the German language.

We didn't even dare to leave the ship after dark, because the local bullies would have loved to beat us up. There was open season on Germans. The wounds were still too fresh, and many years would pass before people would believe that not all Germans were alike, and that not all Germans had committed those horrible crimes.

Our very next trip brought us to England, and I must say, I was very grateful for the fair treatment we received there. The British just treated us like everybody else. They did not single us out just to let us know what the Germans had done during the war. It was good to know that not the whole world was out to get even with a few poor German sailors for all the crimes that Hitler had committed.

My next trip to Sweden definitely brought back my belief in humanity. Here was a country untouched by war. No bombed out cities, no hostile people, I could hardly believe a country like this existed. Our first stop was the beautiful capital of Sweden, Stockholm.

It was a pleasure to walk through clean streets and look at well dressed and well fed people. The shop's were clean and well stocked, unfortunately our Swedish Kronas were in short supply.

From Stockholm we went deeper into the country to a little town named Sodertelje. I could have gone on forever cruising the beautiful fjords. Our bow carving through the calm, deep blue waters. Green forest all around us and a bright blue sky above. The town of Sodertelje was surrounded by forest and water, and even the girls seemed to be just a little prettier than in other places. For all of us it was a world of peace, a world most of us had never known, and we enjoyed every minute of it.

The "Carl Rehder" was to pick up a load of lumber, and the loading was going way too fast for our taste. We could have stayed forever. In all my travels in later years, I never had the good fortune to visit this charming little town again.

One member of our crew was a pig, a real pig. The crew had given her the name of Josephine, but she was actually the captain's pet.

Food was still scarce in Germany, especially meat, which was also very expensive. So the captain had decided that from our leftovers on board we could feed an additional mouth. This is how Josephine joined the crew.

In good weather her playground was the foredeck. Many of us were ready to throw her overboard, because we hated to clean up after her. But Josephine was pretty safe under the protection of her master, our captain. At night and during bad weather she was housed right behind the crew's quarters under the forecastle, in something that looked like a dog house with a door on it. The captain was real fond of her and their relationship was more like dog and master. When she was outside, he would come down from the bridge, pet her and talk to her. She would say "oink, oink" and our captain was a happy man.

On one of our next trips to the city of Malmo, Josephine's life almost came to a violent end.

It is required that crew members declare duty free merchandise like cigarettes, liquors etc. while entering a foreign port. A specified amount is allowed for personal consumption, while any excess is locked up under seal by custom agents. After the ship reaches international waters again, the seal may be broken and the goods returned to their owners. For most sailors however, the sale of these goodies is a source of extra income, and is therefore not declared. The only problem is, it has to be hidden from the custom agents.

Sailors have become very inventive over the years in the art of hiding it, but so have the custom agents in finding it or at least know where to look for it. On this particular trip we had been cleared in another Swedish port and never left Swedish waters. For one reason or another, customs agents had kept our ship under constant surveillance, preventing us from selling our goods.

Knowing that Malmo would be our next port of call, I had decided to play it safe and keep my cigarettes to be sold there. Two cartons were exposed openly in my bunk, and I did not think of the possibility that we might be searched again. It was my turn at the helm when we entered the port of Malmo. The harbor pilot standing in front of me giving instructions in rapid succession as we approached the pier. The lines went over and suddenly I recognized them, standing at the pier and waiting for us. The "black gang" we used to call them. Custom agents dressed in overalls, ready to search the ship.

"My cigarettes," the thought flashed through my mind in terror. I had to get off the bridge before the gangplank went over.

As soon as the ship was tied up I excused myself and raced down to get my cigarettes. I knew exactly where to go. There was no time to waste. Josephine's place was the nearest hide-a-way.

With so much commotion on deck nobody noticed me when I opened Josephine's parlor. She was all exited, because she expected to be taken outside. Today however I was sorry to disappoint her, but I needed her services to protect my contraband. Above the door I had placed a board that could only be seen when crawling all the way in. This place had served me well in the past, and I had no reason to believe they would find it this time.

I placed my two cartons on top of the board, pushed Josephine back and closed the door. What a relief...

The gang came on board, searched the whole ship and to the relief of all crew members found nothing. After the gang left, there was a lot of laughter and everybody was proud of having beaten them one more time. It was like a contest between sailors and custom agents. This time the sailors had won.

We didn't dare to get our goodies out of hiding immediately, because we still didn't trust them. Right after dinner I just had to look and see what Josephine was doing, and of course what my cigarettes were doing.

Josephine was very excited when I opened her door, but so was I when I recognized what she was eating. She was munching happily on my valuable contraband. It is unclear to me how she managed to get them down, or if they fell because of my haste, but there was nothing left except a few pieces of paper and cardboard. If it was not for the left-overs, I would have suspected somebody of stealing.

After recovering from my initial shock, I closed the door and fled like a criminal leaving the scene of a crime.

"She is going to drop dead at any moment," I thought, and if the captain finds out who did it he'll kill me.

That same night I went ashore with some of my buddies, but I was not in a mood for fun. All I could think of was Josephinc probably taking her last breath.

I went back to the ship early, telling the guys I didn't feel good. When I got back I came past Josephine's quarters, and not a sound could be heard. Well, at least she is out of her misery I thought. . . .

I didn't sleep at all that night. I was dreaming about the Russians chasing me and shooting at me, then all of a sudden Josephine came charging after me. I was glad when morning came and it was light again. My first trip was outside to see if someone had discovered the body yet.

To my surprise I heard "oink oink" coming from Josephine's place. Josephine was as alive as I had ever seen her, but I still did no trust the situation. Maybe she would die later.

When Josephine was still alive two weeks later, and the captain even mentioned how happy and full of energy she was, I could not keep it to myself any longer. I told the story and even had the nerve to ask the captain to replace my two cartons of cigarettes. That request was denied, but they all got a good laugh out of it. Two cartons of cigarettes doesn't seem like much today, but at that time I considered it a major economic disaster. As much as I still hated to clean up after Josephine, deep down I was glad she had survived.

The next time on our way from England to Sweden we took the shorter course through the Kiel Canal again. As we approached the mouth of the river Elbe, we came upon a strange looking scene. It looked as if the whole sea was covered with crates or cases. As we came closer, we discovered that we were looking at hundreds of cases of oranges floating all around us.

Since we were still fighting the outgoing tide, the captain was not in a hurry and allowed us to pick up what we could get. After picking up about fifty cases, we started moving again and soon afterward we picked up our pilot to enter the canal. The pilot was not aware of any recent shipwreck and had no explanation for the oranges.

We divided our find into equal parts among the crew of eighteen and everybody was happy. The taste was still good, so they could not have been in the water for a long time.

We had to take on coal at the canal station in Kiel, and that meant we would stay the night in Kiel. It was also Sunday, and as soon as we could get cleaned up and dressed, a group of six of us went to a local dance hall. Not even an hour had passed and the whole dance hall had heard the story of our oranges. People came over to our table and asked us if we would be willing to sell. A taxi was ordered, and I went with another member of our crew to get a load of the precious fruit. Each one of us donated one case and as soon as we got back the party really started.

Oranges were still a rare and expensive luxury in Germany and for us it meant free drinks for oranges. Even the taxi driver got paid in oranges. But what started out as a good idea, turned into a wild party. Alcohol and oranges were not a good mix as people started throwing orange peels at each other, and waiters started slipping on orange peels. The end result was that we were told very politely to leave the establishment or else. We had enough of this party anyway, and preferred to spend the rest of the night in our own bunk instead of the local police station. We still had enough oranges left to pay for our return trip. By taxi of course.

After taking on a load of coal and other supplies the next morning, the "Carl Rehder" left Kiel on it's way to Sweden again.

In a way I was happy on board of this ship. I had made

many friends among the crew members, and the captain was a quiet and friendly man. There was one man however I could not get along with. That man was our first officer. A miserable old grouch, and what made matters worse was that I found myself on his watch.

Our admiration was mutual. I didn't like him, and he didn't like me. There was no specific incident that may have caused our hostility, he just did not like younger people and I didn't like an old grouch. The problem for me was that he was my immediate superior and he made life miserable for me wherever he could. I could always be sure to get the worst job on his watch. When I was at the helm, he would find some fault no matter how straight I was on course.

Things finally came to a clash in our last port in Sweden. It was a nice, warm day, and we took advantage of the weather to get some painting done. I was sitting high up in a bosun's chair, painting the mast, when down on deck the first officer appeared. He was accompanied by an executive of the shipping line.

What had always annoyed me about the first mate was that he would hardly ever talk directly to me. He would make his nasty remarks to a third person. Also, he would not call me by my name, but would call me "Langer," which in German means long one or tall one.

Coming from anybody else this would normally not bother me, but constantly coming from him was getting under my skin.

Since he was fat and short I had decided some time ago, that one of these days I was going to let him have it. That day had finally come.

He was showing off in front of the executive and in the process making some remark about me and the younger generation in general. Then, in order to get my attention he called "Langer."

I completely ignored him so he called again, this time louder. Again I could not hear him. By now it was obvious to him that I was ignoring him and his name calling was getting worse. He even added a few more names to his list. The temptation was great to drop the can of paint on his head, but I kept my cool. Very slowly I secured my paint brush and can, and then proceeded to lower myself to the deck. I stood about five inches from him, nose to nose.

"Mister" I said, "I have a name like you and everybody else, and you know damn well what it is. If you call me Langer only one more time, I'll call you Fatso."

His face turned purple, but he was so stunned that he remained silent.

I turned, climbed back up the mast and continued my job.

From that moment on our relationship was soured forever. We barely spoke to each other, but the name Langer never crossed his lips again.

I was ready to quit anyway, and as we reached the Kiel canal again I signed off. I wanted to get on a foreign ship and this was the place to do it.

"Mary Stone"— Short Lived Happiness

The canal locks on the Baltic side are located at Holtenau, a suburb of Kiel. Since many ships of all nationalities cross the canal every day, there was always a chance to get hired on a ship with a shortage of crew. Some German sailors got lucky and received permission to hire on a foreign vessel. A German sailor was only allowed to sign on with a permit issued by the British military government.

I was glad to find a place to stay at the local seamen's home which was organized and managed by the Lutheran Church. It was a nice and clean house with room for about twenty sailors.

Every day I went down to the canal, sitting at the hiring office and listening to the tall tales of the older sailors. In June of 1949 the Danish steamship "Mary Stone" entered the locks at Holtenau on its trip to Scotland. She had requested a decks hand, and since I was the next in line, here was my big chance.

The British officer issuing the permit made it clear to me and the captain that this permit was only good for one trip. He told the captain that on his return to Denmark he would have to hire local crew and that I was to be dropped again in a German port.

Captain Christensen was a charming man. From the first day I felt at home with him and his crew of nineteen. The captain and many of the crew members spoke German, so there was no problem in communication. I shared a cabin with Erik, our eighteen year old deck boy, and we became immediate friends. With Erik's enthusiastic support I began learning the Danish language. First things on the list was how to talk and what to say to the girls.

The North Sea was smooth as glass like I had never seen it before. The sun was still shining as we entered the Firth of

Forth, sailed past Edinburgh and tied up at the little town of Grangemouth.

Our return trip took us back to Denmark, where Erik made sure that I was introduced to all of his girlfriends. The better I felt about this ship and my new friends, the more I was worried about losing it again.

Captain Christensen assured me that he was not even going to try finding a replacement for me.

"I'll just tell the British I could not find a Danish sailor for this job," he said.

Captain Christensen kept his word as we entered the canal gates again at Holtenau, but so did the British officer in charge. The captain did everything in his power to keep me on board, but to no avail. The British officer insisted I sign off, and the "Mary Stone" had to sail on without me.

I was so mad, and I could have cried at the same time as I stood at dockside, waving good-bye to the slowly disappearing ship and it's crew. I was mad at the British and their stupid regulations, and the temptation was great to throw a few rocks at their headquarters. Only the realization that one day I would need another stamp from them, made me give up those plans.

Being unemployed is a depressing experience, but it is definitely more pleasant to be unemployed in the summertime than looking for work in the cold of winter. There was such a feeling of loneliness when those icy north eastern winds swept across the country. When I was frozen stiff and didn't know where the next meal was coming from, that's when I really felt homeless. In summer the world looked different. As long as the sky was blue and the air was warm I felt more optimistic about my future. If I didn't have a place to sleep, a park bench would do. But again I found a place at the local seaman's home, sparing me the discomfort of having to sleep on a park bench. I had also saved some money and was confident I could wait for a ship, determined it was going to be a foreign vessel again.

Shortly after I was forced to leave the "Mary Stone," the British turned control over to German authorities and it was now possible to hire on for an undetermined time. Unfortunately it was too late to help my cause, as I was convinced that I would still be sailing on the "Mary Stone." This was probably the first time I enjoyed being unemployed. Of course there was the uncertainty of not knowing when the next job would come along, but I enjoyed the warm summer days, and I enjoyed meeting new friends at the seaman's home.

One day, while watching the ship traffic at the canal I came up with a brilliant idea. What if I just walked onto one of those big foreign ships while they tied up inside the locks? It would be just a matter of hiding on the ship until it reached international waters again. The more I thought about it the more I became convinced it would work. The ship movements were posted in the shipping agents office at the canal. It listed the ship's name, its nationality, its last port of call and its final destination. To me it was like going to the local travel agency and study the offers. The canal locks itself were considered a duty free zone which was controlled by custom agents. This posed no serious problem for me. I had always used the canal locks as a shortcut to cross the canal instead of using the ferry, or the even more distant bridge.

As I watched the activities at the canal, my plan began to take shape. The trouble was that a few days before I was going to convert my plan into reality, I took part in a practical joke that would have an effect on the final outcome of my adventure.

One day, while down at the pier, I met a few friends. We came across a little coastal freighter that was tied up at the pier for some minor repairs. My friend Gerd was acquainted with one of the crew members. This fellow was standing on top of the gangway and was busy chatting with us, when I noticed this custom agent about 100 feet away, watching us intensely. "Don't look now," I said to my friends, "but the law is watching us."

Anybody who knows the relationship between custom agents and sailors, will understand the temptation of the moment. Here was an opportunity to win a round for the sailors.

Without anyone turning around we discussed our plan of action. This friend on the ship was to get an empty cigarette carton and throw it down to us at the pier. Then all we had to do was wait and see if the agent would take the bait.

Our friend disappeared and after a short time came back with a carton of cigarettes. Empty of course. He looks around very suspiciously and then tosses the carton down to us. My buddy Gerd grabs it and quickly pushes it under his shirt.

It works. Our Custom agent is there in a minute as expected. "What did you just get from the man on deck?" he wants to know.

"What are you talking about?" says Gerd.

"Come on, I saw it," insists the agent.

"You saw what?" comes the question back.

This confrontation continues for about five minutes, until our agent is about ready to take us all in for smuggling and obstructing justice. Finally Gerd reaches into his shirt and pulls out the empty carton.

"Is this what you want?" he asked the agent.

His voice was pure innocence.

Everybody around is in stitches, except the agent. He doesn't think this is funny at all, but what can he do? We have not broken any law.

This little episode should come back to haunt me a few days later, as the final stage of my operation "Stow Away" unfolds.

On the listing I had spotted the right ship. A 9,000 ton freighter, sailing under the flag of Uruguay, coming from Finland with its final destination Montevideo.

South America was my goal, and I was ready to give it a try.

My friend Gerd was the only one who knew about my plan. I went over the last details with him, and I instructed him where to send my belongings after I was gone for three days. There was no way I could board a ship under these circumstances with a suitcase under my arm. I could take only the most essential items with me.

The next day I was ready. By calling the shipping agent's office, I found out the expected time of arrival at the canal. From a window at the seaman's home I was able to see the ship approach the canal gate, and by the time he tied up inside the lock, I was there.

Standing in the background I kept my eyes on the custom

agents. When I saw two men from the shipping agents office approach the gangway I fell right in step with them. Nobody would have guessed I didn't belong there, because I was dressed exactly like them. I was wearing a business suit, a tie, and an attache case under my arm, containing a few basic necessities. It seemed to be the easiest thing in the world. The custom agent near the gangway was just turned around, talking to someone next to him. A few steps and I was on deck, still following the two guys from the office. As they started climbing up to the bridge, I turned and entered the midships section between what I thought to be the officers quarters.

I couldn't believe it was that easy. While still looking around for my first place to hide, I heard steps behind me and then a voice in German.

''Hey you, wait a minute.''

I turned slowly. The voice had not been familiar, but the face certainly was. I was looking at ''my old friend'' from the pier.

''What are we doing here?'' he wanted to know. Now it was his turn to have that dirty smile on his face, while his voice was as sweet as honey.

My story about visiting the second officer didn't hold up very long. I didn't even know the guy's name. Besides, he wasn't even interested if my story was true or not. I did not have a pass, and the ship was off limits.

He asked me to follow him to the customs office, and after inspecting my attache case it was probably clear to him what my intentions were. Since I could not be accused of smuggling, he just took me to the gate and told me to get lost. I didn't like that smile on his face, but I knew what it meant. It meant we were even, and I had made his day. To this day, I don't know where he came from and for how long he had been watching me. I had never seen him near the ship, but I was convinced that I had paid a high price for our harmless little joke at the pier.

S.S. "Ketty"—Ship of Fate

On September 13, 1949 "Ketty" entered my life. S.S. "Ketty" was a 1,300 ton Swedish steamship, entering the canal on its trip to Rotterdam. She was under the command of captain Strindin and had a mixed crew of Swedes, Finns and two Germans. Our chief engineer was German, and so was one of his machinist. The Ketty also had one thing in common with all my previous ships, she was old.

I was assigned to the 8-12 watch, and my companion was a fifty year old Swede by the name of Olsen. All of us called him Ole for short.

Life on board was easy going, and at first everything looked very harmonious to me. However, very soon I discovered that alcohol was the big problem. I knew that Scandinavians in general like to drink, but I never realized how deep rooted this problem was. The Swedes had even issued a motbook to all citizens over the age of eighteen. Once a month a person could purchase one quart of alcohol at a government owned liquor store, with the purchase being entered into the motbook. Ole, my watch companion, would not rest until I applied for a motbook at the next Swedish port.

"There is no use in wasting the good liquid," he insisted.

We had barely entered a port and secured the ship, when the crew was gone. At first I went along like a good sport, but soon I found excuses not to go. I didn't mind a party and a few drinks here and there, but this was too much for me. These guys were not interested in girls, dancing and just plain having a good time. These guys were just interested in getting smashed. Many times they had to be bailed out of the police station the next morning.

The biggest problem though was the captain himself. Captain Strindin was a jovial heavy set man, very pleasant to be around when he was sober. That was only on rare occasions, because most of the time he was drunk. He also had a relationship with our cook. That's not to say that our captain was gay, but our cook was a female by the name of Anna. She was a fine cook when she took the time, but she spent so much time with the captain that our menu began to suffer. There was one more female member of the crew, a combination kitchen helper-stewardess. She spent most of her time being jealous of Anna.

Around mid October the Ketty was coming from the northern Swedish city of Sundsvall with a load of lumber destined for Liverpool. The captain had been drinking ever since we left Sundsvall and we were just passing the Swedish isle of Gotland. A strong wind was blowing and steadily increasing.

The captain, whose cabin was in the stern section, staggered across the high decks load of lumber to get to the bridge. He remained there for only a few minutes, but by now it was dark when he returned to his cabin. He was about halfway across, when the Ketty lifted her bow, leaned heavy to starboard and came crashing down again. The first officer on the bridge, whose eyes had followed the captain, saw him disappear.

The alarm "Man over board" was sounded.

The idea of bringing a lifeboat to water in the dark of the night, under these stormy conditions had everybody scared. We knew very well that more life could be lost out there, while trying to save someone that was probably lost anyway.

A floodlight from the bridge was skimming the stormy sea. There was no sign of our captain.

The Ketty was now stopped and rolling in the heavy seas. The lifeboat was about ready to be launched when somebody screamed, "Here he is."

They had found him, not in the water, but between the winches on deck. He had fallen between the stacks of lumber, not over board as first believed.

Everybody was relieved that we didn't have to launch our boat, but the crew was ready to hang the captain. The old saying, that nothing happens to drunks and children held up again. He had passed out, but besides a little bump on his head he had suffered no major injury.

When the Ketty entered the Kiel canal after two more stormy days in the Baltic, the captian was sober. The ship was listing slighty to the port side, but all of us were glad to reach the calm waters of the canal. The Ketty was still listing to the port side as we entered the North Sea at Elbe I. Storm warnings were posted. For the North Sea it was the beginning of the winter season and storms at this time of the year were normal.

As we steamed down the German coast toward the English channel our little storm was getting nasty. Captain Strindin was spending more time on the bridge, and he even appeared to be sober.

On the morning of October 22nd we had reached the Dutch coast and the wind was now blowing at hurricane force. When I took my last turn at the helm at 11 a.m. the foredeck was beginning to look like a battlefield. We were beginning to loose part of our decks load. The Ketty was now listing to starboard, a fact nobody had noticed at first. Since she was rolling in heavy seas we had not paid any attention, but now there was no doubt. The ship also felt stiffer and was hard to keep on course. She would not roll as much as before, but just sit in the water like a rock and take a beating.

When my watch was over at noon, the whole crew was at midships. Nobody would dare to cross the fore deck any longer. The captain had discussed the possibility of severing the heavy cables and release the decks-load, but it was too late for that now. It would have been suicide. Whoever would have done it, would have gone overboard with it. The best we could hope for now, was that the storm would blow itself out, but so far there was no sign of it.

When I returned to the bridge at 8 p.m. the Ketty was leaning even farther toward starboard. I was beginning to fear she would capsize at any moment, and in a way I was glad we still had our cargo of lumber. Maybe it would help us to stay afloat, and maybe it did.

When our watch was over at midnight the situation looked hopeless. The Ketty was now crippled and did not respond to the rudder any longer. Shortly afterwards the engine room had to be abandoned.

The first officer had been trying to make radio contact

without any success. Before the radio went dead, we had picked up several distress calls from other ships, but we could not even think of helping anyone else. We had enough trouble of our own. The only thing left to do was shooting flares, and as they illuminated the stormy night it made our situation look even more hopeless. I didn't think our location was more than ten miles from the Dutch coast, but we seemed to be the only people on earth. All of our flares had been fired without any response from anywhere. How much longer could we stay afloat, that was the big question.

The whole crew was huddled at midships, about the only dry spot left on the ship. It was extremely difficult to keep our footing on the slanted deck.

The morning of Sunday, October 23rd dawned, and with the first daylight came relief and new hope. The storm was calming down, and to our biggest surprise we found ourselves only about three or four miles from the coastline. Not only the coastline, but right off the city of Ijmuiden, the entry to the canal leading to Amsterdam.

It still took almost an hour before we saw two tugs steaming in our direction. Just like the cavalry riding to the rescue with only minutes to spare. The Ketty was now hanging deeper and deeper in the water.

The first mate asked me and Ole to come to the forecastle with him to secure the lines from the tugboats. It was hard to keep our equilibrium as we struggled across the fore deck, but eventually we got the line across. I am sure every man of the crew felt a little better at this moment. We were not alone out there any more.

The biggest concern for the captains of the tugboats was to bring the Ketty into the port of Ijmuiden. If she would sink now, she could very well block the entry to the canal leading to Amsterdam. This could develop into a disaster for international shipping. The second tug had quite a job in pulling our stern around as we just barely came clear of the breakwater on our starboard side. Once inside the port a coast guard cutter came alongside to pick up the crew from midships, and we couldn't believe our eyes as we found ourselves surrounded by boats with newsreel cameras and reporters.

Everything came to a climax now. The Ketty was sinking

"Ketty" takes it on the chin.

Foto toont de Neeltje Jacoba, die steeds in de buurt was gebleven, terwijl een gedeelte der Zweedse bemanning haar schip verlaat. Even nadat deze foto was genomen, verdween het achterschip onder water

Photo shows the "Neeltje Jacoba" standing by while part of the crew is leaving the ship. Shortly after photo was taken, the stern disappears under water.

LANGZAAM VERDWIJNT HET ACH TERSCHIP van de onfortuinlijk Zweedse houtboot „Ketty" onder wate

fast. The tugboat captains recognized the danger and started pulling full speed to the port side. They were just able to get us out of the main shipping channel when our stern went under. The three of us had remained on the forecastle, but now there was so much stress on the mainstay of the mast, that things began to pop. We could not stay any longer without getting hurt. All three of us jumped and got picked up by the cutter immediately. Two minutes later the Ketty was down. Only the bridge and mast was above the waterline, because the water was not very deep.

Our next surprise came when we approached the pier. Several hundred if not thousands of people were lining the pier, as it finally dawned on us that we were the main attraction.

We were taken to the local hotel "Augusta" for our first meal in a long time, and especially a well deserved rest for all. I was extremely tired, but I could not sleep. My bed was still heaving and rolling and I had the feeling I was falling out. I must have opened my eyes every five minutes to assure myself I was on land, and I was safe, even though the storm was still howling in my ears.

The following day the crew was taken to Amsterdam to stay at the International Seaman's Home. Reporters were still following us to get the stories of our stormy adventure, but the strangest feeling was seeing the last moments of the Ketty on the newsreel. During our ordeal it had never occurred to me that we might not survive. For the ship itself I would not have bet a nickel, but somehow it never crossed

Gisteren is een drijvende bok begonnen de in de bergingshaven van IJmuiden aan de grond gezette Zweedse houtboot „Ketty" te lichten en leeg te pompen. Zoals men weet raakte dit schip onlangs in moeilijkheden toen het door een Zuidwesterstorm overvallen werd en de deklast in beweging kwam. De kabels van de drijvende bok hebben inmiddels hun werk gedaan; vanmorgen was de Ketty gelicht en na te zijn leeggepompt heeft 't schip de ankers gelicht. Het wordt nu opgesleept naar Amsterdam

Clipping from Dutch newspaper. English translation: Work has started yesterday in Ijmuiden to raise the sunken Swedish lumber carrier "Ketty." The ship got into trouble recently, when its deckload shifted during a fierce southwest storm. The cables of the floating crane have done their job, as the "Ketty" has been lifted and pumped dry. She will now be towed to Amsterdam.

Neue Sturmwarnung für die Nordsee

Schiffsuntergänge — SOS-Rufe

Eigene Berichte

gkl. **Hamburg, 24. Oktober**

Weite Gebiete der Nordsee werden seit dem Wochenende von Stürmen heimgesucht, die im Höhepunkt, in den Regenböen fast Orkancharakter angenommen hatten. Leider hat das Unwetter eine Reihe von Unfällen verursacht. Große ausländische Dampfer mußten Schutz unter der Küste suchen. Ein 5000 t großer Engländer befand sich, während diese Zeilen in Druck gegeben wurden, in der Nähe von Norderney in Seenot. Mehrere Küstenfahrzeuge sind untergegangen. Soweit bisher zu übersehen war, hat der Sturm aber keine Menschenleben gefordert. Mit ungebrochener Kraft rast das Unwetter, das nach dem Wetterdienst erst gegen Abend schwächer werden soll, zwischen England und dem Süden der skandanivischen Gewässer.

Bei dem rapide fallenden Barometer war zum Wochenende nichts anderes zu erwarten: Sturm, der in Böen Windstärke zehn erreichte. Am Sonntag begann er sein Unwesen und erreichte in den Mittagsstunden des Montags seinen Höhepunkt. Sein Operationsgebiet erstreckt sich von Irland bis in die skandinavischen Gewässer. Die Nordsee wurde besonders heimgesucht. Der Schaden ist bedeutend größer, soweit es bisher übersehen werden kann, als man nach der Stärke des Sturms vermuten konnte. Nach Mitternacht wurde eine Reihe von SOS-Rufen gehört. Die Namen aller in Seenot befindlichen Schiffe sind noch nicht bekannt. Es ist zu hoffen, daß die Schiffe, die Seenotzeichen gegeben haben, Nothäfen haben anlaufen können.

Kennzeichnend für die schwere See, die der Sturm aufgewühlt hat, ist der Fall des 5000 t großen englischen Dampfers „Trevaylor" (Reederei Hain & Co in London), der nach Hamburg bestimmt ist. Das Schiff gab heute früh SOS-Rufe. Es hat in der Umgebung von Helgoland Maschinenschaden erlitten und treibt in der hohen See. Bergungsschlepper der Fairplay sind ausgelaufen und gegen mittag wieder zurückgekehrt, da der Dampfer mit eigener Kraft den Hafen erreichen will.

Der Schiffsmeldedienst teilt mit, daß das Küstenmotorschiff „Gisela", in Ütersen beheimatet, bei Norder Till gesunken ist. Über das Schicksal der Besatzung liegen noch keine Meldungen vor.

Der 1138 t große schwedische Dampfer „Ketty", der eine Deckslast Holz hatte, ist ebenfalls in der schweren See gesunken, wahrscheinlich gekentert. Bevor es gelungen war, die Verbände zu kappen, die die Deckslast hielten, kam diese ins Rutschen. Die Besatzung wurde gerettet.

Ein Schiffsunglück, das offenbar nicht auf die Rechnung des Sturm zu stellen ist, ist der Untergang des holländischen Küstenmotorschiffes „Kasana". Es ist auf der Reise von Kopenhagen nach Aarhus auf eine Mine gelaufen und untergegangen. Die Besatzung wurde auf der Insel Fünen in Sicherheit gebracht.

Der ausgehende Schiffsverkehr, auch für größere Schiffe, liegt brach. Viele Schiffe sind vor Anker gegangen, um ruhiges Wetter abzuwarten.

Der Wetterdienst teilte heute früh mit: Ein Sturmtief ist am Sonntag südlich von Irland entstanden. Es hat jetzt Nordjütland erreicht. Der Südweststurm ist in acht bis zehn Windstärken aufgetreten. Er wird heute mittag bei rechtsdrehender Tendenz seinen Höhepunkt erreicht haben. Der Nordatlantik ist durch das Unwetter verschont geblieben.

Eine neue Sturmwarnung ist heute mittag bekanntgegeben worden: „Der Südweststurm, der in den Mittagsstunden des Montags seinen Höhepunkt erreicht haben sollte, wird wieder auffrischen und aus Südwestrichtung wieder Windstärke 10 erreichen. Erst in der Nacht rechnet man mit einem Abflauen.

Gespräch mit „Elbe I"

Kapitän Clausen, der Führer des Feuerschiffes „Elbe I", mit dem wir heute morgen ein Seefunkgespräch führten, teilte uns mit, daß noch immer zehn Windstärken und in Böen darüber gemessen wurden. Um zehn Uhr war der Wind noch nicht abgeflaut. Die See ist 3,50 m hoch, was für die Nordsee bei dem verhältnismäßig niedrigen Wasser schweren Seegang bedeutet. „Elbe I" liegt mit dem Kopf auf die See. Das Schiff bewährt sich sehr gut, es nimmt kaum Wasser über. Der Lotsendampfer hält sich zwischen den Feuerschiffen „Elbe II" und „Elbe III" auf. Schiffe, die einen Lotsen brauchen, werden noch immer bedient. Das spricht dafür, daß die Lotsen ihren schweren Dienst auch in dieser Wetterlage ohne Rücksicht auf die Gefahr, versehen.

Springflut in England

Von unserer Londoner Redaktion

Rh. **London, 24.** Oktober

Einer der schwersten Herbststürme die je über England und den Ärmelkanal hinweggebraust sind, hat Wolkenbrüche von fast tropischem Charakter und eine Springflut an der Küste, wie sie bisher [illegible] selten hier erlebt worden ist, mit sich gebracht. Deiche sind an einigen Stellen des Landes gebrochen. Das Wasser hat Häuser und Land überflutet sowie Straßen überschwemm' Sechs Deichbrüche werden aus der Näh von Folkestone gemeldet. Schwe Regengüsse in London haben Straß und Keller unter Wasser gesetzt.

Headline from a German newspaper. New storm warnings for the North Sea. Ships sinking—S O S calls. The 1138 t Swedish steamer "Ketty," loaded with a cargo of lumber, was also lost in the heavy seas. She apparently capsized before the crew was able to sever the lines and prevent the deckload from shifting. The crew was saved.

my mind that I would not make it out alive.

Since all of our possessions rested with the Ketty at the bottom of Ijmuiden harbor, the crew had to go shopping for new clothing in Amsterdam. We looked like a bunch of bums from skid row as we entered the stores. Word spread that here was the crew of the Ketty, the ship that most of them had seen in the headlines of the local papers and on the newsreel. At first it felt good to be recognized as a hero, but after a while it became a nuisance to tell the same story over and over again. How can you tell anyone what it was like out there, especially people who had never been at sea. After a few days of rest, things began to happen again. There was an inquiry held, to determine the cause of the Ketty's sinking. Then it was time to say good-bye to the shipmates who were going home.

Captain Strindin, knowing I had no place to go, had offered me to stay on. I gladly accepted.

Salvage operations had already started to raise the Ketty, and by mid November she entered dry dock in Amsterdam. Our chief engineer and the other German crew member from the engine room also remained in Amsterdam. During the month of November we enjoyed a well deserved vacation, and by mid December we could move on board again. Since the ship itself was still in the hands of the shipyard, there was nothing else for me to do, so my official job was that of a watchman.

Christmas 1949 in Amsterdam was a lonely holiday for me, and so was New Years Eve. The captain had gone home and so had the chief and the other German fellow, because their home was in West Germany. I was glad, when it was all over and normal activities resumed.

By mid January of 1950 a crew was hired and the Ketty was ready to sail again. This time our crew of nineteen was even more mixed than before. The "Ketty" was taken out in the port of Amsterdam for a trial run, and everything seemed to check out as expected.

With what was left of our cargo we entered the canal to Ijmuiden, and as we entered the locks to the canal, the first sign of trouble again. I was at my station on the forecastle and had just gotten the spring line across. From the bridge I could hear the engine telegraph ringing and I expected the engine to go in reverse, but nothing happened. The Ketty was still moving at considerable speed toward the gate. Still no sound from the engine room, but now cursing and screaming from the bridge.

"Get the line across," came the command from the bridge.

"Line is across," I shouted back.

"Hold on," it came back from the bridge, and I put one turn around the bollard.

The ship was still moving too fast as the heavy steel cable was beginning to burn the inside of my leather gloves.

"Hold the line," screamed the captain.

This was crazy. I could not hold the heavy ship with one line, but obediently I put another turn over.

That was too much. Before I could even move, the line snapped and the heavy steel cable whistled around my ears, missing me by only inches.

The Ketty still bumped into the gate, but it was not hard enough to do any serious damage. It meant however another day in Ijmuiden, with engineers from the shipyard trying to find what went wrong. Finally the Ketty was ready to sail for her ultimate destination, and with no more surprises we reached the port of Liverpool.

Our next port of call was the little town of Fowey. Located in Cornwall, at the end of the English channel, it is one of my favorite places in all of England. The land and it's people have been immortalized in the many classics written by Daphne Du Maurier, the famous writer who lives in this part of the country. Books like *Rebecca, Frenchmans Creek* and others make the land come alive with adventures. I was fortunate to receive an autographed copy of *Frenchmans Creek,* but sadly enough I did not enjoy it for very long.

Our cargo was china clay and it's destination was the Swedish port city of Goteborg. The weather in Cornwall was beautiful, considering it was the end of January. Even as we left the port of Fowey and entered the English channel, the wind was moderate. This was not to last for long, because as we came to the end of the channel the wind started picking up by the hour. Our course was set to the northern point of Denmark, which was also shorter than going through the Kiel canal. If this storm was getting any stronger, it was also safer to go through the open North Sea and stay away from the dangerous German coastal waters.

For two days we battled an ever increasing storm. Weather conditions had deteriorated even more and snow was beginning to fall. Tons of water tore across our ice crusted decks. On the morning of February 1, we discovered to our dismay that our radio directional finder was defective. Without it we could not take a bearing and determine our position in this and turbulent environment.

The "Ketty," also without radar, was stumbling blindfolded through the North Sea. Water and sky seemed to be fused into one gray mass. Because the storm was now blowing with such intensity, we were forced to go at slow speed. There was no way of telling how far we were blown off course. Visibility was down to about zero. From the bridge we could barely recognize any details of the deck in front of us. The lookout was pressing his nose against the enclosure of the bridge, trying to spot anything outside. There was no use in keeping the man outside. With the storm blowing snow in his face at 60 knots an hour, his visibility was even worse than in the protection of the bridge. "If that damn customs agent had not caught me on that ship in the Kiel canal I could have been in Montevideo today," I thought, and I hated the guy even more for spoiling my chances. I was sure he would smile, if he could see me here in the middle of nowhere, being kicked around like an empty beer can. It was now eleven p.m.and I was on my night watch till midnight. My thoughts drifted back and forth between reality and dream land as I stood behind the wheel, digging in my heels to keep my balance. I was dead tired and under normal weather condition I'm sure I would have fallen asleep as I had once before. It always had a hypnotizing effect on me, to stand at night on a darkened bridge, look into a dimly lit compass housing, and try to keep two little black marks lined up. The only sound would be the monotonous sound from the engine and a slight vibration under my feet. Well, I was hardly in danger of falling asleep as the howling of the storm alone kept me awake. I was glad when I could turn the helm over to the next watch at midnight.

Most of the crew slept on the deck of the midship mess room. All I could think of was getting to the forecastle and to my bunk. I just had to try it.

Counting the seconds from one wave to the next, I became convinced I could make it without taking a bath at the same time. I told the guys on the bridge to look out for me, just in case.

They thought I was crazy.

If my attempt had failed, I would have been washed overboard and nobody would have been able to help. But again I was lucky, as I reached my goal with hardly a second to spare.

Although the feeling was that of riding on a roller coaster, I was asleep in a matter of minutes. I had only taken off my heavy coat and my boots, otherwise I did not dare to undress. Being over six foot tall was to my advantage, because my body matched the length of my bunk, and there was less of a chance to be thrown out. The constant rattle of the anchor chain was the last sound I heard before stepping into dream land.

I was awakened by a tremendous jolt. My head was pressed against the headboard of my bunk. For a moment it felt as if the ship was held by a giant hand, than a scraping noise and movement again. After a short while a second jolt that hit at the moment I was trying to get into my boots. Loosing my balance I went down hard, hitting my head against a built-in bench. I was the only one in the cabin, and now I was getting the feeling of being the only one left on the ship. It was quite a relief, when I opened the hatch and saw light on the bridge. My next problem was getting midship. There was no doubt that the "Ketty" had run aground, and was now taking a terrible pounding from the surf. She appeared to be sitting solid on the bottom, but I could still feel the foredeck move when the big breakers came rolling in. The vessel was moaning and groaning under the stress. I knew I had to get to the bridge as soon as possible, before the ship would break up.

Timing my move, I jumped into the runoff from a wave,

knowing I had only seconds before the next one would hit. I could stretch enough to reach for the handrail to the upper deck, when the next wave rolled over me. It took all my strength to hang on. A few more steps and I was safe, at least for the moment.

The bridge was probably the only dry spot left at this time, and the whole crew was taking refuge here. The first mate tried again to establish some radio contact with the outside world, but all we could hear was static. Only for a very brief moment did he make contact with a German station. After that it was more static and soon the radio was silent. We could not see any shoreline. Snow was still falling and visibility remained poor.

At about nine a.m. we saw the dark shadow of what looked like a salvage tug coming up behind us. We watched intensely for about fifteen minutes, wondering why he did not come any closer. Our hopes faded when we saw him disappear again. The surf was beginning to take its toll. There was not a dry spot left on the ship, as the waves were beginning to dismantle the bridge. It was almost ten a.m. when we could make out the shoreline at about two hundred yards.

All of a sudden we discovered an open cutter approaching from the north. For the next twenty minutes we watched in awe the most skillful maneuvering any one of us had ever seen. I was so fascinated and concerned about their survival, that I forgot completely the danger I was in myself.

The cutter had to come close enough to shoot a line across, while at the same time stay far enough so it would not be smashed against the "Ketty." At times he would be towering high above us, and only seconds later we would be looking down on him.

The first rocket with a line attached soared overhead and got hung up in our rigging. We could not reach it. The second one we managed to haul in and soon we had a line established between us. It was now up to the cutter to keep at a safe distance and also try to keep the line tight. Attached to the line was a block and something that looked like a bosun's chair. There was no time to loose. One by one the crew was hauled over to the cutter. The water felt almost warm when I jumped.

Once the last man was hauled over, the boat with it's human cargo returned to the pier of a little fishing village. The whole population was assembled in spite of the bitter cold. One by one we were taken quickly to their homes. We had to get out of our wet and frozen clothing as fast as possible. I had hardly any feeling left in my arms and legs. Like a robot I followed one of the fishermen to his home. After a hot bath and a rub down to get my circulation going, it was off to bed. As soon as I got warm again, I fell into a deep sleep which lasted until the next morning.

My good samaritans introduced themselves as the Madsen family and the name of the village was Thorsminde. We had run aground in the northern part of the Danish west coast

My biggest problem was the circulation in my feet, otherwise I felt fine. After a hardy breakfast I could not stand it any longer. With my host I went down the main street of the village to find out what had happened to my shipmates. The fishermen of the village could not leave port in this kind of weather, so most of us spent the day visiting each other. Of the crew of nineteen only three were taken to a hospital in Esbjerg, the nearest city of any size. None of them was in any serious condition. The rest of the crew recovered quickly and soon we were celebrating our survival.

On this day we also found out how much we had to be thankful for, and how much reason we had to celebrate. While talking to our brave rescuers, we heard the full story of our rescue for the first time. And what a story it was.

The German radio station we had been in contact with for a short time, was apparently able to get an approximate fix on our position. They immediately contacted radio Esbjerg to send out an alert for a ship in trouble in their area. A salvage tug left port to check out the coast up north. This was the same vessel we had seen as a dark shadow behind us. Now we found out the shocking reason, why he did not come to our rescue. They had expected us to blow up at any moment. They knew something we didn't know at the time, because we didn't know our position.

The Germans had installed mine fields to protect against

possible Allied landings during WW II. The fields had never been cleared, but the fishermen knew about them, and it was marked on all charts. It made my hair stand up, just thinking about it. The "Ketty" had crossed over five belts without hitting one and blowing us all sky high. A Danish newspaper called it a miracle and was showing a detailed drawing of our position and the mine fields.

While all this was going on, a bus was leaving early in the morning from our village of Thorsminde. Destination was the city of Esbjerg, about thirty miles to the south. The road follows along the coastline behind the dunes.

Barely out of the village, one of the passengers, a fisherman from Thorsminde, motioned the driver to stop. He thought he had seen the dark shadows of a ship. The few people on the bus would not believe him, but everybody went out looking.

"There it is again," screamed one of them.

The bus returned immediately to the village and sounded the alarm. The lifeboat stationed there for this purpose was under cover on a slip. Ice had to be broken before the boat could be launched, and that took more valuable time. Then the MB 22 under the skillful hand of Victor Jensen and two more experienced fishermen was off to the rescue. The rest of the story we had witnessed with our own eyes.

The fishermen take pride in manning the rescue boat, and only the most experienced men will be allowed on a mission like this one. I could see why, because anyone with lesser skill would not have pulled this one off.

Our crew remained in Thorsminde for two days. Meanwhile a little resort hotel located on the coast about ten miles to the south, opened the doors for us for a few days of rest. This hotel had been closed for the winter season.

Although we had been in Thorsminde for only two days, we had become family, and it was hard to say good-bye. These people that had helped us so much didn't want to hear any thank you from us.

"We can be in that same situation tomorrow, and we know you guys will do the same for us," was all they said.

Before we departed, we took a last look at the "Ketty" or what was left of her. It was like visiting a cemetery. The beach was littered with all kinds of parts from the ship.

There were parts from the bridge, position lights, hatch covers, and even one half of a lifeboat. It was surely a strange sight, and there was no doubt, this was the end of the line for S.S. "Ketty," home port Landskrona-Sweden.

After the days of rest, which were only interrupted by visits from reporters, the crew was taken to Esbjerg for another inquiry. On February 13, 1950 the crew was officially signed off before the Swedish consul in Esbjerg. All of us got a fixed amount of money to cover our immediate needs, the rest would be paid out in the currency of our respective countries. If I was ever superstitious, the number 13 should have told me something. I was hired on the 13th of September and signed off on the 13th of February, on the same ship that went down twice. The only thing I still have not figured out, was it good luck, or was it bad luck. I came out of it alive, didn't I ?

We were all issued railroad tickets to return to our place of hire. In my case this was Kiel, Germany. After a last dinner together we said good-bye, and the following morning all of us went in different directions. The chief, and the other German fellow by the name of Otto Simms travelled with me to Germany. Two dutchmen were on the same train, the rest of the crew went to Norway, Sweden and Finland. Parting from Ole, my good friend and watch companion, was hard for me. He had been like a father figure to me, although I had probably watched more over him than the other way around.

If I had expected a quiet and relaxed trip on the Scandinavian Express, it was not to be. It was all because of my ticket. Since I was hired in Kiel, my ticket was issued for a trip to Kiel. All of my buddies were going to Hamburg, and that was where I wanted to go. According to my own estimate the distance from the Danish border to Kiel was approximately the same as it was to Hamburg. Why should the price be any different? I asked myself. Of course my calculation did not include a German railroad official

"When it says Kiel on the ticket, it means Kiel, not Hamburg," he explained to me, pronouncing every word as if he was lecturing an idiot.

I tried another approach. Poor German sailor, just shipwrecked off the Danish coast, no money, wants to go

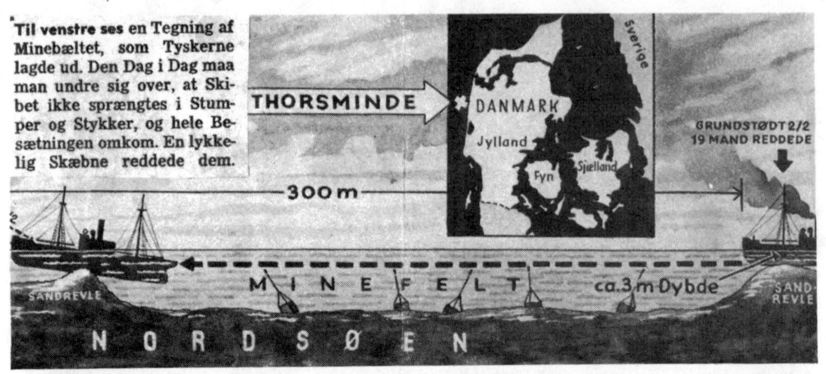

Headlines from Danish newspapers. English translation: A drawing shows the minefields which were placed by the Germans. Day after day one must wonder why the ship was not blown to pieces and the entire crew perished. A lucky star saved them.

HAVET omkring Danmark kan være mildt og venligt paa Sommerdage, men om Efteraaret og Vinteren, naar Stormene raser, viser det Tænder. En af de mest dramatiske Strandinger i det sidste Sekel fandt Sted ved den jydske Vestkyst, ved Thorsminde, den 2. Februar. Den 1200 Tons store Damper »Ketty« af Landskrona, lastet med Porcelænsler til Gøteborg, kom ind i en Brandstorm, og i 72 Timer stod Skibets Fører, Kaptajn K. G. Strindin paa Kommandobroen for at søge at hindre Skibet i at gaa paa Grund. Det lykkedes ikke. Nordsøens granithaarde Bølger spillede Bold med det tunge Skib, og Mandskabet svævede i den yderste Fare. »Ketty« blev kastet ind mod de tyske Minefelter, som endnu ikke er uskadeliggjort, og kun et Mirakel reddede den 19 Mand store Besætning.Da Stormen var forbi, stod den svenske Damper kun 30 Meter fra Land. Strandingsstedet er sørgeligt berømt i Vestkystens Historie. Her strandede Julenat 1811 de to britiske Krigsskibe »Defence« og »St. George«, og en Mindesten er rejst i Erindring om de flere Hundrede Søfolk, der dengang satte Livet til. At der ikke denne Gang kom en ny Mindesten, skyldes Thorsminde-Fiskernes Mod og Uforfærdethed.

English translation: The sea around Denmark can be mild and friendly on summer days, but in fall and winter,when the storms rage,it is showing its teeth. One of the most dramatic shipwrecks of this century took place on the Danish west coast near Thorsminde on February 2nd. The 1200 ton steamship "Ketty" from Landskrona, loaded with china clay , got caught in a hurricane force storm. The ship's captain K. G. Strindin stood on the bridge for 72 hours, trying to save his ship. His effort failed. The crushing waves of the North Sea played ball with the heavy ship, and the crew had to fear for their lives. The "Ketty" was thrown into the German minefields, which have not yet been disarmed. Only a miracle saved the crew of 19. When the storm was over, the Swedish steamer stood barely 30 meters from shore. The location of the stranding is sadly famous in the history of the Danish west coast. Two British warships, the "Defence" and "St. George" stranded here on Christmas Eve in 1811. A memorial plaque has been placed in memory of the several hundred sailors who lost their lives. That a new plaque does not have to be placed this time, we owe to the bravery and fearless effort of Thorsminde's fishermen.

Vraggods skyller ustandselig op paa Stranden. En stor Stabel Vraggods ligger ved Strandfogdens Hus, og mere vil komme til, efterhaanden som Bølgeslaget faar Bugt med Havaristen. I Strandlinien ses en Redningsbøje fra »Ketty«. Skibets Navn træder endnu tydeligt frem. Vestkysten med dens farlige Revler har krævet endnu et Offer.

English translation: Salvage goods keep washing up on shore. A big pile of salvage goods is stacked up near the house of the beach warden, and more will come as the waves keep dismantling the wreck. On the beach is part of a lifeboat from the "Ketty" with its name still clearly visible. The dangerous waters of the west coast have swallowed a new victim.

home, etc.

My talent was wasted on this fellow as my sad story did not seem to disturb him at all. He was following regulations.

While this palaver is going on at the border station the Scandinavian Express is ready to take off. Next stop is Hamburg. My buddies are back on the train while I stand there arguing with the authority. By this time I am convinced that I can not do any business with this fellow. So I just wait until I see the signal going up and the train starts moving. Before he knows what is going on, I take off and jump on the train. The last thing I see is him getting on at the end of the train, and of course he knows where I am.

I ran at once to the compartment where my friends were seated and let them know of my little problem. From there on, all the way down to Hamburg, my "friend" from the railroad is doing nothing but checking out the toilets on the train, while I switch toilets at least twenty times. My buddies keep busy giving me signals. After he checks a toilet and enters the next car they give me a signal and I switch to the toilet he has just inspected. This way he can never find a toilet that shows "occupied" all the time.

We are only about thirty minutes from Hamburg, when

my buddies talk me into joining them in the compartment.

"The coast is clear," they tell me.

Well, the coast was not clear. While I am still standing undecided in the door of the compartment, I hear someone coming, and the first thing I see coming around the corner are the shiny buttons of his uniform. I have no place to go but inside. By this time all people in the compartment have heard of my predicament and are enjoying the game of cat and mouse. A Swedish lady, occupying the window seat, moves over and hangs her coat so I can hide behind it.

There is just enough time to pull up my legs, when the door opens, and the surprised official appears. He was so sure he had seen me enter this compartment that he can not believe his eyes.

"Is there anything you are looking for?" asked the lady. He shakes his head in disbelief, turns around and closes the door.

I could barely control my laughter, because I had watched the scene through the button hole of the ladies coat.

The rest was easy. Since I was familiar with the station Hamburg-Altona, I knew exactly what I had to do. My shipmate Otto passed through the gate with his official ticket and purchased a subway ticket, handing it over the fence to me. The train and subway gates in Altona are all connected. When the checker at the gate complained that my ticket was not validated at any station, I simply told him that was not my fault.

The chief and Otto were both at home in Hamburg and a nearby suburb. We shook hands, and Otto, with a twinkle in his eyes said, "Stay away from me, I am not going to sail with you on the same ship again."

Clouded Future

In Hamburg I found a cheap hotel to be my residence for a few days. I had requested the company to send my last paycheck plus my insurance money to the Swedish consulate in Hamburg. Within a week I was able to pick up my check and could now go out and bring my wardrobe up to standard.

At this moment there seemed to be a lull in the cold war, and I learned it was possible to get a permit to visit my family in East Germany. I had mixed feelings about going home. In a way I needed to be with loved ones. After the events of the last few months and it's emotional stress I was more than ready to go, but I dreaded the idea of crossing the border. What if they didn't let me out again? Who would ask for me? I did some more investigating, but was assured it was safe. Anxiously I boarded the train for home.

There was no visible change, everything looked as dull and dreary as it did years ago. Not many of my old friends were left, and the ones that were, I did not trust to talk to. It was a treat to see my brother again for the first time since 1943. After his release from a British P.O.W. camp in March of 1948, he had followed his natural instinct to go home. I had been unable to meet him and possibly warn him that it would be impossible to get out again. Now it was too late.

He had just gotten married and proudly introduced me to his new bride. He was happy at this time, but I felt sorry for him, knowing he would spend the rest of his life behind the iron curtain.

Mom and dad, after hearing the story of my last close call, tried to convince me again to stay at home. It was a lost cause, and deep down they knew that I would never return as long as there was Communism. I didn't even have the nerve to tell them that at this moment I was a little discouraged with the life at sea, but whatever I was going to do, it would not be in East Germany. That I was absolutely sure about.

After a few days at home I felt restless again. I didn't like to go out, because I always had the feeling I was watched, and deep down was my fear of not being allowed to leave again. The only way to find out was to cross the border again, and that I did without any major incident. It is difficult to describe the feeling of relief when that border is crossed again.

Back in Hamburg I began to make plans for the future. To find a job on land, one must have a place to live and this remained the biggest obstacle. As much as I was discouraged with life in the Merchant Navy, my dream was still stronger than anything else. The dream of getting out of Europe, the dream of starting a new life in a new country. This was the only reason I ever wanted to join the Merchant Navy. I had always seen it as my only way out. My chance to jump ship. If I could only find a ship that was going to the right place. My goal was still South America. Which country I was not sure of yet, but I had to be certain it was a country that would not return illegal aliens. I had only one chance, because if I would be returned by any country I would loose my international seaman's book, and without it I could not be hired again. Finding a ship with destination South America was the most difficult part, meanwhile I had to work.

When the opportunity came to go to Rotterdam to sign on the 16,000 ton Norwegian tanker "Kollgrim," I jumped at the chance. After my experience with the cold and stormy North Sea, the thought of the Mediterranean, the Red Sea and the Indian Ocean was very tempting.

The Mediterranean was nice, the Suez Canal was sand on both sides, and the Red Sea and Indian Ocean was so hot that we could have fried eggs on our deck. If I had any illusions about our destination, the Persian Golf, there was more disappointment. We were tied to a pipeline, and within twenty four hours our belly pumped full of crude oil. The only things we were able to see was more pipelines and more water and sand. There was no place to go and nothing to do, and after twenty four hours the Kollgrim was on her return trip to Rotterdam. From there it was off to Kiel for an extended stay at the Howald shipyard.

That was just right for me, because the crew would not be laid off. We could all stay on board, work a normal eight hour day, and have nights and the weekend off.

Spring was in the air, and with the Kollgrim laid off for at least two months, I had a chance to improve my social life.

The first time I went to a dance on Saturday night I met Anneliese. We danced all night and had a terrific time, but our relationship was doomed from the beginning. Anneliese had signed a contract to work in England. Travel arrangements had been made, and a week later she had disappeared out of my life. . . .

I was still in mourning a weekend later, and my good friend Addie tried hard to cheer me up.

Addie was our steward on board the "Kollgrim." His real name was Adolf, but that name was not very popular in todays Germany, and besides the name Addie fitted his personality better. Among the crew he was generally recognized as an expert on the female species. He was our consultant in all matters concerning love and the ladies, and he had an answer for everybody, always claiming his knowledge came from personal experience. Now Addie was working hard on my case.

"I know just the right place for us to go," he said. "We have to get respectable," he continued. "No more of these sailor hang-outs around the docks. We have to look for class."

"Wait a minute," I protested. "Anneliese had class, and I didn't find her down at the docks."

Addie agreed, "She had class," he repeated, "but she is gone."

This conversation went on for an hour. A little drink once in a while, and soon my pain was not as great any more, the picture of Anneliese was beginning to fade and a new picture emerged. The picture of a nice little restaurant on the outskirts of town, visited only by all the nice girls from the neighborhood. And of course there was dancing on weekends. That's the way Addie described it to me, but I still had my moments of doubt.

"I am not in the mood," I said, "I'll just spoil it for you, and I'm bad company today."

Addie would not take no for an answer, and after another little drink I was ready to give it a try. As far as I was concerned, I was doing Addie a favor.

"If it makes you feel better, I'll go with you," I said.

How could I possibly know that many years later I would remember this day and this place with pleasant memories.

The place was everything it was supposed to be, nicely located, surrounded by green areas and a fairly good size dance floor. A four man band played tirelessly the popular tunes of the time. We also found a table from which we had an excellent view of the local beauties. However, the whole atmosphere and the music reminded me of Anneliese, and I was not in the mood for dancing.

Addie kept calling my attention to different girls in the hall, but I was still not interested. After about an hour or so I had danced only twice, and that was more to keep Addie from pestering me than any real interest in girls.

Then, as my eyes swept across the dance floor again, I spotted her.

She was sitting at a table with three other girls. I pointed her out to Addie, as if I needed his approval to make a move.

"Not bad," was all he said, but the way he said it was very encouraging. As far as I could determine she was not with anybody special, but before I was able to get to her table, she was dancing with someone else. The next dance, and the same thing happened again. There had to be a better way. Storming across the dance hall and knocking over chairs and maybe tables in my wake was not the answer. The occasion called for strategy. Timing was everything, and as the band struck up for "Capri Fisher," I just happened to be only five steps from her table. Nobody was going to beat me this time, and twenty seconds later I held her in my arms. At this moment I did not realize that this was the beginning of a long and happy relationship.

Her name was Luise-Marie, but her friends called her Lu for short. What had attracted me at first was that she looked like Anneliese. After a few more dances I found out how much she was really alike, not only in looks but also in temperament. Before the night was over, I was in love again.

Addie and I had joined the girls at their table, telling tall stories about our adventures in the Persian Gulf. The fact that we never set foot on Arabian soil was never mentioned. The girls found all this very interesting, compared to the other local boys who came to this place. Needless to say, that our story kept growing as the night went on. After the band played "Auf Wiedersehn," signaling the end of the evening, we insisted in taking the girls home. Fortunately Lu was the last one on the line, and I made Addie understand that his services were not required for the rest of the night. Being the expert that he was, Addie got the message.

If I had any grand plans for the rest of the night, Lu brought me back to reality. She informed me that her time limit was 12:30, and that was five minutes from now. Her parents had it all figured out. Dancing ended at midnight, allowing twenty minutes for walking home, which leaves ten minutes to say adios to friends.

Barely did I have the time to ask for our next date, when mom hung her head out of the window.

"Lu, is that you?" she wanted to know.

I didn't even have a chance to give her a long good night kiss. My whole plan of action had been interrupted by this unexpected interference. Here I had not even met my future mother in law, and already I didn't like her. She had messed up my grand finale, the climax of a beautiful evening.

Addie was waiting for me, when I entered my cabin. He wanted to know all the hot details about the closing moments of my new romance.

"In case you need some advice for next time," he said.

"If you want to help, you can keep her mother off my back the next time," I answered.

Addie smiled. "That's the way they are," he said. "They are very protective."

I was always amazed. He was barely two years older than I was, but at times he sounded more like sixty.

Lu and I enjoyed every day we could spend together. She worked in a local delicatessen store, and I would pick her up from work if I could, and take her home. On weekends we would go dancing or to the movies, or just wandering around in the park. After three weeks it was as if we had known each other for years.

Lu's home was located on a quiet street, looking down on a little river. At the end of the street was the terminal of a streetcar line, and at the corner was a charming little garden restaurant, right at the rivers edge. This is where I was waiting for Lu on a beautiful Sunday afternoon.

She was five minutes late, which was highly unusual for her. After a few more minutes she finally appeared. Grandma had come for a surprise visit, and her parents wanted her to stay at home. Her mother, realizing the problem for her daughter, had a suggestion.

"Why don't you invite him for coffee?" she asked.

This offer sent Lu running down the street.

"Would you come?" she asked.

"I know," I said, "the ladies want to inspect the merchandise, right?"

On the other hand I didn't want them to think of me as a coward.

"We might as well face the jury." I said. "Give me a minute."

I went back to the restroom to straighten my tie, because I knew I would be in for a close inspection. The first thing Lu had called to my attention was the fact that I had paint under my fingernails. Small wonder, when all I was doing lately was painting, a never ending job on a ship.

Well, as it turned out, her mother was really a charming lady and so was grandma. With her father I hit it off from the moment I set foot in the door. He worked at the same shipyard where the "Kollgrim" was in dry dock, so we had a lot to talk about. It was like a time long ago when I was still at home. The family life I had not seen and experienced since I left East Germany. When it was time to leave, Lu accompanied me down to the corner. She was beaming.

"They liked you," she said.

"What did you expect?" I asked, but I knew how much it meant to her. It also meant a lot to me.

All good things must come to an end, and so did our summer of 1950. The Kollgrim was ready to sail, and it was going to be the Persian Gulf again. I had seen all the sand to last me a lifetime, and besides it was not the direction I wanted to go. I considered it a waste of time. Although I had met a girl I really cared about, my plans had not changed. Germany was recovering very slowly, and many of the problems remained. There was still a shortage of food and other basic necessities, most of all housing.

When the Kollgrim was ready to sail, I signed off and moved into the seaman's home again. Within only a few days I was lucky to be at hand, when a call came in for a deckhand on the Swedish freighter "Mathilda."

Again it was a ship of only 1,300 tons, but for some reason we had smooth sailing. Our trips took us mostly between England and Sweden, and whenever we crossed the Kiel Canal I had a chance to see Lu. She had to travel all across town to see me for just a few minutes at the locks of the canal. Once or twice we got lucky, because we had to take on coal, and that meant a few extra hours.

One day, while the Mathilda was docked in London, I received a painful lesson in Swedish history. All of my shipmates had gone ashore for a night out, except me. I was the watchman on deck. Shortly before midnight I was down at the pier. The changing tides had caused the gangway to hang up, and I had climbed down to straighten things out. When I was about ready to climb back up, I heard two drunken sailors approaching. They were singing loudly, interrupted only once in a while by cursing. As they came closer and recognized our name and home port, their curses grew even louder.

I recognized the Norwegian language and was sure they belonged to a Norwegian freighter, docked right behind us. Since the Norwegian language is very similar to Swedish, I had no difficulty in understanding. When they spotted me at the gangway, they started calling me a goddamn Swede among other things.

Still thinking these two fellows were just having a good time and were kidding around, I said,

"Hey you guys, watch your language, this is a first class neighborhood."

When I finally realized these guys didn't like the Swedes and were looking for a fight, it was too late to retreat. Even though I had the advantage of being sober, it was still two against one, and they were not exactly lightweights either. If it was not for the first mate coming to my rescue, I might have taken a pretty good beating.

Sitting down for a cup of coffee afterwards, I said to the first mate, "Now first of all I would like to know what I was fighting for."

He was bursting with laughter and said,

"For Sweden of course."

Then he went on to tell me how Norway and Sweden at one time in the early eighteen hundreds had been united, but the union was dissolved in 1905. "They have also never forgiven us that we remained neutral during the last war," he said.

"This is a new one on me," I said, "I always thought you were good neighbors."

"We are," he said, "but show me two neighbors who do not have a little dispute every once in a while."

The next day the whole crew was laughing about our little international incident and my black eye. The captain even declared me an honorary Swede.

"Before I accept, I want to read up on Swedish history," I said laughing, "because so far I have had enough trouble being a German."

As funny as this little incident was in one way, it showed how on old grudge can be passed on from generation to generation, with the last one not even knowing what the grudge was all about.

When we returned to Sweden, I was in for a real treat. I was fortunate to witness one of the greatest shows of nature I have ever seen, the northern lights.

The Mathilda had penetrated deep into the fjords, way up north and very close to the polar circle. It was late in the year, and soon the waters would be frozen solid. The days were getting shorter and shorter.

Stepping out on deck one night, I watched in amazement a spectacle of nature I had never seen before. A luminous arch was stretching across the northern sky with rays extending upwards like searchlight beams. Bright veils were spreading in all directions, increasing the brightness of the night sky a hundred times. Colors seemed to be changing constantly from combinations of green to red, blue orange and aqua. It was an experience to look at a serene scenery of little tree covered islands reflecting in the mirrorlike surface of the water. It was like a dream, and words can hardly describe the beauty of that moment.

After one more trip to England and a return to Goteborg, winter once again draped it's cold blanket over land and sea. Memories of last winter kept flashing trough my mind, and when I heard our next port of call was going to be in Poland, I started making plans again. I wanted to quit, but the question was how to do it in Sweden.

The answer came the following night from an unexpected source. One of my shipmates, by the name of Lars, had asked me to join him for a night out. He had told me a lot about his cousin Margit, who was living in Goteborg. According to him she was a real doll, and since I had nothing better to do I agreed to join him. I had to find out first hand what this doll was really like.

We met Margit and a friend of hers, and from the moment I set eyes on her I was in love. Her sparkling personality and her good looks had me spellbound in a minute. I was a happy man, when I noticed that this feeling was mutual. We talked about a lot of things and eventually came to talk about my past and my dreams about the future. I also told her about my plan. Lars meanwhile seemed to be satisfied when he noticed that his friend had caught fire. When the two girls had to go to the ladies room, he gave me a friendly push and said

"Didn't I tell you?"

At the same time he confessed that he was very impressed with Margit's girl friend.

The night was far too short for us, but we knew that this would not be the end of our relationship. As far as I was concerned, I would do anything to see her again. When we took the girls home, Margit was hanging onto my arm very tightly, as if she was seeking shelter from the cold wind that was blowing in from the Baltic. I could tell she was in love.

"Do I see you tomorrow?" she whispered as we kissed good night.

"You'll see me tomorrow." I said simply.

Back on board I could not sleep all night. I was tossing and turning in my bunk, while a thousand plans flashed through my mind. I simply had to get off the "Mathilda," and do it fast. At best we had only three days left in port.

The temptation was great. Margit was a very attractive young lady. She worked at the local post office and had her own apartment in Goteborg. I knew she could be helpful, but I didn't think it was right to use her to accomplish my goals. That was the last thing I wanted to do. But my thoughts always returned to Margit, not only because I thought she could be helpful, but because I was very attracted to her.

Margit was bubbling over when we met the following evening, just the two of us. Before I could say anything she told me about her plan. The general idea was the same as mine, except that under her plan I was even allowed to stay with her. It would certainly save money for me and make things simpler in one way, but I was still worried.

I told Margit that I had mixed feelings about our relationship. That I had nothing to offer and was in no position to make a serious commitment.

"I know what my chances are," she said very quietly. Then, throwing her arms around me she said, "Let's take it one day at a time."

The two of us sat together until late at night, like a couple of conspirators planing the overthrow of the government. I made no attempt and I don't think she ever expected me to leave that night.

The date was November 17, 1950. I was up early in the morning, eager to get aboard and put our plan into motion. It was all very clear now. I knew exactly what I was going to do. My first step was to tell the first mate that my back was hurting, and that I would like to see a doctor. Anybody seeing me move around would have been convinced I was in pain.

The doctor agreed I had a back problem and said I needed rest. After returning to the "Mathilda" I told the captain I had to sign off for health reasons. To make my point more convincing, I was moaning and groaning in agonizing pain.

The first roadblock I encountered was at the local Immigration Office. In order to stay in the country I needed a stamp, otherwise the company had to arrange my immediate return to Germany. There was only one way to get the stamp. The doctor had to certify that I was unable to travel.

Margit, who had taken the afternoon off, turned out to be very helpful now. Accompanied by her I went back to the doctor. When I told him of my problem he cast an approving look at Margit and nodded his head. He knew, but he signed that most important paper for me and wished us good luck. The first hurdle had been cleared.

The following morning I registered at the Seafarers Union bureau, confident my big break was at hand. Goteborg was a major port city. This was the place where the big ships came in, where I should have the best chance of getting a big, modern vessel, sailing to the far corners of the earth.

My days were filled with waiting at the bureau, only meeting with Margit for lunch in downtown. At night I would pick her up in front of the post office. Those were happy days for us, but the uncertainty was always in the background. After one week I had to return to Immigration for the extension of my permit. So it was back to the doctor for another attest that I was still unable to travel. Stooped low, and with an expression of great pain I entered the Immigration office. Within five minutes I was out with one more week extension. This was repeated one more time. After that I knew my time was running out.

With only one day left before the last extension was expired, I got lucky. There was a chance for a deck hand on a big ship of the Johnson-America Line. Since I was in the possession of a Swedish motbook I was entitled to sign on. There was one little formality to take care of. I had to get a stamp from the Immigration to allow me to sign on. In other words a work permit. Nothing to it I thought, one little stamp between me and the world.

It was late in the afternoon and I decided to go to Immigration early the next morning.

My up-beat mood did not exactly spill over on Margit. She was aware that the end of a beautiful relationship was near, but she also knew that this had been part of my plan all along. I would have loved to stay for at least the duration of winter, but we both knew that Immigration would never go along with that idea. It was time to face reality.

I was in for a rude awakening when I entered the Immigration Office early the next morning. The official on duty told me point blank that according to regulations I could not be issued a work permit and had to return to Germany immediately.

"But I have a job," I argued. "What is it to you, to put a little stamp in my passport and I will be out of here."

He must have stepped out on the wrong side of the bed that morning, because he was definitely in a rotten mood.

"You planned this all along," he said, "Now that you found a ship, your illness disappears overnight."

I tried to remain calm and polite, but even that did not help.

It was ten in the morning and his last word was, "Since you are now in a condition to travel and your time is up, your train for Germany leaves at four this afternoon."

By now it was very clear to me that I was fighting for a lost cause. I gave it one more try, by telling him I had a girlfriend, and that I could not just sneak out on her while she was at work.

"O.K." he said, "I will make you my last offer. You have until tomorrow afternoon, and if you are not on that train I will take you there myself."

I knew, I had reached the end of the line.

When I waited for Margit that night, I tried hard to hide my bitter disappointment. Now that I realized that my plan had failed I had nothing to look forward to. For almost an hour we sat in silence, each one of us trying to accept what we had known all these days.

"We should never have started this," I said. "I am sorry I got you into this."

"Don't say that," she answered. "I knew my chances before, and I still would not like to miss a day we spent together."

There was silence again. Suddenly she looked up, and

there was that spark again in her eyes. She had a new idea, and she was dead serious about it. Her family lived in a small town way up north. Nobody would ask me for any paper or permits up there, and also her father had connections to get things straightened out eventually.

"We could get on the train tomorrow and leave town," she said.

"What about your job?" I asked.

"I'll just quit," she said simply.

All I had to do was say yes, but I could not possibly take the responsibility to go on with this. It had gone too far already and we were both hurting. How could I get her involved any deeper. I had to say no, for her sake.

Neither one of us slept during our last night together. She was clinging to me as if she wanted to hold on forever, and while at first we were still talking and discussing alternatives, it was soon quiet. Each one of us with our own thoughts.

Margit had called in sick to spend the last day with me. The hours were dragging on. I wanted to get it over with, because it was painful to look at Margit and see the hurt in her eyes. There was not much to be said any more. My future was very blurred at this moment, and I did not want to complicate the situation by false promises. At this instant I did not know what tomorrow would bring me.

So it was a relief when it was time to take the bus to the railroad station. It was like going to a funeral. The time had come to say good-by, and one last kiss. I will never forget those sad eyes, and the tears streaming down her cheeks as the train moved slowly out of the station.

The whole journey was like a bad dream. I hardly noticed the train entering the ferry to take us over to Denmark, nor did I notice the picturesque countryside as we passed through.

At the pass control on the German border I had to force myself to be polite to the official, because on this day I was mad at the world and especially at public officials. I blamed those guys for everything that ever went wrong in my life.

Arriving in Kiel a few hours later, I moved in at the Seamen's Home again. A light snow was falling on this cold and dismal December day. Soon it would be Christmas again.

For a few days I lived withdrawn from everything while trying to re-establish my options. At this moment I had invested three years of my life in the Merchant Navy. I had no interest in making it a career. All I wanted was a place to call home and live like normal people again. But I also realized that my dream of making it to the new world was still very strong. I was going to give it one more try. The coming year 1951 was going to be the year of decision. I was not willing to waste any more time crisscrossing the North Sea or the Baltic, these trips would lead me nowhere. I had to get a ship that was going in my direction, no matter how long it would take.

For the last few weeks I had been on an emotional roller coaster. My short lived romance with Margit, the planning and high expectations and the promise of a good ship. Then came the big let down, when my carefully laid out plans fell apart. But with my goals in place again came new optimism, and with it a strong desire to see Lu again. I needed a friend, someone to talk to.

Lu was happy to see me again when I picked her up at work, and since I had met her parents already before, I was invited to stay for dinner. It was almost like last summer again. Only there was that feeling of guilt. The memory of Margit was still too fresh in my mind.

After dinner we talked for a long time. There was talk about renewed hope for Germany and of better things ahead. Also the inevitable question came up,"Why don't you stay on shore?" I said I needed one more year. I never explained for what. How could anyone understand how I felt? How could anyone understand that I wanted to make it on my own terms, according to my own plans. If I had told them of my plan to jump ship in South America, they would have thought of me as a crazy adventurer.

When I met Lu the following day, she had some exiting news. The family had a little spare room under the attic. If I wanted, I could have it for as long as I wanted to stay. Realizing that this would give me extra staying power, and with the added bonus of being close to Lu, I gladly accepted

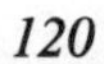

M.S. "Ellen Hugo Stinnes" 1951

S.S. "Kollgrim" 1950

S.S. Carl "Redher" 1949

the offer. There was of course never the carefree relationship that I had enjoyed in Sweden. Mother made sure of that, and since it was in the middle of winter, our activities unfolded mostly under the watchful eyes of the family. At the same time I enjoyed becoming more and more a member of the family and the feeling of belonging somewhere. It was a pleasure meeting grandma again, a great old lady who was more liberal and understanding than mom and dad. As we celebrated Christmas of 1950 I was thankful for the new home I had found. It was hard to imagine that my old home town and my parents and relatives were not more than 60 miles away. Separated by barbed wire fences, mine fields and watchtowers.

We celebrated the new year with family and friends. Even though I did not spell it out, my new years resolution was a promise to myself, that 1951 was going to be the year to make it or break it. I was determined to make one last effort to reach my elusive goal.

Ship of Destiny

The year started with great hope and expectations. The German Merchant Navy was allowed to own bigger ships, and sooner than expected I came up with a solid lead.

The German Stinnes Line had purchased the 7,000 ton M.S. "Pacific" from a Swedish line. While it was not a new ship, it was considerably more modern then any ship I had sailed on before. At this moment the ship was in dry dock at the Howald shipyard in Kiel for minor repairs and renovation. The new owners had renamed her the "Ellen Hugo Stinnes," and when she was ready to hire a crew, my name had reached the top of the list at union hall. When I also found out that her destination was the Caribbean, nothing could hold me back. This was going to be my ship of destiny.

Friday January 19, was the day for the crew to sign on, and I noticed with great relief it was not Friday the 13th. We spent the following week with general cleaning and taking on provisions. On January 27th we were ready to cast off.

So for the second time in a few weeks it was bidding farewell to a loved one again. I had tried very hard to keep this relationship from getting out of hand. As much as I liked Lu, I didn't want to bind her with promises I was not likely to keep. If my plan was going to work, I knew I would not return. As far as Lu was concerned, I was leaving her with the idea that she would see me after my return trip. For her it was just a little longer wait than previous ones. For me, the anticipation and joy of finally going where I wanted to go for a long time, was greater than anything else.

On Monday, January 29th we dock in Rotterdam and here the news hits me with devastating force. Our destination has been changed to east coast U.S.A. with a cargo of steel. I am beginning to believe I can't do anything right, but it is too late. We have reached a foreign port, and I can not sign off. We sail from Rotterdam on Saturday February 3rd. Our first destination is Baltimore, and after leaving the English channel we are running into a good size winter storm in the Bay of Biscay. A few days later we have reached the Azores, and with it comes spring, blue sky and sunshine.

The crew is shedding the heavy winter clothing and generally everybody seems to be in a better mood. Everybody except the captain and the chief engineer. There are problems with the starboard engine, serious enough to shut it down. After a few days we are beginning to have trouble with our port engine, and for the next two weeks we are limping across the Atlantic with only one engine at a time. On Sunday February 25th we have reached Bermuda, and as if to celebrate the event, the one engine running at the time blows a cylinder.

The Ellen Hugo Stinnes is towed into St. George harbor, and for the deck crew it is the beginning of two beautiful weeks of relaxation. For the engine room it meant overtime to clean up and get things moving again. Parts had to be ordered and flown in from Germany. Since we had just left the shipyard in Germany, there was not very much to do for us, not even painting. So we spent our time with practicing lifeboat maneuvers and other emergencies.

On the first Sunday in St. George I went with two other shipmates to explore the island. As we left the little town, we were joined by a friendly little dog that was determined to come along. None of us had any objections and our little friend had a marvelous time returning sticks and rocks we had thrown. After about half an hour we got to an area that was dotted with little ranches. As we passed close by one of these little ranches our friendly little dog turned into a raving maniac. Before any one of us knew what was happening we heard a chicken scream and saw feathers flying, and our dog returning to us with a dead chick between his teeth. The next thing we saw was a heavy set black lady, screaming bloody murder and swinging a big stick at us. We had a hard time understanding her, and she had a hard time understanding us. It took a long palaver to declare our innocence and convince the lady that this was not our dog. The dog meanwhile had dropped the dead chicken at our feet and decided it was not safe to stay in this neighborhood. We never saw him again.

On March 14th our good time on the island came to an end. With both engines repaired we were on our way to reach our destination, Baltimore. Late on Sunday the 18th, we picked up the pilot off Cape Hatteras and at noon the following day the "Ellen Hugo Stinnes" had arrived at her first port of call in the U S A, the city of Baltimore.

The United States Immigration Service boarded our ship immediately and started handing out long questionnaires to all crew members. They set up shop in our mess room, and we were asked to come in with our papers and the filled in questionnaire.

While I was helping my shipmate Felix with his form, we came across the question, "Are you, or have you ever been a member of the Communist Party or it's affiliates?"

Felix stopped for a moment.

"What's the matter," I asked.

He told me a long story about how he had joined a Communist youth group in the early thirties.

"It was kind of experimenting," he said. "After six months I was completely disgusted and left."

"Big deal," I said, "be honest and put it down on that form."

I wished I had never said it, because I had several days to feel guilty about it. To me it was a new experience to find out how ignorant the Immigration Service was, but I had also never heard of a Senator McCarthy and his witch hunt for Communists.

When Felix stepped over to the table, the officer must have looked at this all important question first. He reacted as if Felix was the carrier of a very infectious disease, by calling for the captain immediately.

The captain was informed that Felix was to be retained on board and was not going to be issued a stamp for shore leave. He protested by saying that Felix had committed no crime, that he had no authority to force him to remain on the ship during his time off, but to no avail. It all ended when the Immigration Service posted a guard on the ship, watching over poor Felix twenty-four hours day and night.

I blamed myself for talking him into being honest about a part of his life that happened twenty years ago. As far as Felix was concerned he was a family man, not really wild about going to town for a good time.

"It would have been nice if I could go downtown for some shopping," he said.

The ridiculous part about this incident was that we had three crew members on board which had been former members of the Nazi party. They had also stated this honestly in their questionnaire, but had received no attention whatsoever from the Immigration. Felix however, who was branded a Communist, was probably the most anti-communist on the whole ship. Not only had he left a Communist youth group in disgust after only six month of membership, but he had lost his whole family at the hand of the Russians. The family farm in Eastern Prussia was lost. His father and mother killed by the advancing Russians, and his sister after being raped repeatedly by soldiers of the Red Army, had died in a refugee camp at the age of sixteen. So when Felix told me one night that he didn't really care about going ashore, I knew he was telling the truth.

"What hurts me," he said, "is that these guys think I am a Communist."

During our stay in Baltimore I was approached by two crew members.

If I would be interested in jumping ship with them, they wanted to know.

"What's your plan?" I asked.

They had no plan. The only reason they wanted me along was because I spoke the language.

"I will help you," I said, "not by joining you, but by giving you some good advice.

"First of all, jumping ship is not a group project. It is an individual effort. Anybody can leave the ship and hide out for a few days or even weeks, but then what?" Sooner or later you have to come out of hiding and become legal.

"I would love to stay in this country, but this is not the way to go about it. If I should ever do it, it will be on my own, and with at least a pretty good chance of success."

I had the feeling they were not listening, and as it turned

out, I was right about that too.

Our last stop was Newport News in Virginia. The first man to come aboard was an agent from the Immigration Service, looking for Felix the Communist.

I tried to make a joke out of it by referring to his celebrity status, but Felix was not laughing. He took it very hard that somebody had classified him a Communist and was watching him twenty four hours a day like a dangerous criminal.

On the morning of our departure from Newport News we had two crew members missing, the same guys I had talked to a few days ago. Our captain was furious, because all kinds of reports had to be filed, and of course it is expensive to have a ship of this size delayed. When we finally cast off for our return trip to Rotterdam we were two men short on deck.

Our engines performed flawlessly as we headed East, although I wouldn't mind a little breakdown, maybe at the Azores?

In Rotterdam we received word that our two buddies have been caught and returned to Germany. All at the expense of the shipping line. I knew they would not last very long.

There was also another bit of news, and this was the best news I had in a long time. Namely that our next destination was going to be the port city of La Guaira-Venezuela. Finally South America, land of my dreams.

After unloading our cargo in Rotterdam, it was just around the corner to Antwerp, and here I realized it was true. We started loading for South America. As a last minute surprise we found out that we would have ten passengers on board, a fact that caused a lot of comments from the crew. Most of them negative, because freighter crews don't like to deal with passengers. They consider them intruders and the cause of many restrictions, including watching your language.

I must say, I shared their feelings completely. How was I to know that one of the passengers in particular would turn out to be of great help to me.

On Saturday April 28, 1951, the "Ellen Hugo Stinnes"

was ready to sail. It was late afternoon as the pilot came aboard to guide us out. Two days later, while I took my turn at the helm, the beacon of Ushant was fading into the horizon. The last light of Europe is gone.

Within a few days we had again reached the warmer region of the Atlantic. Life on board was beginning to be more relaxed, and even the relationship with our passengers was better than anticipated. They were not the snobbish kind of people one might find on a first class passenger liner. These were people that took a real interest in our lives and our work on a ship. So it was no surprise that we got to know each other better every day. The warm weather and the sunshine made everybody spend more and more time on deck.

Among our passengers was a friendly elderly German lady traveling with her daughter. Mrs. Borman was returning to Venezuela after many years of absence. She was a widow now, and was returning with her daughter Lisa to live in Venezuela again. The family had lived there all their lives, and Lisa now twenty four, was actually born in Caracas. For me the two ladies became a real source of information. I could not hear enough about the land and the people I was going to meet soon.

Several of my shipmates were openly talking about jumping ship in Venezuela, but I kept my mouth shut. I knew that most of the talkers would be apprehensive when things got serious. Since I was not interested in a partner, there was no reason for me to talk about it.

With only three days left before reaching the coast of Venezuela, I decided to confide in one person. This person had been of great help to me already, but I needed to ask a few more important questions.

I met Lisa alone on deck after my watch, and again we got into a lively conversation. When the moment was right I asked the big question.

"Can you keep a secret?"

She said she could and I trusted her. I told Lisa of my plan, and how serious I was to accomplish my objective.

"Don't try to talk me out of it," I said. "I have my one chance, and I am going to give it a good shot."

Lisa did not make any attempt to talk me out of my plan, in fact she was fascinated by the prospect of becoming part of my preparations. My intuition was right. Not only did she keep her word, but she also supplied the missing link to my plan, the contact I needed on shore. After this conversation with Lisa I felt more confident than ever before that I was going to make it.

Shortly after noon on May 18th, the dark shadows of the coastal mountains appeared on the horizon. For most of us it was the first trip ever to South America, and for the next few hours we watched intensely as the coast grew larger and larger. Soon we could recognize details on shore. By the time we reached La Guaira, it was dark and too late to enter the harbor. After dropping anchor we had time to look at the lights and the life of the town before us.

The ship was almost motionless in the water, and above us the star studded southern sky. The temperature even after dark was still above 90° F. It had all the ingredients of a romantic travel poster. The beat of latin music drifted across the water as I watched the night life unfolding on shore. What would the future hold for me over there? Now came the realization that I was about to take an important step in my life, but there was no apprehension on my part. I had dreamed about this for too long and had invested a lot of time in this.

Since we did not enter the port we kept our normal watch rotations, which for me was eight to twelve. During my turn, Mrs. Borman and Lisa came up to the bridge to talk for a while and say good-bye. There would be little time in the morning. The passengers would disembark as soon as we would dock, while the crew would be busy securing the ship.

Mrs. Borman wished me a safe return to Europe. Lisa, who knew better, just wished me good luck.

"Let me hear from you," she whispered, before the two retired to their cabin.

There was no romance between us, although I found her to be attractive and have a charming personality. For one thing there was no opportunity for any romance, and also we were worlds apart. She was from a well-to-do family, while I was a man without a country, and in the process of becoming a beachcomber.

Early Saturday morning the pilot guided us into the port of La Guaira, where most of our passengers were greeted by friends or relatives. After securing the ship, the crew was ready for a weekend on shore. Permits were issued to all of us to enter and exit the port area. The gangway was staffed day and night by members of the National Guard, which in Venezuela controls all ports, airports and even highways entering cities.

I used Saturday afternoon to explore the town of La Guaira, and collect information on bus lines and schedules to Caracas. My big day would come on Sunday, when I would attempt to contact my first lead.

What had looked so romantic and beautiful from a distance, turned out not to be so beautiful after all. The town was dirty and noisy, and there was dust everywhere. Shortly before our arrival the coastal region had been hit with a devastating tropical storm. Half of the homes clinging to the hillsides had been washed down, and people had found temporary shelter in large warehouses along the waterfront. La Guaira consisted only of a few blocks of city buildings, after that the coastal mountains started climbing all the way up to about 6,000 feet. On the other side was the capital city Caracas. A modern autopista was under construction, but would not be finished until the end of 1953. Until then the only connection with Caracas was a winding two lane highway with over 300 curves and about twenty miles long.

Venezuela—Land of My Dreams

As I boarded the bus to Caracas the next day, I was in for a new experience in traveling. It was worse than riding a roller coaster in an amusement park. Our driver was driving like a mad man, barely taking the time to slow down in a sharp curve. On several occasions I looked straight down a cliff with a drop of at least a thousand feet. Some of these curves were littered with little crosses and candles, put there in memory of victims who had not made it safely around. Nevertheless it did not seem to worry most of my fellow travelers. Only once in awhile would I see someone making the sign of the cross.

My first stop was the Plaza España in Caracas. From there I took a bus to the little village of Baruta, located up in the hills beyond Caracas.

It was not difficult to find my first contact. Everybody knew el Señor Seiferman in the village. He was of German Bavarian background and the owner of a fairly good size hacienda in that area.

I conveyed greetings from the Borman family and told him of the background of our acquaintance. Señor Seifman, who still spoke fluent German, invited me to stay for lunch. Surrounded by a profusion of colors, I enjoyed his hospitality on the terrace of his comfortable home. After another cool, refreshing drink, I came to the purpose of my visit.

Señor Seiferman listened attentively as I told him of my background and my plans for the future. When I came to the end of my story, he looked at me for a brief moment in silence and shook his head.

"You've got quite a program there," he said. "I don't want to discourage you," he continued, "but there are a few things you should know about this country."

For almost an hour I was captivated by his expose on Venezuelan history, its politics, people and local customs.

Only once in a while I interrupted with a question. I had previously heard a lot about the country and it's people from the Borman's, but Señor Seiferman was undoubtedly more up to date on the latest political situation. It was certainly not the promised land he was describing, but a land of political intrigue and corruption.

The government was in the hands of a military junta since 1948. The president of that junta, a colonel by the name of Delgado Chalbaud, had been murdered recently in November of 1950. At this time there was a struggle, involving another colonel by the name of Marcos Perez Jimenez and Llovera Paez, and any time there was a struggle for power, there was uncertainty.

Corruption had always been a way of life, and influence was sold down the line from the highest authority. Everything had its price. Connection was a valuable commodity which changed with the rise and fall from political power.

Señor Seiferman also told me that he had in the past been involved in helping people like me, "but my contacts have dried up lately." he said. "Right now I don't know the right people."

For a moment I sat in silence, just sipping on my drink. Everything he had said so far was discouraging, but I was not ready to give up. How could Señor Seiferman possibly know how I felt. Granted, he was not painting a pretty picture, but I had never held any big illusions about the new country. On the other side, what was I giving up? When I started thinking about my home town being occupied by the Communists, and a Europe in ruins, I was more determined than ever that I was going to stay. I had invested too much to abandon my dream at this stage.

I told Señor Seiferman that I did not have the luxury of getting on an airplane, flying back to Europe and trying again in six months.

"My time is now or never," I said.

"You might just have the right ingredients to make it," he responded, "I certainly wish you good luck." Then he went on to tell me about Pepe's place in Baruta, the hangout for the Germans of Caracas.

"There you'll find some people who can help, just tell the

owner I sent you,'' he said.

Again he apologized for not being able to be of more help to me, and after thanking him for his hospitality I was on my way to Pepe's. At least the trip had not been a total loss.

Pepe's place was only about half a mile down the dusty main street. The first thing I heard when I entered was German music. In spite of it's Spanish name, Pepe's place was about as German as sauerkraut. It was owned by a friendly Bavarian from Munich, who had converted it to a typical German restaurant. Most of the activities took place outside in the garden, where only the bright colors of bougainvillea and other tropical plants would remind one that this was not Germany. All around me I could only hear German spoken. This place was well known among the German colony of Caracas and was a favorite spot for a Sunday afternoon drive.

I introduced myself to the owner by telling him only that Señor Seiferman had recommended his place, that I was new in town, and that I would like to meet some new friends. At this time a young couple, who seemed to be well known to the owner, walked in. After greeting them with a friendly hello, he introduced me to his newly arrived guests.

I had met my first good friends in the new country. I had met Gretchen and Jorg.

The two invited me to join them at their table and soon we were engulfed in a lively conversation. Both of them were in their late twenties, not married and had been living in Caracas for many years. Jorg was the quiet type while Gretchen was very alive and outgoing. As the questions turned to me, and what I was doing in Caracas, I told them my story. I told them where I came from and what I was planning to do, and suddenly I had the feeling I had come to the right place. Nobody made an attempt to talk me out of my plan. Here was a definite interest in my dilemma and an honest effort to help me find a solution.

Gretchen was the first one to come up with a possible answer to my problem. She knew a German engineer by the name of Gorland. This man, accompanied by his wife and two small children, had sailed across the Atlantic in a small sailboat. He was now living with his family down at the coast, in a place called Laguna Caribe.

Gretchen gave me a good description on how to find this place. She was convinced this man would understand my problem better than anyone else, and would help. That was encouraging news and a real lift to my spirits. After spending the rest of this eventful Sunday afternoon with my new-found friends, they dropped me off at the bus station in Caracas. We promised to meet again the following Sunday in Baruta for a progress report.

I returned to La Guaira on that same winding road, with darkness mercifully preventing me from looking down those steep canyons.

Some of my shipmates wanted me to join them for a night out on Monday, but I declined. Since I was not looking for a partner in my upcoming adventure, I was not about to let somebody look over my shoulder. I pretended to have a girlfriend in Caracas, and everybody guessed I had an affair with Lisa. My relationship with Lisa had not escaped their attention, but this was fine with me as long as they left me alone.

On Monday night it was too late for me to travel the twenty miles down the coast to find this Laguna Caribe, but on Tuesday I was on my way. A ramshackle old bus took me past the resort town of Macuto to a little village called Caraballeda. During this trip I experienced first hand the devastation the last storm had left behind. Huge sections of the mountain had come floating down to the coast, with trees still standing upright like an island. The bus had to cross deeply carved out riverbeds, and so it took considerably longer than expected to reach our destination.

The little village of Caraballeda was situated at the foot of the mountain. When I got off the bus at the end of the line, I was immediately approached by a little boy, who was trying to sell me something.

"Laguna Caribe, donde esta?" I asked the boy, using up my whole Spanish vocabulary in the process. His answer was a long speech, of which I understood absolutely nothing. With his hand he pointed down to the coast, and right below us, at less than a mile distance I could see the lagoon. Gretchen had given me a pretty good description of the area. Along the beach was a grove of coconut palms, and inside the lagoon I could see several sail and power boats at anchor. On the east side was the only building, a little wooden cabin.

I gave the boy a medio, (25 cents) and he showed me the only way to get down there. Only a narrow little trail was winding it's way through the brush. Again the boy said something in Spanish, with his hands pointing down the trail. Then he disappeared into the village.

Night comes quickly in this region so close to the equator. Within a matter of just a few minutes I found myself in total darkness, about half way between village and the lagoon. At first I was not worried about it, but soon I started loosing the trail. Even here the storm had left it's destruction behind. Certain sections of the trail were washed out. The light at the cabin below me was still visible and was now my only guide for direction. Strange noises came from out of the darkness around me, and thousands of fireflies filled the air. This was not exactly a walk in the Black Forest I thought, and for the first time I got the feeling of being in hostile territory.

Suddenly the darkness around me fell silent. My heart was beating faster as I had the unmistakable feeling of imminent danger. A strange sound made me turn my head to the right, and there, less than ten feet from me I stared into the glowing eyes of a big cat. All I could think of was tiger, while I stood there absolutely petrified like a monument in front of city hall. It was too dark to recognize any markings or color on this animal, but its size was still impressive. I must admit, I was scared stiff like seldom before in my life. The feeling was that of complete helplessness, without even as much as a stick in my hand. "This is the end of your Venezuelan adventure," I thought, while the big cat stood just as motionless as I did. To me it seemed like hours, but it was probably not more than seconds. The cat appeared to be undecided on what to do with me, just as I was undecided on what to do with her. She must have been able to hear my heart pounding. It was like a confrontation in which nobody wants to give an inch, although I would have gladly given up my position if I could. But I did not dare to move. With her big paw she started clawing the ground in front of her as if to say "Come on you bastard, lets fight." A soft growl was the next thing I heard.

"Now she is going to attack," I thought, but nothing happened. Only those big glowing eyes kept staring at me. Then as suddenly as she had appeared, she turned and vanished into the night.

When I began to realize she was gone I started pondering the question of continuing to the lagoon or return to the village. I decided in favor of continuing on the trail, because the distance in either direction was about the same. Once I found my way back on the trail I reached the lagoon and the cabin without further incident.

Now the Gorland family was in for a surprise, because they were not accustomed to have visitors after dark. After I had introduced myself, we settled down for refreshments and a long conversation, and once again I noticed how Gretchen had been correct in her assessment of the Gorland family.

First of all I told them about my meeting with the big cat and got a good laugh out of it. The cat, I was told, was a puma, a relative of the mountain lion. They live in the mountains and come down at night, even to the coast. According to the Gorland's there were not many reports of humans being attacked, but who knows. Maybe this one had already eaten and was on his way back.

The Gorlands were eager to hear the latest news from the old country, and in the course of our conversation emerged the story of their adventurous journey. While listening to their account, I became convinced they would understand my plight. Compared to Señor Seiferman, this family had seen what I had seen. They had endured what I had endured, and they had essentially done what I was about to do.

Accompanied by another boat, the family had crossed the Atlantic in their 28 foot sailboat called the "Dugong." The other boat was called the "AJAX" and was also of the same size. It belonged to a German family, which had now settled in the interior of the country in a government sponsored and newly developed agricultural community.

Their boat was still moored in the lagoon and was cared for by the Gorlands.

Mister Gorland had signed a contract with the Tanaguarena Yacht Club. A contract which called for him to build a dredge that was capable of deepening the lagoon and reopening access to the open sea. This yacht club had only recently been formed, but the disastrous storm had closed the lagoon and trapped all of the bigger boats.

When I told him the real reason of my visit, Mister Gorland was not surprised at all. I did not even have to ask the question if he was going to help me. He reacted as if this was the most natural thing in the world, and again I had the feeling of being on the right track.

"You can stay with us for as long as you want," he said. "It will be at least a month, before we can start work on the dredge. Until then you can spend some time with the children and help me with the boats and certain other preparations. Also, I can not pay you anything until we start dredging, but you can eat with us and sleep on the Ajax."

I got up from the old box I had been sitting on and walked over to him. A firm handshake and a "thank you," was all it took to seal our agreement. I felt very grateful to this man I had just met less than an hour ago.

Only one question remained to be answered.

"How do I get back to the village?" The last bus left at eleven.

Mister Gorland understood my problem, and offered to accompany me back to the village.

"Thanks," I said, "I appreciate this. Because until I get a little better used to these big pussy cats, once a night is enough."

He took a flash light and a long machete and without incident we reached the village. We talked about a few more details about my move, and then it was time to get on the bus for my return to La Guaira. Another step in the right direction had been taken on this Tuesday, May 22nd, 1951.

Two days later I started moving part of my belongings to my future home, the sailboat Ajax. This was not exactly as easy as it may sound, because I could not carry a suitcase under my arm. I had to carry it all on my body and get past the National Guard. What made this very uncomfortable was a temperature of 100° F plus. In this brutal heat even one pair of pants and one shirt was too much. I was also careful to get an early start to reach the lagoon before darkness. The last encounter with the big cat was still vividly on my mind. I had learned my first lesson well. After one more trip on Saturday the stage was set for the final act, and on Sunday I met my friends again in Baruta.

We celebrated my success and late afternoon we drove to Caracas, where I was introduced to Gretchen's family.

Mama and Papa Klampferer lived in one of the old colonial homes in downtown Caracas. Several rooms in their home were rented to single men, all of them Germans. If it was not for the different style of architecture, with the big, open inside patio, one might have thought to be in Germany. It was like one big family in the Klampferer house, and everybody made me feel part of it. Two of the tenants had similar backgrounds to mine, and all offered to help me if the need should arise. When I returned to the ship that night, I was beginning to feel secure in the knowledge that I was not alone any more. I had friends in Caracas.

The Moment of Truth

Our time in La Guaira had been estimated at two weeks, so it was important for me to be ready. It required two more trips to get my belongings off the ship, and now I was down to bare necessities. I also told Max about my plan to jump ship.

Max was my good friend and watch companion. We shared a cabin and it had been very difficult to hide my preparations from him. Although he had noticed my coming and going, he had attributed the activity to the girlfriend in Caracas. Now he was surprised.

"You never talked about it, while almost everyone else was talking about jumping ship," he said.

"You should know that barking dogs seldom bite," I answered.

I knew that I could trust him not to talk to anybody about my intentions. I had to confide in someone. There were things I had to leave behind, things I could not carry, and others I would not need any longer, like warm winter clothing.

By Friday afternoon I got the information I had been waiting for. The ship was scheduled to leave La Guaira on Monday. My date was set. On Sunday, June 3rd I would make my final move. That giant last step which would change my life forever.

I can well understand why so many sailors talk about jumping ship at one time or another. There are exotic places and tempting opportunities, but when it comes down to that final moment of truth, not very many dare to take that final step. I was well aware of the decision I had made, and how it would effect my whole future. That I would leave the world that I knew behind, and face a strange land with alien people, speaking a foreign language. Nevertheless, this was not a spur of the moment decision for me, and I did not expect it to be easy and without hardship. All I had to do was think of the past four years. Of winters at sea and fight for survival, and there was no hesitation to take this next step. Max would have loved to come with me, but he was married and had a family in Germany. Besides, he was from West Germany and had a place to call home.

So it was Sunday afternoon, when I shook hands and said good-bye to my good friend and companion, presented my permit to the guard at the gangway, and disappeared into the streets of La Guaira. One hour later I joined the Gorland family for a picnic at the beach of Laguna Caribe.

That night I slept under the open sky in the cockpit of the Ajax, my new home. I didn't really sleep at all. The strange noises around me, and the starlit sky above me was something to get used to, and a thousand thoughts flashed through my mind. Every time I opened my eyes and looked at those millions of stars above me, I was sure this was all a beautiful dream.

The Ellen Hugo Stinnes left La Guaira on the 6th of June, not as scheduled on the 4th. Mister Gorland, who had to go to the port city for some parts, witnessed her departure. Meanwhile I enjoyed my freedom and the tropical paradise around me.

Work on the dredge advanced rapidly. I also made the acquaintance of some of the other inhabitants of the Laguna Caribe. The most colorful of them was Captain Busch.

His boat, a schooner named the "Jutta," was by far the biggest vessel in the lagoon. Everything about the Jutta was mysterious. It was said she came from Germany with several paying passengers, but she was apparently at home in the Caribbean. Captain Busch told me himself, that he had sailed these waters for the last thirty years. He told me stories about smuggling and political intrigue, and seemed to have a close relationship with dictators in Haiti and Santo Domingo.

I could never verify the truth, but he sure told a fascinating story.

The captain was seventy years old and very seldom left his ship. Three former crew members remained on board with him, two Germans and one Spaniard. All three had been working with Mister Gorland on the construction of the dredge.

There were about ten other boats in the lagoon, all of them pleasure boats. Their owners came down from Caracas and spent the weekend on the boat. Within two weeks I had met most of them. A very close friend of the Gorlands was an American by the name of Jim Baker and his charming wife Carol. He was an executive of a Texas oil company, living in Caracas. When I was introduced to the Bakers, they were told about my situation, and he promised to see if there was anything that he could do to help.

Early one morning I went with Mrs. Gorland to the mercado libre in Macuto. This mercado libre is something like a farmers market, where all the little farmers come out of the hills to sell their goods. It was here, where I received my first lesson in horse trading Venezuelan style.

In Germany prices would be marked on merchandise, or if the vendor named his price, it would be paid without questioning. Not here. In this country the naming of the price was only the beginning of a time consuming act of haggling. In the weeks that followed I managed to hold my own against the toughest, when I went shopping by myself. What I lacked on language, I made up for by showmanship. All I had to do was let him name the price, walk away in disgust at least five times, let him pull me back and pay a reasonable price after that. Like I said, it is time consuming, but it works.

Once in a while I would spend a weekend in Caracas at the invitation of the Klampferer family. Their home had become my headquarters for "Operation Venezuela." In this short period of time we had known each other, they made me feel like family. I will always be grateful for their help and support when I needed it most. All of them tried their best to find any possible solution to my problem.

On my way to Caracas I had to go through La Guaira. Not only was it strange to look at the harbor and not see my ship there anymore, but I was also keenly aware of my status as an illegal alien. Every time I saw a policeman, I was convinced he had seen my picture in the post office and was out there looking for me. The next stop that made me nervous was the alcabala (police check point) on the city limit of Caracas. All vehicles had to slow down, and depending on how hot the political climate was, could pass or had to stop for a complete search. At the moment the political situation was unstable, but buses would rarely be searched. The Guardia Nacional would be satisfied by just sticking their head in and look very important.

In early July the dredge was ready for operation. She was not a beauty but was doing the job well. The dredge consisted of a basic steel pontoon with an outrigger on one end. The heart of this vessel was a Ford V-8 engine connected to a pump. With the outrigger we were able to lower a snorkel to the bottom of the lagoon, scooping up the sand. A pipeline would carry the sand over to the beach. Very simple, but effective.

My days would now be filled with activity from early in the morning till late at night. Three times a week I would go to the mercado libre for supplies. At nine I would start school for six year old Einar, my only pupil in the class, while Mrs. Gorland would take care of little four year old Helga. From one until nine p.m. I would work my turn on the dredge, and here for the first time in Venezuela I got paid for a job. The money came just in time to freshen up my meager reserves.

On the "Ellen Hugo Stinnes" I had been allowed to withdraw only a certain amount of my earnings in foreign currency, thus I had not been able to collect all my money. Even though I had saved a few dollars from our previous trip, my starting capital in Venezuela was still less than 300 Bolivares (about 90 dollars). Now I was paid 200 Bolivares a week.

The Ellen Hugo Stinnes returned to Venezuela in August.

I received a letter from Max, postmarked in Trinidad, in which he notified me of their arrival. When we met in La Guaira we had a lot to talk about. He wanted to know how I was doing, and I was anxious to hear the story of my disappearance from the other side.

Max told me how the captain had at first believed that a girl had something to do with it, and that I would be just late in returning to the ship. However, as the time passed and the ship was ready to sail, he got suspicious. When he finally had my locker opened and found most of my belongings gone, he began to realize that I was gone for good. He had no choice, but to report me missing to the authorities, which in turn caused a delay in his departure by almost two days. During this time and the following week the skipper was in such a foul mood that it was best to avoid his company.

"The entire crew was rooting for you," said Max. "You had done something they all wanted to do, but didn't have the guts to do it."

I invited Max to come up to Caracas with me and meet my friends. On one of the following nights Max arranged a meeting with a few of my old shipmates in La Guaira. The guys were anxious to see me again and hear my story. Before leaving I gave Max a picture that showed me in front of a fancy car in Caracas, and he was dying to show it to the captain. I would have loved to see the skippers face when he did.

This was the last time I saw the "Ellen Hugo Stinnes" in La Guaira.

A few miles down the coast was the little town of Naiguata, and once every year this town celebrated the birthday of their patron saint.

My three friends and co-workers on the dredge had invited me to join them to watch the festivities at night, and I was eager to go along.

It was already dark when we arrived. The party was in full swing. The entire population was in a frenzy. Men, women, children and animals filled the dusty streets. Some of the animals, mainly goats and chicken, were slaughtered on the spot and roasted over open fires. The smell and the smoke was awful. An old jukebox was blaring a popular tune all over town at full volume. The Catholic Church tried to compete by transmitting a sermon from a loudspeaker, while at the same time setting off firecrackers and cherry bombs from the steeple. It was sheer bedlam. Many of the natives seemed to be in a trance and not aware of their surroundings.

For the first time I realized how different their religion was from ours. To me the Church and its rituals had always been something very solemn and dignified. Here it was adapted to the native population and mixed with old indian and even voodoo rituals. The spectacle was so spooky that I felt completely out of place.

Although we stood out in the crowd, nobody tried to harm us or pick a fight with us, in fact nobody even seemed to take notice of our presence. Neither I nor any one of my companions had the courage to eat or drink any of the local offerings, but I found it most fascinating to observe the people and their activities at this wild celebration.

The hour was late, and many of the revelers had passed out wherever they dropped, but the music and the noise continued. For almost an hour we had been searching for some kind of transportation. We had found a few taxis, but no drivers. The party had swallowed them all.

When we were finally able to locate one that was halfway alive, we paid the demanded fare without argument. He was the only thing in town, and with a sigh of relief we left the scene of the wild celebration behind us.

I had written a little note to Lisa, just to let her know where I was and what I was doing. Her response came a few days later. She asked me to join her and her mother for dinner on the following Sunday.

I knew the address was Country Club, but it was quite a culture shock for me to come out of the wilderness and go dining in a big villa in the most fashionable district of Caracas. Somehow it didn't seem right to ride the public bus, get out at the next stop, and then walk up to a fancy villa. That's not the way I had seen it in the movies. It was however a very pleasant evening.

The two ladies did everything to make me feel comfortable and the dinner was delicious. After dinner they wanted to hear what I had been doing and about all the people I had met so far. We also discussed the political situation, which was one of the obstacles to getting my papers in order.

Lisa also told me that she and her mother would travel to Europe again, and not return until Christmas.

"I hope you'll have all your papers in order when we return," she said.

I had all my papers in order when we met again, but two years would pass before this day became reality.

At the end of September Mister Gorland's contract was abruptly canceled. An old Venezuelan captain had convinced the management of the yacht club that he could now take over the dredge and do the job for less money. On the first day of October he took over the project.

There was a certain satisfaction in watching those guys pumping clear water over to the beach for hours. They had no problem in operating the equipment, but they would pump the same spot for hours, without moving the dredge and lowering the snorkel. We could laugh about our replacement, but we didn't get our job back. The time had come for all of us to plan our next move.

The Gorlands were restless again and wanted to sail to Haiti, and from there, who knows. They offered to take me along, but I declined. I had come this far and was confident that I could make it in Venezuela.

Jim Baker came through with a plan for me. His oil company had operations in the Orinoco delta, a region called Delta Amacuro. He had talked to one of his people down there and everything was set. All I had to do was get on a plane and fly to Tucupita. His contact had connection with the governor of the state. He was our man.

Before I left I wanted to go up to Caracas, spend some time with the Klampferer family, and tell them about my good fortune. We agreed that the Bakers would take me up to Caracas when they returned the following Sunday.

When the Bakers came down the following weekend they brought bad news. Something was brewing in the capital, and the Guardia Nacional was on alert. All vehicles entering or leaving Caracas were being searched. Jim thought it might be better to wait another week and let things calm down.

In a way I felt sad that life in this paradise would now come to an end. There was the uncertainty about my papers, but I had never known such carefree existence in all my years. A person hardly needed any money to survive. If I was hungry, I could always get a coconut from one of the many palms along the beach.

I still treasure the nights on the "Ajax," when I slept under the open sky, listening to the pounding of the surf and the occasional beat of the drums coming from the village of Caraballeda. The children and I spent a lot of time roaming the beach, or go sailing in our little dinghy. At night I could sit for hours, listening to Mister Gorland's stories about his life and travels of the past, and his plans for the future. He was a brilliant man and highly intelligent. His wife also enjoyed the carefree life, and it was probably for this reason that they never got settled. I only felt it was not fair to the children, because sooner or later they would have to attend school.

Jim Baker did not come down on Saturday, and I was beginning to get worried. Some of the other boat owners however reported that the political situation in Caracas was calm again, and that inspections at the alcabala were back to normal.

Early Sunday morning Jim arrived without his wife. She did not feel good and had decided to stay home. I helped him repair a few minor things on his boat and in late afternoon we were ready to leave. During the day I had said good-bye to old captain Bush and his crew, as well as some of the other new friends I had made in Laguna Caribe. After thanking the Gorlands again for their help and wishing them God speed in their upcoming journey, we put my meager belongings in the trunk of Jim's car and went on our way.

We talked mostly about my upcoming trip to the Orinoco region, while we were climbing the winding road to the capital. Jim gave me some last minute information about the land and the people I was going to meet down there. He had been living in the country for many years and had a good understanding how things worked here.

Traffic at this time on Sunday was always heavy, as thousands of motorist returned from the beaches. So when the traffic in front of us came to a standstill we didn't think much of it. Accidents and crazy drivers were a common occurrence on this road.

Jim brought the car to a stop, and when nothing moved after five minutes, we got out of the car to stretch our legs.

Nobody in front of us seemed to know what had happened.

All of a sudden we started moving again, but only a few yards. Then it was stop again. After about twenty minutes we had barely moved a hundred yards, and now the bad news had trickled down the line. There was no accident up front. There was trouble in the capital again, and the Guardia Nacional was searching all cars. We had at least a mile of cars ahead of us, and by now probably a mile of cars behind us. Turning around was now impossible. Steep mountains covered with dense jungle on both sides.

"Don't worry, we will make it through," said Jim. "They can't keep this up. The line will be backed up to La Guaira in an hour," he said.

He had a point. Not only was the line getting longer, tempers were also getting hotter. Someone in the line started honking his horn, and within seconds the noise of hundreds of automobile horns filled the air. It seemed to help, because we moved a little faster.

As we finally rounded the last corner we were able to see what was going on at the alcabala. The guards, realizing they were unable to search every vehicle, began to make spot checks by stopping only every third car. As we got closer and closer I started counting. I was afraid we would be the third car.

Jim was calm.

"Just sit tight," he said. "Don't say anything, and let me do the talking."

I was hoping it would not come to the talking.

The last car to be searched was given the clear sign. Two cars in front of us started moving slowly. As we approached the guard he lifted his hand, but Jim looking straight ahead kept moving.

The guard shouted something, Jim stepped on the gas and the car jumped forward.

"Hang on," he screamed.

In less than ten seconds we scraped around the next curve and disappeared in the streets of Catia, the first barrio of Caracas.

For awhile we kept away from the main street leading to the center of Caracas, because we did not know if a patrol would come after us. In the meantime the lights came on as darkness fell over the city.

Our next stop was a bar where we had a cold and well deserved drink. Jim Baker had taken a hell of a chance for me. Otherwise I might have been behind bars by now, and during a political unrest, that is not a good place to be.

"Why did you do it?" I asked.

Jim smiled. "Temptation" he said, and continued. "When I saw the short distance to the next curve, I just could not resist. Furthermore, it had dawned on me that I would have a hell of a time to explain our relationship."

I knew he was right. There was a good chance we would have both been in jail by now.

Jim dropped me off at the Klampferer's house, where I told the story of our narrow escape. Nobody had heard about the unrest yet, but this was no surprise. The radio stations belonging to the government never admitted to any unrest in the country. Father Klampferer was sure that this would be over in a day or two, not to worry.

In the meantime I could not risk to fly to Tucupita, as long as this state of alert existed. In order to get out of Caracas, I had to get past the alcabala again. The airport was in Maiquetia, which is located next to La Guaira at the coast. Not only did I have to get past the alcabala, but there was a checkpoint at the airport. Also I was certain there would be another check of all incoming passengers at Tucupita.

The next day the city of Caracas was filled with rumors, but nobody knew what was really happening. There was a lot of military movement and everybody was nervous. This was no climate to strike any deal for legalizing my immigration. A week passed, and nothing had changed. I was trapped.

Every Sunday morning the Klampferer family attended mass at the church of San Jose del Avila. This church was nestled against the coastal mountains, and part of the complex was a monastery. It's inhabitants were mostly German speaking Christian Brothers. When the Klampferers returned from church this Sunday, they brought exiting news. They had talked to one of the brothers about my delicate situation, and he had offered to help. Since I am not a Catholic, I was at first hesitant, but my friends convinced me in a hurry that the Catholic Church would be the only party willing and also capable to assist me. They had even set up an appointment with brother Alfons for the following Wednesday night.

Gretchen dropped me off at the monastery, and I wished she would come in with me to hold my hand. I met brother Alfons, a friendly, elderly man with a warm smile and a heavy bavarian accent. After only a short time I felt comfortable with him. We sat down, and for about twenty minutes I answered his questions about my past, and my plans for the future. I was relieved that religion was never discussed.

Brother Alfons excused himself and left the room. When he returned he handed me an envelope and said, "You have an appointment with Monsignor Henriquez at the palace of the Archbishop on Saturday morning at eleven. He is the personal secretary of the Archbishop, and this letter will introduce you."

I don't know what I had expected, but certainly not this.

Brother Alfons noted my surprise and shock.

"Don't worry," he laughed, "the Monsignor is not going to eat you. In these times we need all the help we can get, and he will be your best hope."

Before I left, brother Alfons advised me to be on time for my appointment, and then wished me good luck for the days ahead.

Even the Klampferers could hardly believe what I told them. An audience with Monsignor Henriquez? Mother Klampferer was excited.

"I wish I could go with you," she said.

"I wish you could," I answered. "I need someone to hold my hand."

Although I was nervous about my upcoming visit, the two days passed slowly.

On Saturday morning the whole household was up early to give me some last minute advice.

The palacio was located in the heart of Caracas adjacent to the Plaza Bolivar. Since brother Alfons had given me good instructions I had no problems in finding the right gate and deliver my letter of introduction. After waiting for about fifteen minutes, I was led down a long hallway and into a large ornate room.

The Catholic Church with its pomp an ceremony had always been a mystery to me, so I really felt out of place in these surroundings. How was I going to address this man? What was expected of me? Those questions flashed through my head as I stood there admiring the elaborate furnishings and impressive paintings.

My anxiety vanished as soon as Monsignor Henriquez entered the room. His handshake was firm, and his smile was sincere. Since his English was better than my Spanish, we settled on English. It was also apparent that he had been briefed about my status.

"We seem to have a little problem with Señor Morrison?" was his first question.

But it was more a statement than a question. Señor Morrison was the Director de Extranjeros, the equivalent to chief of immigration.

Monsignor Henriquez told me about his previous interventions and the reactions of Señor Morrison. Through Morrison's secretary he was apparently well informed about what was going on at the Department of Immigration. "The politicians don't like it when the Church gets involved in government business," he said. Referring to the political situation at the moment, he said: "They don't know how long they are going to be there, but the Church has survived many governments through many centuries."

He continued to ask questions about my past and about my plans for the future. Then he sat down behind his beautiful desk and proceeded to write two notes. One was addressed to Señor Morrison, Director de Extranjeros, the other one to Morrison's personal secretary, Gabriela Arivalo. He told me to got to the Department of Immigration and deliver the note to Señorita Arivalo first. She would then instruct me on what to do next.

I was overjoyed. With the blessings of the Church, what could possibly go wrong? For the first time I felt that an organization of power and influence was on my side.

"I am very grateful for your effort and the support you are giving me Monsignor," I said.

Monsignor Henriquez nodded, and with a friendly smile responded, "Vaya con dios, y buena suerte my son."

A firm handshake, I turned and left the room. I was clutching my two notes as if I was carrying a million dollars.

When I returned to the Klampferer house, I found all of my friends anxiously waiting to hear the story of my historic meeting. There was no doubt in anybody's mind that the rest would only be a mere formality.

On Monday morning I was on my way to the Immigration department to deliver my first note to Señorita Gabriela. She was not surprised at all, and I could tell this was not the first time that Monsignor Henriquez had requested her help. Judging by what I had heard from him, she was his confidant in this dėpartment.

She asked me to return at four p.m. because the time was not right, as she put it.

I was certain she had her reason for it, and promised to be back in time. When I returned shortly before the hour, I found two people still waiting. Señorita Gabriela asked me to take a seat and wait. After the last man had left, she took my note, which was addressed to Señor Morrison and disappeared behind the big door. It took almost five minutes before she returned with a big smile on her face.

"El Director is now going to see you," she said. The smile on her face made me relax a little, but when I entered and looked at the serious face of Señor Morrison I was not too sure anymore. He asked me to sit in front of his desk and studied me for a long time without saying a word.

I felt very uncomfortable, and was glad when he finally began to talk. He noticed my problem with the Spanish language and switched to English.

"So, you are the one," he said.

I didn't know which one he meant, but I figured it would be best if I agreed with him.

"Yes," I said, "I am the one."

He shook his head and smiled for the first time. "How did you do it?" he asked.

"What do you mean, Sir?" I questioned.

"I mean, how much did you have to pay?" I still did not understand what he meant, but he started explaining that he was sure I had paid someone to let me off the ship.

Now I got the message, and I told him how I had removed my belongings piece by piece while the ship was still in port. I also told him what I had done since the ship had left La Guaira, without implicating any of my friends. We talked for almost fifteen minutes, and since I was the last man for the day, he did not seem to be in a hurry.

Finally he picked up the phone and called for someone. When a man appeared he said to me,

"Please go with him, he will take care of the paperwork."

After thanking Señor Morrison, I followed the man down the hallway into another smaller office. He introduced himself as Señor Sanchez as he sat down behind a typewriter.

We had some difficulties with the standard forms, because they were obviously not made for illegal entry. At five p.m. Señor Sanchez asked me to go home, and return the next day at nine in the morning.

Again it was time to tell about the events of the day, when I returned to the Klampferer house. The unanimous decision was that I had conquered the biggest hurdle. Although I had experienced many disappointments before, this time I wanted to believe it. I had seen the top man at Immigration and had apparently passed inspection. What could possibly go wrong now.

There was no indication of any change, when I returned the following morning. Señor Sanchez sat down behind his typewriter and continued to ask questions, just like he did the day before. When he was finished, he asked me to wait while he was gone for about ten minutes. He returned with another man and told me to go with him, because his part of the paperwork was finished.

I followed the other guy outside, where a car was waiting. My escort said something to the driver, and we were on our way. At no time did I have any suspicion of trouble ahead. The two fellows looked like secret police to me, but since nobody had taken any fingerprints or photograph of me, I was certain they would take me to police headquarters. Only when the driver turned in the direction of Catia was I beginning to have my doubts.

Where are we going?

A terrible thought crossed my mind.

"What if they take you down to La Guaira and put you on the next ship to Germany?" I thought.

As we approached the intersection in Catia, the driver turned left instead of right.

"It's not going to be La Guaira," I thought with a sigh of relief. A few minutes later we came to a stop in front of a large building complex. "CARCEL MODELO" the big sign said.

Even when my escort asked me to get out, I had no idea of the trouble ahead. Only when he handed me over to the reception and left, did I come to the realization that I was now in jail.

If I had been on cloud nine during the last few days, I came crushing down to earth again at this moment. "What had gone wrong?" I asked myself. For the first time the lack of a fluent command of the Spanish language was frustrating to me. I wanted to protest and demand to make a phone call, but perhaps it was better I kept quiet.

After the check-in procedure I simply followed the guard to the compound that was going to be my home for a while.

The guard had barely left, when I was surrounded by a number of inmates. I was the new kid on the block, and the questions came in rapid succession. Questions that are probably asked in every jail in the world. Questions like "Where are you from, and what are you in for?" Those were the questions on the top of the list, and within an hour I had made the acquaintance of a wide variety of inmates.

I was amazed. The whole world seemed to be represented. There was Carel from Czechoslovakia, Antek from Poland and Boris from Yugoslavia. All three spoke German. There was Alberto from Italy, and a fellow from Greece as well as Marcel from France, and a Columbian general. We all had one thing in common. We were the Musius, which is the unflattering name given to all foreigners by the natives.

Many of the foreign inmates had committed the same crime I was in for. The most discouraging news was that Antek, the Polish fellow, was the last one in before me. He was in there already for three months. However, I discovered one thing which gave me hope. I had left a trail behind. Someone would ask questions, I was sure.

Most inmates had little connections to the outside world. They did not know any influential people which might be able to help. There were people in there absolutely lost in the system, and nobody on the outside asking questions. I was also told by several fellow inmates that I should consider myself lucky to be here at the Carcel Modelo instead of the older and infamous Obispo. They told me horror stories about Obispo.

One thing I had to agree on. This place was clean. It did not take me very long to find out why.

An inmate, who seemed to be a person of respect, stopped by to inform me that I had the honor of working for him. Since everybody showed him a lot of respect, I found it to be in the interest of self preservation to do the same.

After he was gone, I was told that he was in there for murder, with a maximum sentence of fifteen years. He also had a very low opinion of Musius. It was no coincidence that most of my new friends worked for him on the cleaning gang. All of us Musius.

I never knew his real name, we just called him ''Jefe'' and he seemed to like it. There were several big shots in there, all of them murderers with long sentences. They held a position of trust and even seemed to be supported by the guards. If they were not in charge of a work detail, they would own some kind of a franchise in jail. One of them would have the coffee concession, while another would sell empanadas or tamales. No other person would dare to infringe on their territory. The general opinion was that the big shots never had it so good in their lives. Before coming here they had been the nobodies, the losers, living under miserable conditions in the slums of Caracas and other cities. Now they had become a person of respect, with a roof over their head and three regular meals a day. It was mostly the long term convict who occupied his own cell, while the little guy, and especially the foreigner, slept on the floor in the open hallway. I heard horror stories of killings inside the jail, committed by the big boys for only one reason. Their term was up, and they did not want to give up their position of respect. I had every reason to believe it, because there was a killing during my time in Carcel Modelo.

One of the first things I learned from my fellow inmates was, "Don't go to the restroom alone, especially at night." At six p.m. there was a head count in the exercise yard, and after that nobody was allowed out in the open.

My first meal in jail was not too appetizing, but I was hungry. Later on that night we had a heated discussion in our international group. The topic was politics, and the biggest mouth in town was our Columbian general.

He was a fiery fanatic, leader of a leftist band of revolutionaries. His dark eyes sparkled as he spoke. His problem was that he could only see the world from his narrow perspective. The reason he was in jail, was that he had to flee from the Columbian Army and cross into Venezuelan territory. To prevent him from causing any trouble between the two countries, the Venezuelans had transferred him to Caracas.

There was one man in our group I liked from the moment we met. It was Carel, who took me under his wings and instructed me in all the things I should know about. Like the who is who and what to do and what not to do, and just how to survive in this place. He spoke fluent German, and I was awful glad to have him around. His reason for being there was also political. He was a victim of the times and of jealousy at the work place. Someone at the company he worked for, had reported that he had made an anti government statement. Nothing more, and the Seguridad Nacional had picked him up. No official charges had ever been filed. No trial, just taken to jail and left there. That was two months ago.

My first night in jail was a nightmare. I kept thinking about my friends on the outside. Would they find out where I was?

They must have guessed it by now that something went wrong.

A thousand things went through my mind, as I lay there, listening to the strange noises of this place. What a difference from the paradise of the Laguna Caribe. At 3,000 feet the night is cool and one blanket is not really enough to keep a person comfortable.

I was sleeping on the floor, right in front of the cell

block. Only a four foot high wall separated me from the exercise yard. I didn't sleep at all during this first night, and I was glad when the first rays of the sun appeared slowly over the eastern mountains.

Shortly after head count and breakfast, I was on my knees scrubbing floors. It was not so much the job which was bothering me, but the spectators. El Jefe was strutting around like a peacock, bellowing orders to the delight of the native population. The temptation was strong to dump the pail of dirty water over his head, but self preservation told me to swallow my pride. My buddies on the cleaning crew had learned to live with it, even laugh about it.

All of the long term inmates had their cell doors open day and night, but one section of our compound housed a special breed of criminal. Their doors were looked at all times.

Carel told me they were political prisoners, and had something to do with the assassination of the last president. When we scrubbed the floor in front of their cells, a guard was standing by to prevent us from talking to them.

All day long I waited for someone to call me and tell me the whole thing was just a mistake. That I was free to go, but nothing happened. Another sleepless night and another day of scrubbing floors. Nobody called for me, and slowly it began to sink in, that this was going to be more than a one night stay.

On Saturday my name was called and my heart started beating faster. A guard led me to the front of the building where I found two visitors, Gretchen and Jorg.

What a relief to see a familiar face from the outside world. They brought me some food, some personal belongings like a toothbrush, and most of all good news. After several days of inquiries, they had finally discovered where I was.

At first nobody had admitted to know of my existence. They had called brother Alfons at the church, to let him know of my disappearance. He in turn had notified the office of the Archbishop. On Friday morning Gretchen got through to an embarrassed Señor Morrison, who promised to look into the matter. By Friday afternoon he informed her of my whereabouts, and made arrangements for her visit.

To see Gretchen and Jorg gave a tremendous lift to my spirits. At least I knew I was not forgotten. The family had discussed the possibility of talking to a lawyer, but I advised against it.

"Let's wait another week and see what happens, before we spend any money on lawyers," I said.

I could not see what a lawyer could do, short of spending large amounts of money to buy my way out. That was the system.

Four more days of scrubbing floors, and four more miserable nights went by. On Thursday morning a guard called my name, and led me to the front office where a man from Seguridad Nacional was waiting for me. I was told that I was not released, but would be taken to Immigration for a hearing of my case. A car was waiting outside and within the hour I was sitting in front of Señor Morrison again.

He almost apologized, and told me that he had nothing to do with my arrest. According to him, the chief of control of the Seguridad Nacional had ordered my arrest.

I knew he was telling the truth, because the Seguridad Nacional was in control of every part of the government.

After a short conversation he informed me that I would be sent to the city of Carupano, to be confined there for a period of one year. "Confinado" he called it, and it was something like being on probation for one year. I would be free, but not allowed to leave town.

He described Carupano in glowing terms to me and told me that his entire family came from the region. Again he apologized for having to return me to jail, but promised I would be on my way within a few days.

I thanked him for his help and promised him I would be a good citizen of his home town. All I wanted was a chance to be free to work, and eventually get my legal papers. We shook hands and parted like good friends. My escort was waiting outside to return me to the Carcel Modelo.

I almost felt guilty when I reported to my friends in the international section, because I knew that many of them had been in there much longer than I had.

It was Monday, when I was escorted to the Direccion de Extrajeros again. Señor Morrison was all smiles, and acted like a travel agent who had just completed all the arrangements for a trip to the French Riviera.

With my escort, I was told to go to the Department of the Interior at the Capitol, to pick up my papers and airline ticket. Once I had these in my possession, the guard had instructions to release me. All I had to do was promise to be on the plane tomorrow, and report to Seguridad Nacional at my arrival in Carupano.

Señor Morrison wished me good luck, and with my escort in tow I was on my way.

At the Department of Interior we ran into the first snag. The paperwork was not ready until two in the afternoon. It was not even eleven o'clock and the question was what to do with three hours. My escort called his boss and was told to let me go, with the understanding that I was going to pick up the papers at the specified time.

Mother Klampferer was at home when I got there. She promised to have a special treat for lunch, but after a refreshing shower I had a brilliant idea. There was enough time to return to Carcel Modelo and pick up my belongings.

The guards were not surprised at all to see me return without my escort.

"Estoy libre," I said proudly, pointing at my chest.

They laughed, and let me in to get my personal things.

My fellow inmates at the international pavilion, as I called it, were glad to hear my report. Maybe it gave them hope that they might be next.

When I returned to the main gate, I realized I had made a terrible mistake. Word of my release had not yet reached the administration. The guards absolutely refused to let me go.

"Please call the Interior Department to confirm my release," I insisted.

They just laughed.

When I refused to return to my section, I was taken there by two guards.

I had given my word to pick up the papers, but two p.m. passed and I was still in jail.

To make matters even worse, El Jefe had made it a

special point to request my services on this day. I was ready to strangle that little son of a bitch, but again I kept my cool.

That night I heard that Alberto, the Italian, was going out every day with an escort. He was allowed to liquidate his business in Caracas, before being expelled from the country for alleged anti government activities. I asked Alberto if he could manage to call Señor Morrison as soon as he got outside the next morning.

He must have been able to make that call, because at ten the following morning I was picked up and taken to Señor Morrison's office again.

He handed me the paper and the airline ticket and said, "I am sorry, but your plane leaves at one."

Since it took over an hour to get down to Maiquetia I had barely one hour to get my belongings. There was just enough time to say "hello" and "good-bye" again to the Klampferers, then I was on my way to the Maiquetia airport. All the way down the winding road I was thinking about the people I had left behind in prison. What would the future hold for them?

From only two of them I ever heard again. The Columbian general was killed by Columbian troops a few months later, when he tried to return to Colombia. He had been released from prison under the condition to stay away from the Columbian border. I read about his end in the paper, and I was not surprised.

Carel and I met again in Caracas, where we became good friends and even neighbors, but that was years later. From the carcel modelo he was sent down to the infamous El Dorado penal colony, which is located in the jungles of the Orinoco. Only through the intervention of good friends in Caracas was he finally released.

The pass control was still on in Maiquetia, and I was glad to have my little piece of paper. A DC-3 of the Taca Airlines delivered me safe and sound to Carupano. I thought it was funny that the first time I had ever been on an airplane in my life, was to be at the expense of the Venezuelan government.

At the airport in Carupano I was received by a man from

Seguridad Nacional, who gave me instructions for my residence in town.

I was free to do what I wanted to do, except I was not allowed to leave the city limits, and I had to report to Seguridad Nacional once a week.

"Confinado"

That part was easy to live with, what was not so easy was how to survive in town. Even though Carupano was a city of about 60,000, there was no industry. The town's economic survival depended on the surrounding area, which consisted mostly of coffee and cocoa plantations.

Carupano was the seaport for the shipment of those products. Otherwise it was isolated. The road from here to the next city of Cumana was about 100 miles of dirt road.

Faced with an uncertain future, combined with low cash reserves, I had to stretch my money as far as possible and live as frugal as I could.

Probably the cheapest hotel in town was the hotel Colon, located in the port area. It was small, dirty and cheap. It's rooms were only six foot high partitions of masonite board. The wallpaper pattern was alive and constantly moving. They called them cucarachas here, also known as cockroaches.

My first meal was a fish soup. The taste was not bad, but all I could see was a big head in the middle of the plate and a pair of eyes staring at me. The other distinguished guest's of this establishment seemed to be the local winos. Language was another problem. These people talked so fast, that a whole sentence sounded like one word. Yet in spite of all adversity I was not discouraged at all. After just being released from prison, I considered this a step forward. Within days of my arrival I had made some new friends. After walking up and down main street a few times, I had the feeling everybody knew me.

The first person I talked to was Pepe, a Spaniard and owner of a dry cleaner and laundry. Pepe promised to keep his eyes open for a possible job for me. He also told me about Señor Popiolo and Wladimir, and their jewelry store on main street. I decided to pay them a visit, and was surprised that both of them spoke German.

Popiolo was a Russian Jew and Wladimir was a former Russian P.O.W. who had decided not to return to Russia after WW II. Although our countries had been enemies, there was no sign of it in our relationship. We had so much in common when we talked about the old countries we had left behind. Politics never entered into our discussions. We became good friends, and both of them have been a great help to get me over the first hurdles.

The first contact had been established, and after a few days I landed my first job.

Pepe knew the owner of Taller Bermudez, a auto repair shop. He did not have much to offer, but it was a beginning. Since I was pretty good at painting I was soon engaged in putting a shiny new coat of paint on those old country buses. I also moved out of hotel Colon and moved into a little empty room in the garage. The room was bare. A hammock to sleep in was the only piece of furniture. Besides a free place to sleep the owner could only pay me five Bolivares ($1.75) a day, but I was able to survive on this. I had discovered the Comedor Popular, where I could eat for only one Bolivar. Lunch and dinner was mostly rice and black beans, with a little meat and a baked banana. Since I liked black beans and baked bananas, I was not complaining. Breakfast in the morning consisted of a french roll and bananas. Furthermore, the place was sponsored by the government as a public kitchen and was fairly clean. A tremendous improvement over hotel Colon.

That was the beginning of my early days in the city of Carupano.

I thought about what Señor Morrison had told me and I had to agree. The city was beautifully situated and I liked the people.

One day Popiolo came over to the shop and was all exited.

"Get dressed," he said. "I got a job for you."

"What is it?" I asked.

"Manager of a hotel," he answered.

"Are you crazy?" I asked. "I have never managed a hotel in my life."

Popiolo, undisturbed, went on to tell me about Señora

Dora, the owner of the hotel. How she was going on a two months trip and had nobody to run the place. He also confessed that he had told la Señora about me and that I had previous hotel experience. Popiolo convinced me to give it a try. What did I have to lose?

I got cleaned up and dressed, and followed him to be introduced to Señora Dora. He had given me precise instructions on how to act. After he introduced me to the Señora I said politely, "Mucho gusto Señora."

From there on it was one long speech, of which I understood considerably less than half. Whenever she paused, and I thought it convenient, I would throw in an occasional "Si Señora, como no." The introduction lasted maybe fifteen minutes, then we shook hands and I said, "Adios Señora." Once we got outside I could not wait any longer. "What did she say?" I asked. "You got the job," said Popilio. "She wants you to start on Sunday." He also gave me a little bit of the family background. The hotel was actually owned by three sisters. Dora, Providencia and Hortensia.

Dora, the oldest at about forty, was running the hotel. She was attractive and had a very outgoing personality.

Providencia was younger, very beautiful, and she knew it. She worked on it all day and had no intention of doing any other kind of work. Her day never started before noon. She was cool and arrogant, and had even the most trivial things done by servants.

Hortensia was the black sheep of the family. She was completely different from the other two. Not very pretty and not very smart, she was treated with disrespect by all, including personnel.

That was the family background presented to me by Popiolo.

The hotel Madrid itself was located at the waterfront, looking out at the Caribbean Sea and the port of Carupano. Built around a large inside patio it had only 20 rooms. Carupano was too remote and isolated for tourism, and the only guests were travelling businessmen and one airline crew every night. Most of our guest had been coming here for years and it was like one big family. Everybody knew everybody. This was Hotel Madrid when I started my career as a hotel tycoon.

Dora never found out how shaky my hotel background really was. She left the following day for a two months' absence.

Most of our guest were foreigners, so language was less of a problem for me. With most of them it was English or German, and even the Spanish speaking people spoke a more civilized Spanish that I could understand. If I had any problem in communicating with personnel, I also found a solution to this. If I did not possess the vocabulary to give long and detailed instructions, I would just grab a broom and say "Limpiar." They would always get the message.

One thing took some time to get used to. Both of the girls working in room service, had babies and were not married. They would bring their babies to the job. I found out that this was customary all over the country. Otherwise I learned fast, and I never had any serious problem with the people I had to work with. Their interpretation of cleanliness and punctuality were not the same as mine, but we always managed to get things done. I enjoyed talking to them and learned a lot about the country and the people.

A week after beginning my new job it was Christmas. That's what the calendar said, otherwise I would not have known. Of course there was a Noche Buena and the country being strictly Catholic, celebrated the birth of Christ. But it was so different from what it used to be back home. Snow would now cover the landscape over there, and church bells would ring in the holidays. The songs would be solemn like "Silent Night, Holy Night."

Here the temperature was 98° F and the music had a distinctive latin beat. Fire crackers had been going off all month long.

However, I was not homesick. All I had to do was remember the last years and the Russians back home, and I was glad to be here.

We had hardly any guests on Christmas eve, only the airline crew arrived as usual. The captain was a dutchman, and we had a few drinks together and talked about the old country. During the day I had prepared a few goodies for the limpiabotas (shoe shine boys). I felt sorry for these poor eight and ten year old boys, who had never known their fathers. They would sit all day in front of the hotel, trying to support their mothers. Some of them were pretty smart, although they had never been inside a school. It was all knowledge picked up on the street.

The oldest, called Pepito by his friends, talked like a 60 year old man, but was only twelve.

Pepito and his gang caused me a lot of grief during the average day, mostly because of their foul language. Any person going in or out of the hotel had to endure a barrage of smart and obscene remarks. I had tried both ways, by friendly persuasion and by getting tough, but nothing seemed to work. At least not for long.

New Years Eve turned out to be quite an international event. I had invited Popiolo and Wladimir and we were joined by two airline crews from Taca and Aeropostal. One captain was an American, the other was French. The two copilots were both Venezuelan, one stewardess Hungarian, and the other Columbian. It is not a big crowd, but we are having a good time.

At the end of January the President of Venezuela is visiting the city. It causes quite a commotion. A few days in advance we get some high ranking guest from Seguridad Nacional, and on the day of his visit his personal pilot and crew stay at our hotel. The President himself is guest in the house of a long time personal friend.

Those are hectic days, but very interesting. In connection with the visit I am introduced to the chief of Seguridad Nacional in Carupano. He is without any question the number one man in town. From this day on he calls me amigo, while I make sure that he is never charged for anything he eats or drinks in hotel Madrid. As soon as his subordinates find out that I am a friend of the boss, I am treated with respect and mucho cuidado.

The fringe benefits of this friendship are many. Since we are seeing each other at least three times a week, there is no need for me to report to his office any longer.

Dora returned at the end of February, just in time for the carnival season. She had no intentions of running the hotel again, and was enjoying her freedom.

Here in Carupano I got my first taste of carnival Venezuelan style. It all started out very harmless, by local businessmen driving down main street and throwing candies to the kids. The following day was called ''Bandera Negra'' (black flag), and things were getting out of hand. People started dumping pails of water over other people with no consideration of how they were dressed or what they were doing. A guy driving a motorcycle got hit while riding his bike down the main street. Blinded by the water he smashed against the sidewalk and had to be taken to the hospital. An old lady, who had trouble enough to walk on her own, got soaked by one of our ten year old limpiabotas. While he thought this was funny, the poor old lady lay helpless in the gutter. Not satisfied with using clean water, people resorted to all kinds of liquids, including paints and even gasoline. Many homes were barricaded to prevent others from entering and causing damage.

Dora found it especially tempting to initiate me into the local custom by dumping a large bowl of water over my head. I retaliated hours later by dumping her into a previously prepared bathtub. She was a good sport, she never got mad.

My friendship with the chief of police was tested when Hortensia got into an altercation with a ten year old limpiabota. It all started when she returned from the dry cleaners with a formal dress draped over her arm. The kid made a smart remark, which was answered by Hortensia with a reference to the kids mother. While she entered the building, the kid grabbed a handful of dirt, followed her into the building and unloaded the dirt all over her dress.

I had just entered the building and observed the whole scene. When he turned and wanted to run, I grabbed him by the arm and held him. Hortensia, infuriated, reached out and slapped his face.

Screaming obscenities, the kid disappeared down the street.

This should have been the end of the story, but it was not. About an hour later, a policeman entered the hotel, followed by at least a dozen men and women of all ages, and the kid. The kid had assembled the whole clan. Mother, grandmother, uncles and cousins, everybody is there.

A big palaver in the lobby, and the funny part is that nobody is talking about Hortensia hitting the kid. No, it's the big bad foreigner, El Musiu.

The policeman, knowing of my relationship with his boss, is clearly embarrassed. In order to find a solution to the problem, he asked me to follow him to the jefatura.

The clan is delighted, and the whole procession marches down main street to the jefatura. We all sit outside in the hall, while the policeman enters the office of the big boss to deliver his report. After a few minutes he returns, asking me to enter.

Dora had already called and explained the situation to the chief, but he still had to satisfy the mob outside.

"Listen," he said. "Whatever I say to you, please keep your mouth shut, and please look guilty. I don't want a riot on my hands."

I promised to do whatever necessary and he called in the clan.

Again the screaming started when they tried to explain to the chief the terrible crime I had committed. The crime had by now grown out of all proportions, and it was a miracle the kid was still alive. I sat there biting my tongue while they called me every dirty name in the book.

Finally the chief spoke up. "You have committed a very serious offense." he said to me, trying to look very official. "We can not allow a foreigner to come in here and beat up our children," he continued.

The clan loved it.

Oh, how I would have loved to really slap this kid myself and wipe that dirty smile off his face, but I remained calm and just looked at the floor. After threatening me with at least a ten year prison term if this ever happened again, he let me go. The clan is satisfied. Followed by a barrage of profanity I left the room.

The chief came over the same night to apologize, but I understood his problem.

The hotel was now always filled to capacity, and I had an excellent opportunity to meet influential people. There were sales managers of international corporations and business people from Caracas. I was certain that some of them could be helpful later on. All I had to do was wait for my confinement to come to an end. In the meantime I was not exactly suffering. Although I didn't draw a tremendous salary, I had all the food I could eat and I had a room of my own. I had also been introduced to many important people of the community and was now a respected citizen, even though I was still a confinado.

Exploring the Jungle

In April some new guests arrived at the hotel who did not fit the standard mold of business traveler. Three Americans from New York, with plans for an expedition to explore the feasibility of opening sulfur mining in the region. They came well prepared with maps and film equipment, except one little item. Nobody spoke a word of Spanish.

Since Dora happened to be in town, she had no objection to run the hotel for a week, giving me a chance to join the Americans on the expedition.

We rented a jeep and drove to the little hamlet of El Lazo, where we hired a guide, two helpers and several mules for the trip into the jungle. Not only did we encounter dense jungle, but the terrain was extremely steep at times. Coming from a rural area I had been exposed to horses since early childhood, but these mules were a different breed. They seemed to change their mind every five minutes. At one moment they would stubbornly refuse to move at all, while only minutes later they would climb the steepest mountain with the enthusiasm and ambition of a race horse. It was frightening to ride these animals in places with hardly enough room to set one foot. The mountain seemed to be a challenge, because the rougher it got the better the mules performed.

One of the Americans, without any doubt a city man, and also a little bit on the heavy side, became the biggest problem to our progress. He was always convinced that his mule was more stubborn than mine, and he wanted to switch. As soon as we had traded mules, he wanted to swap again, because now my mule was acting up. What he did not understand was that his nervous behavior was driving the animal crazy, no matter which one we gave him.

Juan, our guide, had a ball just watching him. Here I had a unique opportunity to study the characters of two different worlds. On one side was a highly intelligent geologist from the big city of New York. He was completely misplaced in this environment and acted more like a bungling idiot. On the other side was a man who grew up in the jungle. He had never seen a school, never read a book and had never been to a big city. The jungle was his backyard. He knew every plant and every animal and he knew how to handle them. I gained even more respect for this man a few hours later, when I was thrown off the mule and came face to face with a big snake.

The mule got spooked when he almost stepped on the snake, while I got caught admiring all the beautiful flora of the jungle. I sat there paralyzed, not knowing what to do. Juan dispatched the snake with one powerful swoop of the machete.

When I first entered the jungle, I had expected a tiger or a big cat lurking behind every tree. The puma of Laguna Caribe was still fresh in my memory, but I never saw a big cat in all these days. After hours of nothing happening I became fascinated with all the beautiful plant life and the colorful birds. This incident with the snake brought me back to reality.

We made several attempts to reach the sulfur springs of Mundo Nuevo from different points. After trying it from El Lazo, we went by jeep to another place called Agua Caliente. Again we hired a guide and mules, and tried it from this side. Along the way we made notes and filmed the terrain. Another day we drove to the little village of Columbia where we got only donkeys to ride. We were never able to make it from that side. The mountains were so steep that we gave up and returned. Agua Caliente appeared to be the best location for a starting point, and so we returned one more time.

The three Americans with their rear ends worn out, decide to stay behind and let me, Juan and three men go it alone. Although my own rear end is hurting, I am still a lot younger and in better shape than they are.

This time we move a lot faster. Juan takes a slightly different course and we come across a little rancho in the middle of the jungle. The rancho is inhabited only by an old man, several chickens and a goat. The old man is delighted to have company and offers us some kind of a home brew. My companions never say no to a drink, and I don't dare to refuse it, no matter what it is and what it looks like. The old man has never seen a blonde, blue eyed aleman before, and he watches me like a rare animal. He is very pleased when he sees me gulp down his drink, even though I have a hard time keeping a straight face. The only glass he has is covered with a sticky mess and the contents are still burning my intestines, but I keep smiling.

Juan is getting restless and is now pushing to get to the mines. I am greatly relieved, because I am afraid the old man might offer me another drink, and I am not sure my stomach can handle it. When we reach our goal we set up camp for the night.

All around us are little springs, and I discover that the temperatures are quite different from one to the next. They range from luke warm to steaming hot. I search for the lowest temperature I can find and climb in to soak my tired bones, just in time before total darkness. It is very relaxing, but the mosquitoes are having a feast.

Early the next morning we start collecting rock samples. Juan is very concerned that our animals get properly loaded, and soon we are on the march again. Our return trip is without incident, although the mules are heavily loaded. In Agua Caliente we load as much as possible into our jeep, but leave most of the samples behind for a later pick up. Juan and his crew get paid for their services and the four of us return to Carupano.

A few days later the Americans return to New York, while I make the arrangements to have the samples picked up and shipped also to New York via the Grace Line.

Dora can hardly wait for my return because she has travel plans again.

Her absence does not disturb me, but the constant fighting between the other two sisters is getting on my nerves. The last thing I want to do is get mixed up in a family squabble, and yet they always succeed in getting me involved. It always becomes a public spectacle, much to the delight of the personnel and to the horror of many of our guests.

Exploring the jungle, Venezuela 1952.

Several times I have talked to Dora about it, but she just shrugged her shoulders and said, "Don't worry about it."

While Dora is out of town, I receive an offer that is hard to refuse. Right next to us is the hotel Victoria, the biggest and best in town. It is twice the size of hotel Madrid, and is managed by a Spaniard who is ready to retire. The owner is also a Spaniard, although he is from Barcelona and prefers to be called a Catalan. Since we are not exactly hostile competitors, we have been talking to each other on many occasions, and there has always been enough business for both of us. So when Señor Casas offers me the job at twice the money, I see this as the best chance for advancement I ever had.

When Dora returned I gave her the bad news. Immediately she offered me the same pay, but for me it is not the pay alone. I told Dora that I was unhappy with the family fighting I was getting involved in, and that I was going to leave anyway once my time as confinado is up.

She promises to correct all the things I am complaining about, but I know that nothing is going to happen. She accuses me of being ungrateful, and in a way I feel guilty about it. I feel honestly sorry for her. She is a wonderful person, but she also has to live with her family.

Never before had I seen this many characters in one clan. Dora was as different from her sisters like the day from the night. Even from her own mother she was light years apart.

I had only met her old lady once before, when I thought she was in the process of burning down the hotel. Only the timely appearance of Dora saved me from an embarrassing situation.

I found the old lady one morning right in the middle of our lobby. She had poured some kind of liquid in a circle and put a match to it. In the center of the circle I found some burning candles and other ingredients, which I could not immediately identify. I was about ready to grab the old lady, when Dora appeared on the scene and pulled me aside.

"For God's sake, leave her alone," she said.

"Mama still believes in the old traditions, and she is now cleaning this house of all evil spirits."

She went on to tell me that her mama had her own little hotel at the end of town. Every once in a while she was coming over to take care of spiritual matters.

I also noticed that our personnel had an enormous respect for her, and her temper was feared by everyone. So I was only too glad that Dora caught me just in time before I could extinguish mama's holy fire and throw her out of the hotel.

The job at the hotel Victoria was tempting for another reason. It was organized and managed in the more disciplined european tradition, something that I would never be able to accomplish at the Madrid, no matter how hard I tried.

Dora was still pouting, but I remained firm. On the first day of May I took over at the Victoria.

It was a strange feeling to work next door, but after a few days I got over it. My amigo, the police chief, was a customer in both hotels anyway, so there was no change in our relationship. Both hotels followed the same policy of not charging the chief for food or drink, although we always kept the appearance of propriety

With a grandiose gesture the chief would say, "Send me the bill amigo," and I would respond, "No se preocupe señor." (Don't worry)

Shortly after I changed jobs, an event of historic proportions took place in Carupano. La Virgin de Coromoto, the patron saint of the country came to visit. Accompanied by ranking members of the Church and government, the statue of the Virgin was flown around the country for the first time in history. The statue of the Virgin is normally kept at the shrine in Guanare, where she first appeared to the indians of Coromoto.

Any politician would have been proud if he could draw a crowd only half as big as the one that came out to honor the Virgin. I had never seen such devotion in my life. From the youngest baby to the oldest person, the whole town was at the airport when the plane of Aeropostal Venezolana landed.

On the following day the city of Carupano rolled out the red carpet again. Flanked by little girls, dressed as angels, the holy statue was mounted on a special carriage and led through the narrow streets. As the procession moved slowly down the main street it was mass hysteria. Many people were overcome with emotion and fainted. The town was completely paralyzed during this visit. All of our personnel was out there somewhere on the streets, and there was nothing I could do about it. I would not even have tried it. For weeks and months after, the visit of the Virgin de Coromoto was the talk of the town. I was glad when it was all over and things began slowly to normalize again.

One day I had a surprise visitor. A young German with a background very similar to mine. He had also jumped ship, and he was also confined to Carupano. Actually he had been in Carupano two months longer than I had. The limpiabotas had told me a story about a German, but nobody could tell me anything specific about him. I had always thought of it as a fabrication.

Well, it turned out that Hermann Adler was for real and he was living on the other end of town with another confinado, a young Yugoslav. Both of them had a hard time to exist and could just make a living doing odd jobs.

I helped these guys as much as I could, but I was never able to get a decent job for them. All they could really do was wait for the year to pass, and return to Caracas where the action was.

I was told that the idea behind the confinement was to get newcomers out of the capital. Almost every immigrant coming to Caracas found a job and remained there. The city of Caracas was a boom town, bustling with activity and bursting at it's seams. There was a saying in the country: "Caracas is Venezuela."

The rest of the country was still in the 19th century.

The government had no control over these immigrants and could not dictate where they should settle. The illegals however, that was a different story. They could tell me to go to Carupano, or else. But what could we do? We did not have a nickel to invest, and there was no industry to make use of our talents. So with rare exceptions, we just became another bum in town.

Carupano had settled down to the slow pace and easy going lifestyle of the past. My biggest problem of the day was always to get things started in the morning. Fernando, our

Italian chef, had to get up at five in the morning to go to the mercado libre for fresh produce. If I did not call Fernando, he would not get up. One airline crew had to be awakened at six for the first flight out of Carupano. The waiter had to serve their breakfast at 6:30, and if I did not get up, nothing would move. This happened only once, and the airline raised hell with me because the flight left one hour late. A few times we had close calls, with the crew getting dressed in the car that took them to the airport.

Since almost all of our guests were repeat customers, I had developed a close relationship with many of them. Some of them expected me to go out with them for nightly entertainment, and that meant only one place.

A few miles out of town was a cute little restaurant called El Copey. It was nothing spectacular, but its location was idyllic. Situated right at the water's edge, framed by coconut palms and a white sandy beach, it was a setting fit for a movie. Music was supplied by a jukebox and there was plenty of room for dancing. I had been there several times with my amigo the police chief and his buddy the colonel, commander of the garrison. However, my favorite people to take out there were still the airline people, mostly because they would always bring their own girl. Some of the pilots had some kind of a relationship with a certain stewardess, but not all. If the captain or his copilot did not show any interest, it meant she was available to be courted by ordinary folks like me.

What I missed the most was the carefree relationship with the opposite sex, which I had experienced in the European countries. In Carupano it was impossible to ask a girl even to go to the movies at night. This came very close to asking for her hand in marriage and would always involve taking big brother or some other chaperone along. Anybody sneaky enough to get around these old customs would run the risk of being invited to a shotgun wedding. As tempting as some of these local beauties might be, I was too scared to try it. At age twenty-four, I was not ready to settle down in Carupano.

None of the girls working for the airlines was a native Venezuelan. They came from Italy, Germany and many from East European countries now under communist rule.

Through my position at the hotel it was easy for me to get to know many of them, and over a period of time a friendship developed. We had many things to talk about, and with two of the girls it became more than just a friendship.

One of them was an Italian girl called Nina, but everybody called her La Condesa. Our romance lasted only two months, when she was transferred to the international division of the airline. The other girl was Hanna. She was ten years older than I was, but we had a lot in common. She was from Czechoslovakia and had fled from Communism like I had. My relationship with Hanna lasted a little longer, but ended the same way it did with Nina.

All these relationships could not bridge the loneliness I felt at times. I was looking forward to their arrival, but it hardly ever amounted to more than a one night stand. We could never make any plans or spend a weekend together. It was just coming in at five in the afternoon and leaving early the next morning. Even when she was there I could never get out of the hotel before nine at the earliest. Some times we would see each other once a week, and some times three weeks would pass before I would see her again.

It was now a year ago that my ship had arrived at the port of La Guaira. A lot had happened since that day, but I was satisfied with the progress I had made. I was a confinado, but I had a job and was able to make a living. I had learned the language, and I was no longer afraid of being returned to Germany. Also, I had met many people and I was certain I had laid the groundwork for a new life. I had every reason to be content, and yet something was bothering me. More and more I became aware that I missed Lu. The memory of pleasant hours we had shared in Germany became stronger and stronger, until one day I decided to write her again.

The last time I had written was shortly after my arrival in the Laguna Caribe. At that time everything seemed so remote and my future so very uncertain. I felt guilty of keeping alive a relationship that might not develop into anything. I was convinced that I had no right to have her wait for some day that might never come, nor did I want to bind myself with promises which could not be fulfilled. So I wrote her honestly about my situation, and asked her to go out and meet other boys. I was also convinced, that her parents would never encourage her to follow me to this far away, little known land. I was relieved and saddened at the same time when I received her last letter. She told me that she had met another young man, and she wished me good luck for the future. Now I could not bring myself to write that first letter again, afraid to open old wounds. "What if she is married?" I asked myself. "What right do I have to interfere in her life again?" My life remained unsettled and uncertain, not much had changed in that respect. But the more I thought about her, the more I missed her, and one day my letter was on it's way to Germany. I started counting the days and waited anxiously for the mailman. Two weeks after mailing my letter the suspense was building up. Would she answer? I must have acted like an expectant father, or like a criminal waiting for the sentence to be pronounced. Again and again I asked myself if I should have written this letter at all. My question was answered a week later, when a letter arrived with the familiar handwriting. Somehow I had the feeling that whatever this letter said, it would have an effect on the rest of my life. The fact that she had answered at all was a good sign.

In the privacy of my room I opened the letter and read it over and over again. She was not married, and she missed me as much as I missed her. In fact she had also wanted to write again, but was afraid she had no current address. When my letter arrived it was like the answer to a prayer. Lu's letter put a new spark into my life. With renewed hope and enthusiasm I was looking forward to the end of my confinado days and a new beginning in Caracas. In my next letter I reported in detail about my life in Carupano, but leaving out the part of my days in jail and the confinement. She would not have understood, and reading it on paper was not the same as telling someone face to face. Furthermore it would have given ammunition to mama's contention that I was an adventurer.

Otherwise not very much was happening in Carupano. Life would have been pretty dull, but the hotel kept me on my toe's with many little things that required my attention. It was a balancing act between keeping the hired help happy, and on the other side keeping the customers satisfied. A job not always easy to do. There was Señor

Contreras, who had reached a low point in the standings with Carlos, our waiter. Señor Contreras always arrived in the dining room at five minutes before closing time, demanding service. Carlos would serve what was ordered, but served in a manner which left no doubt that Carlos was displeased. This in turn would result in a complaint about the outrageous service in our dining room. As diplomatic as I could, I suggested that maybe the food and the service might be better at an earlier hour, but Señor Contreras never seemed to get the message.

Then there was Señor Fuentes, who brought chef Fernando to a boiling point with his never ending complaints about the food, no matter what was served. The spaghetti was either too hard or too soft, the coffee too strong or too weak. I was afraid Fernando might poison him one day.

My biggest confrontation with Fernando came one day when a delivery was made. It all had started very innocently when I went dancing to our favorite nightspot of Copey. I was in the company of two pilots and a stewardess from the airline.

All of a sudden there was a commotion down at the beach. Some of the natives had caught a giant sea turtle. These animals are fairly easy to catch once they come up on the beach. The natives would just turn them over on their back and they would be helpless, unable to move.

One of the guys asked me if I wanted to buy this monster, but I just laughed and declined. What I did not notice was that a deal was made behind my back.

The following day Fernando came storming into my little office. It took a while before I understood what he was talking about. He wanted to know why I had purchased la tortuga, and what I wanted him to do with it.

"What turtle?" I asked.

"The one on the truck outside." Fernando replied, adding a few carambas and worse.

Suspecting foul play I ran outside, and there was a truck with two guys I had met the night before, unloading the big turtle.

"Hey you guys, what are you doing?" I demanded to know. "I told you last night I don't want to buy it."

"Don't worry Señor," one of the guys answered. "It's all paid for."

He was all smiles.

The turtle was still alive, and Fernando refused to touch it.

As far as I was concerned, I had never killed a chicken in my life. I was not even getting close to this monster. The monster was already on the street and both fellows refused flatly to load it again. They were about ready to leave, when I realized I had to make an offer.

Meanwhile several of our guest had assembled and followed with great interest the ongoing palaver. There was talk about the delicacy of turtle soup and turtle eggs and everybody wanted turtle for dinner. While the poor animal was struggling on it's back, a heated debate over it's fate ensued.

Fernando wanted to take it across the street and release it on the beach. I was also in favor of this solution, but nobody else voted for it. All of our assembled guests insisted it was a shame to throw away a gourmet dinner so close at hand. Finally the fate of the turtle was sealed. A compromise was negotiated. The two guys who had delivered it agreed to slaughter the turtle and carve it into small pieces. Fernando declared himself willing to take it from there.

As far as the gourmet dinner was concerned, it was a big disaster. The meat, after hours of cooking, was as tough as shoe leather. The animal had also produced a bowl full of eggs which looked like little ping pong balls, but tasted more like cotton balls. I wished I had insisted in returning this giant animal to its natural habitat, the Caribbean Sea. It was too late. . . .

Again it was November, and I felt I had fulfilled the conditions of my contract with the government. Proudly I informed my amigo the police chief of this important date.

I don't know what I had expected to happen at this moment. Perhaps the chief would sit down behind his desk, fill out an official document, and declare me a legal citizen?

Nothing like this happened. The chief just laughed as if I had told him a joke, and said, "What do you need papers for amigo? Is anybody bothering you?''

''No,'' I said, ''nobody is bothering me, I just want to be legal.''

''You are legal, if I say so,'' was his answer.

''As long as I am the police chief here you don't need any papers. We all know who you are,'' he said, walking out of the room.

My second Christmas in Carupano dawned and still no papers. I had never received a package from anybody, but this year the mailman delivered a small package from Lu. Later in the afternoon I was sitting in front of the hotel and looking across the sea. In the distance I could see the Isla de Margarita, the pearl island, and somewhere over there behind all this water was Europe and Lu. I missed her more than ever, but I was not homesick for Europe. I wanted her here with me. When I thought about the cold and the snow that would cover the land now, I was glad to be here. I had to talk to the chief again about my papers, as long as he was in the Christmas spirit.

He was in a good mood all right, but he still didn't want to hear anymore about my papers. No matter which way I presented my case, his answer remained the same. His charm was disarming. I could not even get mad at him, yet I was scared that my future had been put on hold. I was flattered that everybody liked me and wanted me to stay, but this was not the way to go about it.

The chief had made several remarks about meeting some local girls and getting married, but I pretended to be busy with my job. He would have never understood why I was scared of the local girls, while at the same time being very attracted to them. I had never told him about my girl in Germany out of fear he might think I was a snob. As if the locals were not good enough for me.

Christmas had come and gone. It was almost Easter of 1953, when I decided to take things into my own hand.

Carlos, a Spanish friend of mine, who represented a big pharmaceutical company in the eastern part of Venezuela, arrived in Carupano shortly before the Semana Santa (Easter week). He was one of the few people who travelled by car in this region, mainly because he carried a lot of samples. His plan was to return straight to Caracas to spend the Easter week with his family. When I told Carlos of my plan, he agreed to take me along, glad to have company on this long and hazardous trip. My next trip was to see the chief again. I had my story all ready for him.

A close friend in Caracas was getting married and had requested my presence on this special day. What I needed was an official paper, allowing me to travel to Caracas.

The chief promised to take care of it.

What I did not tell the chief was my mode of transportation. In case of any difficulties I was prepared to go without the paper. For this reason it was better he didn't know.

Next I told my boss about my impending departure, also that I might not return.

Three days before Easter was our scheduled day of departure. Carlos had one more call to make in the morning and was ready to leave right after lunch. We wanted to get as far as Puerto La Cruz by nightfall. The paper was on the chief's desk, but had not been signed. Finally at 11:45 a.m. I got a call. The chief had just come in and signed my document. I was there in five minutes to pick it up.

"Thank you very much, and I will see you next week," was all I said.

"Vaya con Dios," he responded, wishing me a safe trip.

There was so much more I wanted to say, but did not dare. I liked this man and I owed him so much. He had made my life so much more pleasant and easy in Carupano, yet I did not know how far I could trust him.

We left town shortly after one. Not exactly the coolest time of the day, but if we wanted to reach Puerto La Cruz before dark, we had to get started.

I looked for a long time at the town disappearing slowly in a cloud of dust. In spite of a few rough days in the beginning, Carupano has always had a special place in my heart. I had met many decent people and made many good friends.

"You know," I said to Carlos, "I feel as if I have lived in this town for at least ten years."

He nodded his head and said."I bet it wasn't always easy for you."

The strangest thing was that I talked as if everything was settled and I was on my way to a new beginning in Caracas. The fact was that I did not even know if I had to return to Carupano or if I would manage to get my papers in order.

The scenery was spectacular as we drove along the Gulf of Cariaco. Only the cloud of dust trailing behind us spoiled the beautiful landscape. There was very little traffic on the road until we reached the city of Cumana.

Cumana was still a small quiet town but the site of historical importance. It was in 1523 when the Spaniards established their first permanent settlement in this part of the new world. I would come back many times in later years, but now there was no time to visit historic places. On this day our goal was Puerto La Cruz before nightfall.

We reached the city at the time the sun was slowly sinking into the Caribbean as a big red ball of fire. Carlos drove straight to a little hotel at the beach where he was a regular customer. After dinner we enjoyed a cold beer at the veranda and talked about the trip ahead of us the next day. Carlos was nervous about the second phase of our trip and wanted to get an early start.

It was six in the morning when we left Puerto La Cruz. For a while we had the luxury of a paved road until we reached the city of Barcelona. From here we had to go in a big sweeping circle, the only way to get to Caracas. Soon we had reached the hot desert region of the Llanos, and I was beginning to understand what Carlos was so worried about. The car and it's passengers were taking quite a beating. We could taste the dust between our teeth as the sun was burning without mercy from a bright blue sky. This was before the time of air conditioned automobiles. The one thing nobody wanted to do was swallow the dust stirred up by someone in front. So when a driver saw a cloud of dust coming up behind him, the race was on. He would try at all cost to avoid being overtaken. This of course led to some pretty wild contests, until one of the drivers would give up and keep his distance. What made this especially dangerous was the fact that the next village might be 100 miles away. In between there was nothing but heat, dust and some dry desert brush. It was a tremendous relief when we finally reached San Juan de los Morros and a paved road for the final stretch to Caracas.

The traffic was getting heavier and heavier as we approached the capital. For me it was a shock to enter the noise and traffic chaos of the big city again. After an absence of a year and a half in a remote, sleepy little town, it was almost frightening. Only the joy of having returned to civilization and the prospect of seeing my friends again was greater than anything else.

I had written to the Klampferer's about my impending return and was glad to know they had a room for me. Carlos dropped me off at their place, and as we pulled my suitcase from the dust covered trunk of his car, I looked at him and had to laugh. He looked like a coalminer just returning from a day at the mine.

"You don't look much better," he said smiling. My throat was so dry, I could barely talk. It was embarrassing to face my friends like this, but they knew where I was coming from. There was no way I could clean up on the busy street.

After greeting the Klampferer family and a refreshing welcome drink, I went to the backyard to dust off my belongings. Even inside the closed suitcase I still found a layer of dust. A nice shower made me feel like a human being again, but by now I was more than ready for bed. I was dead tired, yet I was laying awake for a long time, unable to sleep. My thoughts wandered back to that quiet little town and the people I had left behind, while I was listening to the noise of the big city outside.

A New Beginning in Caracas

After the Easter holidays my first trip was to the Immigration office. When the girl at the reception asked me for the purpose of my visit, I simply replied I came to pick up my papers. What I expected was a run through different departments and a lot of questions. Instead she took my confinado paper and disappeared for a few minutes. When she returned, she simply handed me an envelope which had my name written on it.

"This has been ready for several months," she said, "but nobody requested it."

I could not believe my ears. Was this for real? Would anything be this simple in the land of mañana? I had expected all kinds of trouble, but not this.

Well, I was not going to argue with her. All I had to do was go to another department, have my picture and fingerprints taken and a cedula (identification card) would be issued. I had taken a giant step forward.

When I returned home that afternoon, I was the proud owner of a cedula. A legal resident at last. A new phase of my life was about to begin. I was on my own. Free to do what I wanted to do and live where I wanted to live.

Top priority was finding a job, and now my hotel connections should prove helpful.

Many of the people I had met in Carupano could not be reached, because they were out of town. A few people I was able to make contact with, offered me a job in outside sales. These jobs called for extensive travelling.

I wanted to get into sales, but for the time being I wanted to remain in Caracas and get settled. So when I met Don Raimundo again, I accepted his offer for a territory in Caracas.

Don Raimundo was the owner of Perfumeria Arisart, the makers of several lines of soap, perfumes and colognes. He was also a shrewd businessman who did like to make a lot of money, but did not believe in paying his hired help. For that reason there was a tremendous turnover of personnel. After only two months on the job I had reached the top and was named sales manager. When I confronted Don Raimundo with the question of what the salary of a sales manager would be, he did not appreciate the question. In his opinion I should be grateful for the title.

I had seen enough to realize there was no future in this job, and kept my eyes open for a better opportunity.

This opportunity presented itself in the form of Señor Casas, the brother of my former boss and owner of the hotel Victoria in Carupano. I had met him once before, when he had spent a vacation at the hotel. He was a charming man, and I had actually liked him better than his more arrogant brother Alfonso.

We met at the corner of Avenida Urdaneta, and it was like old friends meeting after a long separation. He invited me to a nearby restaurant, and over a cafecito and we talked for almost an hour. He wanted to know all about my experiences since I left Carupano and showed a real interest in my life in general. I told him about Lu, and my preparations to bring her over to this country as soon as possible. When we parted he had offered me a job in his company, a job I knew I was going to accept.

This meeting could not have come at a better time. I had seen enough at Perfumeria Arisart to be convinced that Don Raimundo's way of doing business was not my style. With all our turnover of personnel there was no stability, and although I enjoyed a good relationship with Don Raimundo, I was certain this would change sooner or later. If I ever wanted to be successful in my job, I had to disagree with him on a number of issues. But he was not the man to appreciate it, and I was not the man who enjoyed fighting with the boss. Accepting the offer of Señor Casas was my way out before it was too late.

It was a move I should never have to regret, because Señor Casas proved to be the gentleman I had always expected him to be. He became more to me than just a boss. He became a real friend and adviser. I benefited greatly from his extensive knowledge of the import business, when I joined him and his two Dutch partners at Comercial Venezolana. This agency represented many European and American companies in Venezuela. We represented famous lines of food from Denmark and Holland. Bicycles and radios from England and lingerie from the United States. There was a lot to learn. Not only did I have to know the merchandise I wanted to sell, but I had to be familiar with pricing, shipping regulations and import duties for a variety of items. I also had to be able to convert foreign currency like the British pound and shillings into Bolivares. But most of all I had to learn doing business Venezuelan style. I had to learn that price was not always a deciding factor when it came to who was getting the order. It was a matter of knowing the right person and pay the proper dues.

I had seen this system already at work in the daily life with public officials. Where I would pay a certain fee for a drivers license, while taking no test at all. A policeman always expected to be paid, so that he could forgive a traffic violation, justified or not. I had experienced first hand how business was conducted with the authorities, but in the private business sector it was a new game for me, a way of doing business I had never learned. The trick was to get to know the right person and gain their confidence. Some times the introduction of a friend would open the door. Otherwise time and persistence would bring eventual success.

One of the first things I had done after returning to Caracas, was to start proceedings to bring Lu into the country. I could not very well expect her to travel the same way I did.

There was also the question of receiving her parents' permission. Lu was going to be twenty one this year, but we both felt better if everybody agreed. Now I was glad that I had met her parents before.

In a letter to her parents I asked for their permission and understanding while promising to do everything to take good care of their daughter.

It was a difficult decision, I could understand, because Lu was the only child they had. In 1946 I never thought about how parents would feel when their children leave home for an uncertain future. I was so obsessed with the idea of escaping from Communism that nothing else was important to me. Only years later did I even think about how my parents must have felt. Not only because I left home, but because they certainly knew the danger involved in trying to cross the border. All this went through my mind, when I wrote my letter to Lu's parents. A lot had changed since 1946. Lu did not have to cross any hostile borders. However it was an insecure future in a country barely known to most people. A country with a lot of potential, but still mostly undeveloped.

I was very happy, when I received word of her parents consent. In June I had all the necessary papers for Lu's immigration. It was a happy time on both sides of the Atlantic, spent with preparations for a big journey on one side and with anticipation of a happy reunion on the other. At a time when nobody in Germany was thinking of trips to the sunny Riviera, Lu was getting ready to travel to Genova-Italy where she was to board the Italian liner "Castel Bianco" for the trip to the new world. We began to count the days.

Caracas was growing fast. There was construction everywhere, but new apartments were rented faster than they could be built. So far I had been unable to find any place I was able to afford. When a bigger room at the Klampferer house became available, I gladly accepted the offer. It was no luxury, but it was conveniently located. Also the fact that the other members of the family spoke German, would make it a lot easier for Lu to get over the first culture shock.

When the day finally came, the Klampferers were almost as excited as I was. There was no lack of last minute advice, and a lot of kidding about our approaching reunion. Stories about happy and not so happy reunions made the round.

Sleep didn't come easy that night. I was tossing and turning, while a thousand questions flashed through my mind. It was hard to imagine that Lu was already so near, and tomorrow we would be together again. Would she like it here? Would we be happy? Only time would be able to answer those questions.

I was up at dawn, unable to stay in bed any longer. All of a sudden I was afraid the ship might enter La Guaira and I would not be there. Poor Lu would be in panic.

The new autopista Caracas-La Guaira was not yet finished, and again I had to travel the old winding highway down to the coast. I still did not own a car and had decided to take a taxi. It was not very expensive, once I got past the price negotiating stage. For a foreigner this was always a little more time consuming, because he had to prove that he spoke the language and knew the facts of life in this country. Once this point was settled, I was on my way.

The driver was burning rubber as usual as he negotiated the over 360 curves.

"Slow down" I said, as we drove past the most dangerous of all. Looking at all those crosses and candles of past victims I was getting scared.

"What if something happens to me, and there is no one to take care of Lu," I thought. She would be all alone in a strange country.

"Don't worry Señor," said the driver and began telling me a long story of how good a driver he was.

The ship was only a tiny spot on the horizon, when I arrived at the terminal in La Guaira. Most of the arriving passengers were Italians and the terminal was filled with the sound of Italian speaking relatives by the time the ship finally entered the port.

All passengers were lined up on the starboard side of the "Castel Bianco," waving wildly and screaming. The same was repeated on our side, as people began to recognize each other.

All I could see was a mass of cheering people. No sign of Lu. What deck was she on?

Finally, the fellow next to me grabbed my arm.

"Signorina" he said, pointing over to a spot on the promenade deck.

Lu had recognized me first and desperately tried to get my attention, without success. She finally caught the attention of my neighbor, and he understood.

There she was, just the way I remembered her, wearing a white summer dress with bright colored flowers. What a relief to see her.

Now began the long wait before she was cleared through

immigration, but shortly before noon I could finally hold her in my arms. Two and a half years of waiting had come to an end. The moment we had both waited for so long was here. A journey had come to a happy ending. A new journey was about to begin. This one we would travel together.

For the next two hours everything was closing down for the siesta. We had to wait for the luggage to be unloaded, and decided to go for a little walk, just to get away from the crowd. The temperature had climbed past the 100° F mark. Lu was getting her first taste of tropical climate, but we hardly noticed the sweltering heat as we walked hand in hand to the edge of town. A lot had happened in our lives since I left two and a half years ago, and we kept looking at each other to see if we had changed. For me it was as if I had left her yesterday. The only thing unusual was to see her in these new surroundings.

"I can't believe it," I said. "Is it really you? Are you really here, or is it just a dream?"

"It is me," she answered, "and this time you will not get rid of me again."

We had only eyes for each other, and so it was no surprise when Lu's foot got stuck in the pavement, resulting in a heel broken off her right shoe. Walking barefoot on this scorching pavement was out of the question, so a temporary repair job had to hold up until we returned to the terminal.

Once we had retrieved Lu's belongings and finished fare negotiations with a taxicab driver, we could rest our tired feet in comfort. As we started climbing the winding road to Caracas, the temperature became also more pleasant. We had so much to talk about, that Lu did not even have the time to observe all those steep cliffs and dangerous curves. She did not see all those little crosses, placed there in memory of unfortunate travelers who did not make it. When we entered the traffic chaos of Caracas however, she admitted that she was glad to have escaped the twisting mountain roads. Her stomach was beginning to react.

Lu felt right at home with mother and father Klampferer, who had been waiting anxiously for our arrival. When Gretchen and the rest of the family came home that night a lively conversation about the old country got started. They all had roots over there and were still deeply concerned about what was going on in Europe.

Lu answered their questions as good as she was able to, but the excitement of the day caught up with her at last. Her sparkling eyes were beginning to show signs of losing their sparkle. No wonder she was tired. It had been a long day, filled with many new impressions. A day were she stepped ashore in a new country with exotic people, and the unfamiliar sound of their language. A hot climate she was not used to, but also the day of a happy reunion.

I was encouraged by the way she had mastered the first day, and I was hopeful she would adjust to the new world around her.

Although coming from a nice average middle class family, she had never been spoiled with material things. She also had the misfortune to grow up in a time of war and destruction. Her home town of Kiel had been an important base for the German Navy during World War II, and as such had become a prime target for allied bombers. When the ever increasing air raids made it necessary to send the children to safer areas of southern Germany, she had been sent away from home and family with other children. She had endured the hardship of the years immediately following the war. Only now as she was leaving Germany, the country was very slowly beginning to lift itself from the ashes.

In the days following her arrival, it was a real pleasure watching her adjust to the new life. Many relationships like ours had failed miserably after only a very short time. A lot of girls came to this country criticizing everything just because it was different. They never gave it a chance to learn and try to understand why it might be different. Once we met a young couple, and during the conversation the question came up "How do you like it here?"

"Fine," said Lu, "I love it."

The other women looked at her in disbelief.

"Are you serious?" she asked.

Meanwhile Lu was happy exploring her new world, discovering things she had never seen or tasted in her life.

Avocados, papayas, guavas, and mangoes, all these things were new to her and she enjoyed them. She tried to communicate with people in spite of the language barrier. It only created a greater desire to learn the new language.

I took her down to the mercado libre to teach her the finer points of bargaining. Within a short time she was able to go on her own and handle it very well. The only thing she would never get used to were the cockroaches, and those we had plenty of. They were everywhere, and spraying helped only for a few hours. No matter how clean a person was, it was impossible to keep them out of the house, especially in the old downtown section with the old colonial style open homes.

On one of the weekends following Lu's arrival, Gretchen and her boyfriend invited us for a ride to Baruta. They thought it was only fitting to introduce Lu to the place which had also been the first stop after my arrival, and also the place of our first meeting.

Pepe's place had not changed, and Lu was surprised to find herself among so many German speaking people. Here was a little corner of Germany, a home away from home.

Our lucky break came barely two months after our reunion, and it could not have come at a better time. I had been calling on some accounts in the downtown area and was on my way home for lunch. Walking down the few blocks I was approached by a little boy who tried to sell me a lottery ticket. It was nothing unusual to be pestered by all kinds of individuals, from a dirty beggar showing off his open sores, a shoe shine boy, or a variety of salesmen peddling everything from newspapers to stolen goods. Little kids selling lottery tickets were also a normal part of the street scene. The kid following me this day was persistent. He didn't take no for an answer. Again and again he pulled my coattail and held the ticket under my nose. "Compre Señor," he insisted. "Buy this number, it's a lucky one," he said. "It's the first prize."

"Sure," I said, "that's what they all say."

"No Señor," he replied, "not this one."

My resistance broke down. Who could resist this cute

little charmer.

I had said no a hundred times. I had told him to get lost and even threatened him with bodily harm. All to no avail, this kid was tough.

So I reached into my pocket and came up with three Bolivares (about 1 dollar). That was all I had in small change and I figured that should be enough to get rid of the kid.

These lottery tickets consisted of one number being broken up into 20 coupons. The whole ticket sold for 20 Bolivares or each coupon for 1 Bolivar.

The kid was happy. His tenacity had won again and he was all smiles.

"Muchas gracias Señor," he said, as he handed me the three coupons. "You will see, it is the first prize," he screamed as he disappeared around the next corner.

I shoved the three coupons into my pocket and forgot all about them for a few days.

Walking down the same street a week later, I found myself looking at a little newspaper stand. My eyes focused on a list filled with numbers. "Loteria del Estado Miranda," the heading said in big bold letters.

Reaching into my pocket I pulled out my three coupons and started looking for the number 1326.

"Boy, that was close," I thought as I looked at the number 1327 with a win of 500 Bolivares.

All of a sudden I stood there, unable to believe what I was seeing. There it was, printed vertical in bold black print. Number 1326, Bolivares 40000.00.

This meant 2000.00 Bolivares per coupon. I had won 6000.00 Bolivares (about $2000.00). That was a lot of money in 1953, especially for a young couple of immigrants, starting out in life with nothing but what they carried in their suitcase.

I stood there absolutely dumbfounded, looking at the number over and over again. Was this really true? Was this really happening to me? I had never won anything in my life.

When I looked at the ticket, I discovered the main office of the lottery was only a short three blocks away.

"You might as well find out if this is for real or just a

dream," I thought.

I was almost running to get to the lottery office, and barely 20 minutes later I held a bundle of brand new 500 Bolivar bank notes in my shaking hands. No taxes deducted, 6000 Bolivares in cold cash.

The next thing I wanted to see was Lu's face, when I showed her the money. It was about time for lunch anyway, and I hurried home with a tight grip on the bundle of money in my pocket.

Lu looked at me, then at the money, and then at me again with a big question mark on her face.

"Count it," I said.

She picked up the money and started counting aloud, "fifty, one hundred, one fifty, two hundred."

"Wait a minute," I said. "Count it again."

"Fifty, one hundred," she started again, but then her eyes lit up.

"Where did you get the money?" she wanted to know.

"Don't tell anybody," I said in a whisper, "I held up a bank."

She just couldn't picture me as a bank robber, and when I started laughing, she joined in.

"Now I know," she said. "You collected the money for your office."

"No," I said, "we are filthy rich, the money is all ours."

Half the fun of winning the money, was planning what to do with it. At this stage in our lives it was like a gift from heaven.

I had just paid for Lu's trip, and most of the things we needed now required larger amounts of money. After careful consideration we decided on two things. Our first priority was a place of our own. For a house we did not have enough money, but at least we had the money for a rental deposit on a new apartment and some furniture.

Priority number two was a car. Our first automobile, to give us some mobility.

The apartment situation in Caracas remained difficult, but our money proved to be helpful. Only a few days after our good fortune we discovered a beautiful studio apartment in Colinas de Bello Monte. It was located in the modern eastern section of Caracas, in a building only a few years old. The reason it was not swallowed up in five minutes, was that the owner wanted to sell his furniture with the apartment. The price was right, the furniture to our liking, and we were the lucky renters of a modern studio apartment. Our first place we could really call home, our own little paradise.

The Klampferers were sad to see us go, but they had known all along that this was only a temporary arrangement. We had become part of the family and we will always be grateful for the help and support given to us. We remained good friends and visited frequently during our stay in Caracas. In October we had finally collected all the papers required to get married. The wedding date had been set for Saturday, November 14th. Since neither one of us had any family in the country, we had decided on a quiet and simple ceremony.

Lu had selected her good friend Inge as a witness. The two had met on board the "Castel Bianco" where Inge was returning from a vacation trip to Germany.

I had asked my friend Hans, also a young German businessman, to be my witness. He was also living in Caracas, but we had actually met in my early hotel days in Carupano.

With all the necessary arrangements made, we arrived at the precinct of El Recreo at the given time of twelve noon.

The first official act took place downstairs. It reminded me of a movie I had seen once, where the client had to pay the madam first, before he was allowed to go upstairs. In my case, I was told that his honor El Jefe Civil was now on overtime. So was his deputy, and both had to be paid in cash. The price was twenty Bolivares each. After paying the secretary in cash, we were allowed to proceed upstairs.

His honor was on the phone when we entered, and he hardly noticed us. His conversation was definitely very private, but our presence didn't seem to bother him. His deputy sat there, playing with a pencil and at the same time almost undressing the two girls with his eyes. When his honor finally finished his conversation, he was all smiles, welcoming us to his humble office. Probably in the knowledge he was dealing with a cash paying customer, his first official act was to put his jacket on. His second official act was to order his deputy to do the same. Once these minor formalities were taken care off, the ceremony could begin.

After reading about five lines of his text, he abruptly stopped.

"Does everyone understand Spanish?" he demanded to know.

"No," I answered, "La Señora does not speak the language yet."

For a moment I was afraid this might cause some more problems.

"I should not have said that," I thought. "I should have kept my mouth shut.

His honor however was not going to let a little minor detail like this spoil his act. "Bueno, no importa," was all he said, as he continued to read from the two pages of script.

When the time came to say "I do," I gave Lu a gentle push with my elbow, and obediently she answered, "Si."

"I now pronounce you man and wife," said his honor.

His honor shook our hand and wished us a long and happy life together. When the deputy followed his boss, he could not let the opportunity go by without looking down into Lu's cleavage, instead of looking into her eyes. He also spent considerably less time in congratulating me.

As we left the building, another young couple was just in the process of paying their dues before being allowed upstairs. Business was booming.

A little luncheon with our closest friends at the luxurious Tamanaco hotel, and afterwards a little party at our new apartment. That was our wedding day. No honeymoon trip was planned, because I could not afford the time off from work. The last few weeks had been our honeymoon.

One of the first events of the new year 1954 was the purchase of our first automobile ever. A friend in Carupano had taught me how to drive in his jeep. I had purchased the drivers license as was customary, so the only thing missing was the car. In the used car section of El Universal, we found the car in our price range, a 1951 Henry J. The seller was a lawyer, although the car was registered under his wife's name.

I was in for another lesson in the customs of Venezuelan society.

Señor Cardoza, that was the lawyers name, had asked me to return to his house the following day and pick up the registration papers for the car.

"My wife has to sign it," he said.

When I rang the doorbell the next day, a maid answered.

"May I see el Señor Cardoza?" I asked.

"He is not in," she replied.

"What about la Señora?" I asked, "Is she in?" I thought since she had to sign the papers, she would know what I was talking about.

The maid disappeared and la Señora herself appeared on the scene.

"Buenas dias Señora," I said very politely, and then I went on to explain the reason of my visit. At first I got a blank stare.

"What car?" she inquired.

"The green one," I said, "the Henry J."

"Oh, that one," she said, and her eyes began to turn hostile.

"I have nothing to do with that car," she said.

"But you are la Señora Cardoza," I said, "and the car is in your name."

"I am la Señora Cardoza," she said in a tone of voice that would cut steel, "but if you want those papers signed you have to talk to that whore in Sabana Grande."

Wow! That was strong language, and I stood there like an idiot, unable to figure this one out. She looked as if she would slam the door in my face at any moment, while I was desperately trying to find out what I had done to deserve this kind of treatment.

She finally noticed the look of despair in my eyes and must have felt sorry for me. "He lives with another woman," she said. "The car is in her name."

When I continued to stand there motionless, undecided what my next move should be, she asked me to wait and disappeared into the house. When she returned, she handed me a piece of paper with an address written on it.

"I am sure you will also find my husband there now," she said.

I found the address she had given me in the district of Sabana Grande. The doorbell was answered by a little boy, about five years old.

"Papa, Papa," he screamed, when I asked for Señor Cardoza.

He came to the door and didn't even seem to be surprised to see me there. In a minute he returned and handed me the signed papers. When I told my boss about this episode, he just laughed and said that was common practice.

Otherwise the car gave me little or no mechanical trouble, but I had not seen the end of the other kind of trouble.

The former owner, although a lawyer by profession, seemed to have very little respect for the laws of the land. I was about to find this out very soon.

Driving down the Avenida Urdaneta one morning on my way to the office, I noticed a police car following me. Lu was with me, as I was about to drop her off at a friends house.

After trailing me for two blocks, the car pulled alongside and one of the officers signaled me to pull over to the curbside. They parked right behind me and one of the officers approached the car.

"May I see your driver's license?" he asked politely. I handed him my license.

"What did I do?" I asked him, unaware of any infraction I might have committed.

"We are looking for this car, Señor," he said. All he could tell me was that my license plate number was on his list of wanted automobiles, and that he had to bring me in to the jefatura. I knew, that I could not buy my way out of this one. However, after a short consultation with his partner and a small fee of course, the two had no objection to take Lu to the friends house first. They followed right behind me, and after dropping off Lu, they delivered me and my car to the jefatura. Immediately after arriving there I asked for permission to use the phone, which was granted. At least I could call the office and let them know I would be late.

Now the waiting began.

The desk sergeant explained to me, that he only knew that the car and driver was wanted by the Department of Motor Vehicles.

"All we can do is call them and let them know we have the car," he said. "They will send somebody to pick you up," he said.

"When is that going to be ?" I asked him.

"Quien sabe, Señor," he replied. Who knows?

I was still sitting there at noon, when the officer who had arrested me, returned to the precinct.

"You still here amigo?" he asked.

"I like it so much, I don't want to leave," I said smiling, but inside I was getting desperate. Suddenly I had an idea.

"Where are you going from here?" I asked.

"I am off duty now, I'm going home," he said.

"Why can't you take me down to the Department of Motor Vehicles?" I asked, and then added, "I'll buy you lunch on the way over."

That sounded good to him, and he went to talk it over with his superior. Since I was apparently not classified a dangerous criminal, his boss had no objections.

I was glad my friend did not stop at a very expensive place. He was satisfied with a few empanadas at the next street corner. We had plenty of time, because until two in the afternoon everything was closed for the siesta.

When we arrived at the department I was handed over to a desk sergeant, and from there taken before a traffic judge. My file had been pulled and was now placed before the judge.

He studied it for a moment and then started writing down some numbers.

I wanted to say something, but decided to keep my mouth shut for the moment.

The judge had hardly looked at me, and even now without looking up he pronounced sentence. "Three hundred and thirty Bolivares," he said, and read all the different laws I was supposed to have broken.

I stood there in silence, waiting for him to look at me. When he finally did, I said, "Señor, when a driver breaks the law, who is getting charged, the driver or the car?"

The judge was not amused. Why was this guy wasting his

valuable time with stupid questions?

His reply was kind of snappy when he said, "Well, the driver of course."

"In that case I would like to plead not guilty" I said. Now the judge was clearly upset. I could tell, he was not used to many "not guilty" pleas.

"You better have a good explanation," he said, shaking his finger at me.

"Forgive me Señor," I said, "but I can prove to you that I did not even own the car at the time these infractions were committed."

After proving that I was telling the truth, I was released. It had cost me a whole day, a small fee, and one lunch to prove my innocence. Halfway out the door I turned around and walked back to the judge.

"Please Sir," I said, "make sure my license number is taken off the search list."

He smiled for the first time and said, "No se preocupe Señor." Don't worry.

I had heard these same words before. My friend, the police chief in Carupano used them all the time.

Our life now settled down to a more normal routine, as far as one can call life in this country normal. We were happy in our little apartment. On weekends we would explore the surrounding area. Naturally one of the first spots I had to show Lu, was the coast around Macuto, Caraballeda, and of course Laguna Caribe. The site of my first adventures. I was surprised how much things had changed in two years. There was a paved highway now, stretching all the way to Naiguata. The village of Caraballeda had so far seen little change, but on the hillside between the Laguna and the village, construction had started. The biggest change was in the Laguna itself. Not many of the old boats remained. The "Jutta," with old captain Busch was gone. A friend told me she had sunk off the coast under mysterious circumstances. Nobody knew the exact details, but there was a lot of talk about insurance investigations. Judging by captain Busch's past life style, I didn't doubt that he might have had a hand in the sinking.

I also did not find the "Ajax" anymore, my first home in

Venezuela. Many of the old friends were gone. Jim Baker's boat was not there any more. He had been transferred, someone told me. The old familiar cabin, home of the Gorland family and workshop, had been torn down. Only the old dredge was still there. She was tied up in a far corner of the lagoon and looked abandoned and neglected. A lot of memories came back when I looked at her. It was only a little over two years, but so much had happened. The once quiet lagoon had become a busy resort area.

While I was lost in my memories of the past, a car stopped next to us.

"Are we checking out the old neighborhood?" said a familiar voice in German.

I looked up and recognized some old timers of the early day Laguna Caribe, the Gutmann family. The Gutmanns were German-Americans. He was a good dentist, who practiced in Caracas without a license. His patients were all Germans and Americans. They had also been close friends of the Gorland family. That's how I met the Gutmanns and their two girls. The youngest girl was with them on this day. The older girl was a flight attendant with a major international airline.

I was so glad to see them at this moment, because they were so much part of my early days in Laguna Caribe. We sat down under a coconut palm at the beach and talked about the old times.

The only thing that cast a shadow over our reunion was some disturbing news about the Gorland family. The Gutmanns were apparently the only ones who had kept contact with the Gorlands, after their departure from Venezuela.

After stopovers at several little islands of the Caribbean, the Gorlands on their little "Dugong" had reached the Panama canal. That was the last time they had heard from them. After crossing the Panama canal, they had set sail for British Columbia. They never arrived.

That was all the Guttmans knew, but it was certainly disturbing news for me. I have never found out what happened to the "Dugong" and the Gorland family. One thing I knew, Gorland was an excellent sailor and navigator.

When we returned to Caracas that night, hardly a word

was spoken for a long time.

Lu finally broke the silence.

"You are thinking about them, don't you?" she asked.

"I sure do," I said.

I could not get the picture out of my head, with cute little Helga playing on the beach, her blonde locks flying in the breeze and her bright blue eyes smiling.

"They should have stayed here," I said.

As far as my job was concerned, I was making good progress in learning all the finer details of the import trade. I loved my job and the people I was associated with. Señor Casas and his wife Angelina had invited us to their home and made great efforts to make Lu feel comfortable in her new country. Language was still a problem for Lu, but she was learning fast. She was not afraid to talk, even when it was wrong. She was never discouraged to try again.

We had so much fun, the night Señor Casas invited us for a ride down the new autopista which had just opened for traffic. It was an event of historic proportion for the city, connecting Caracas with it's port of La Guaira and the airport of Maiquetia. What had been a nerve racking obstacle course of over 360 curves, was now a modern four lane freeway of only twelve miles, including two tunnels. In spite of heavy traffic, it took less than 30 minutes to get down to the coast. Only a person who had travelled the old road to La Guaira, would be able to appreciate the new marvel.

With more and more responsibility at the office came the need to travel. I was taking over the eastern part of the country in addition to certain lines I represented in Caracas. Lu didn't exactly enjoy being alone for a week at a time, but she had made some friends in the new neighborhood, which made the separation less painful.

Personally I had mixed feelings. I enjoyed being in our new home with Lu, but I also liked the challenge of the job and the opportunity to see the country. The lack of good roads, and the distances involved made it necessary to fly. Most of it on good old DC-3. There were places where I thought the landing strip was too short, but somehow we always made it. There were violent tropical storms which threatened to shake the airplane apart, but we always came out of it in one piece. But on many of these trips I did not only enjoy the unspoiled beauty of nature, but I also had the pleasure of meeting the simple, native people of the interior of the country. They always reminded me of playful, happy little children with not a worry in the world. How sad it was to see these people come to the big cities one day, and linger in the slums of those cities, looking at a life they could never have.

Calling on customers in the smaller towns of the remote regions was quite different from selling in the big city. Life in the big city was as hectic and fast paced as in any other big city of the world.

Visiting a customer in the small town was more like a social call. The salesman was his contact with the outside world. There was a lot of small talk, before getting down to the subject of business. First I would inquire about the welfare of the family, and then it would be my turn to report about the latest from the capital. Only then would I dare to talk about merchandise and prices.

Eventually I made contact with some of the bigger boys, including the buyers for some of the government agencies. It was a slow process to gain the confidence of these people, but once established it could mean lucrative business. The cost of the bribe was really paid by the government and did not come out of our profit. A certain fee was simply added to the price of the goods. The added amount would then be paid to the purchasing agent in cash.

I never felt very comfortable about it, but it was the only way to get the business. I guess I was using the same reasoning a thief would use for stealing. The line, "if I don't steal it, somebody else will take it." Besides, I was not the one who was stealing, I was only helping out.

The real big boys did not even try to conceal the fact they were taking kick backs. Their position was so strong, and their connections reached all the way into Miraflores, the presidential palace. I am sure these fellows did not invent corruption, they only followed a tradition which had been practiced through generations. It was a system to pay off loyal supporters of a dictator.

The dictator now in power was colonel Marcos Perez

Jimenez. He had succeeded in ousting the civilian head of the junta, and was now in full control. Like all dictators in Latin America he was backed by the armed forces, and so it was no surprise that the lucrative jobs went to high ranking military officers. Anybody could see that these officers were living in a lifestyle they could hardly afford from a military salary, yet very few people talked openly about it. Nobody wanted any trouble with the secret police, La Seguridad Nacional.

Someone asked me once, if it reminded me of Hitler and Germany, but I could never really compare the two dictators.

Perez Jimenez never had the power that Hitler possessed. He did not have one strong party, except the military behind him. He did not have a political ideology, like Fascism in Germany, or Communism in Russia, which dominates every facet of life. Like every dictator however, he tried to stay in power, and in the process dealt harshly with his political enemies. To his credit I must say that the country was moving forward. The city of Caracas was a gigantic construction site. New buildings were rising like mushrooms. New streets, sewer lines and telephone lines, and traffic was a mess. The government was very active in promoting national industries. It was also creating a new petro chemical industry. Not all construction was commercial or industrial however. For the first time a government tried to solve the problem of housing for the poor.

The natives called them ranchos, we would call them shanty town or slums. The hillsides of the city were dotted with those ramshackle buildings of the poor. Made from old boxes, crates, or whatever building material they could find. With no running water, no sewers and sanitation, they posed a threat to the entire community. Those big new buildings erected by the government looked very impressive, but they created new problems.

First there was the problem of clearing the land. Section by section the government would serve notice to clear the area. Before construction could begin, the big earth moving equipment had to prepare the site. It meant that all ranchos in this particular area had to be torn down. The problem was that nobody wanted to move, and it required troops of the Guardia Nacional to oust the last holdouts.

The rent in the new buildings was extremely cheap, but even the lowest rent was too much for people who had never paid a nickel for rent before. People who had always lived under primitive conditions could not get used to polished floors and modern facilities. Guards had to be posted to prevent the kids from playing with the elevators, although playgrounds had been provided. It could not be done overnight, but at least it was a beginning.

Life for a latin dictator was not easy. For every citizen made happy by one program, there was another one offended by it. This in turn led to the eventual demise of the regime. I call it the dictator cycle, and it goes something like this.

A dictator rises to power by deposing another dictator. He is then called a hero and a liberator. Once in power he has to prove that he can deliver what he promised, which is not always easy to do. In the process of implementing his programs, if he has any, he steps on toes and makes some new enemies. As time goes on he is forced to arrest some of his opponents in order to stay in power. This creates even more enemies, because the people arrested have friends and family. Finally our dictator has now become a villain and will be disposed off shortly by another dictator, who will be called a hero and a liberator. The cycle will be repeated.

The best thing the average citizen could do was not take sides. Once involved he would rise and fall with the regime. A smart businessman would try to have a good relationship with the people in power, without being too deeply committed. Connection was everything in this country. I found this out very early, when I got help from the church. My good relationship with the police chief of Carupano was certainly helpful. A man without connections was in trouble.

I heard the stories of people who had been arrested for a minor traffic violation. They spent days and some times weeks in jail, not because they were guilty, but because nobody asked for them.

One day, while driving in Caracas, I had the opportunity to try out another one of my own connections. In this case a man in the upper ranks in the Department of Motor

Vehicles. I hate to think what would have happened without my contact.

I was coming down Avenida San Martin and was just crossing one of the intersections when the light turned yellow. A policeman standing on the other side blew his whistle and waved his arm, signaling me to pull over.

"Here we go again," I thought.

As always I had a folded twenty Bolivar bill with my drivers license, but on this day I was in a fighting mood. There was something in the way he came strutting over and leaned against my car that raised my temperature.

"Drivers license," he demanded.

"What did I do officer?" I asked.

I could see in his eyes what he was thinking.

This musiu was questioning his authority.

He started writing, and I knew that the first paragraph on the ticket would be "falta de respecto." (lack of respect)

"You crossed while the light was red," he said. By this time I was determined not to pay this guy. I was curious to find out what he would do.

He was writing very slowly, waiting for me to make the first move.

To help things along I took out my note pad and wrote down his badge number.

"What are you doing?" he asked. His voice was now threatening.

"I want to make sure I have your number," I said, adding, "in case I have to go to court."

That was too much for him.

"You are under arrest," he said, and his eyes sparkled.

He walked around to the passenger side and got into the car.

"Let's go to the jefatura," he ordered.

"Which one?" I asked.

"Quinta Crespo," he replied. We had about two miles to go to the jefatura, and I chose the shortest distance I knew. With only a few blocks to go he changed tactics. He tried the nice guy approach, willing to listen and make a deal.

I played dumb, just didn't get the message. We were now getting closer and closer to the jefatura.

"Turn right here," he said.

"Why?" I asked, "the jefatura is to the left." I kept right on course and his attitude changed again to belligerence. When we arrived at the jefatura, he made his report to the desk sergeant.

There was not much talk about running a red light. Listening to his report, I got the impression I was a hard core criminal who had resisted arrest and had not shown any respect for the law at all. The desk sergeant inspected me from head to toe and started making notes.

"May I make a phone call capitan?" I asked very politely, promoting the sergeant to captain at the same time.

"You can't call now," he said. I knew I had to make that call now, before I ended up in jail. Once in jail it would be very difficult to get to a phone.

"I would like to call colonel Alfredo Martinez," I said, pronouncing the word colonel.

"What for?" he asked."

"He is a friend of mine," I said, "and I have the feeling I need to call a friend."

Again he looked me over, and it was obvious he was thinking fast.

"Muy bien," he said, "go ahead and call."

I dialed the number, got to the switchboard and then to the colonel's secretary. The sergeant and his subordinate looked at each other. I could tell, they were getting nervous.

A terrible thought flashed through my mind.

"What if the colonel was not in his office?"

Thank God he was in, and I was glad when I heard his voice.

"What can I do for you amigo?" he asked.

"Well," I said, "I have a slight problem," and with the two policemen listening to every word I said, I told him of my delicate situation.

"Put the sergeant on the phone," he said.

I handed the phone to the sergeant. Before he took it he looked at his accomplice and his look said it all. "See what you got me into?" His face was red, and his hand was shaking when he answered the phone. He almost stood at attention and for the next few minutes I heard nothing but "Si mi colonel, Si mi colonel." When he put down the phone, he turned to me and expressed his regrets.

"We have made a mistake Señor," he said. "You are free to leave."

"Thank you very much capitan," I answered.

I knew the policeman was in for a sermon from his superior, but it might do some good to cool him down a little bit. He was definitely getting too ambitious and too greedy.

With the chaotic traffic conditions in Caracas it was not very difficult for the average driver to break the law. At times the traffic got so strangled that drivers became frustrated and took the law into their own hands. This of course resulted in even more chaos. I became more and more inventive and found all kinds of shortcuts, but whenever I got a ticket, I paid my dues and did not complain. Only when it became obvious that I was picked on because I was a musiu, did I use all the connections I had. I never abused my relationship with the friends in higher places.

One of the nicest friends we had in Venezuela was Hannes Thompson. He represented the German Horn Line in the Caribbean and had lived in Caracas for many years. His wife Luise was also German born. They had a son and a daughter, born in Venezuela.

I met Hannes Thomsen for the first time when I tried to find passage for Lu from a German port. The Horn Line was all booked up and Hannes could not help me, but coming from the same region in Germany we had a long conversation about the old country. It was the beginning of a long friendship which still exists today. Since I worked in the import business, I would recommend the Horn Line whenever I could.

One night the Horn Line was giving a party for good customers, on board one of their ships in La Guaira. The Thompsons had invited us to be their guests. It was the first time I had set foot on a German ship since the "Ellen Hugo Stinnes."

All ships of the line were basically cargo ships, but with the capacity to take a few passengers. Although these ships did not employ the services of a chef who had learned his trade in a famous french restaurant, we were treated to a superb array of German delicatessen. Afterwards we had a choice of many of the old German names in beer,schnapps and other liquors. The conversation was heating up. We covered topics from German politics to the inevitable tall stories of ships and the sea. Someone brought up the subject of sailors jumping ship.

"Ah," said the captain, waving his hand, "they are all talking about it. "Hardly anybody has ever done it," he added.

I saw the twinkle in his eyes, when Hannes Thomsen spoke up.

"Let me show you one who did," he said.

All eyes turned to Hannes. "He is sitting right next to me," continued Hannes while pointing at me. Now it was the captains turn to look at me.

"You?" he asked.

"That's right," answered Hannes, before I could even open my mouth.

The captain didn't know what to say for a brief moment, then he asked, "what ship?"

"Ellen Hugo Stinnes" I said.

"That's funny," he said, "I met the 'Ellen Hugo Stinnes' three months ago in Antwerp."

"Well, if you see her the next time say hello from me," I said.

Later that night, when we said good-bye to the captain and thanked him for his hospitality, he said jokingly, "Don't let the word get out that it works, I have been telling everybody it doesn't."

"Don't blame it on me if you come up a man short tomorrow," I replied.

So many things on this ship had brought back memories of the past, but more than ever before did I realize how much my life had changed in the past three years.

As the year 1954 faded into history, I was looking back with satisfaction and a sense of accomplishment. In November Lu and I had celebrated our first anniversary. Happily married, with a good and promising job, I had a lot to be thankful for. At noon of New Years Eve, we got together at the office for a drink and a toast to a successful year. We talked about the outgoing year and about our hopes for the coming year. Señor Casas was feeling good, and even Angelina came in to wish us all a happy New Year. The mood was festive and as we parted, we talked about our plans we had made for the last night of 1954.

We were awakened on the morning of New Years day by the ringing of the doorbell. It had been after three in the morning when we came home from our party, and it took a while before I could think straight. The time was almost nine a.m. Who could be at the door at this hour?

Sleepy eyed I opened the door and stood face to face with my two associates, both of them dressed in a dark suit. "Is it not too early for a new years visit?" I wanted to say, but the words stuck in my throat when I looked at their serious faces.

"What happened?" I asked.

The two looked at each other, as if undecided on who was going to say it.

"It's about Señor Casas," one of them said. "He is dead."

I stood there like someone hit by lightning. How could he be dead? We had left him in good spirits just a few hours ago.

"Dead?" I asked, still unable to comprehend what was going on?

Again I looked at their faces, perhaps for a sign that this was just a joke, but I knew that nobody would make a tasteless joke of this kind.

No, it was no joke, and it was not a bad dream either. My colleagues came in, and as Lu and I sat in silence we listened to their story.

The Casas family had gone to a New Years Eve party at a friend's house. When they returned home at one in the morning, Señor Casas became ill while driving. His sixteen year old son Jose took over the wheel and continued to drive home. They had barely changed positions, when Señor Casas had a massive heart attack. His son drove to the nearest hospital, but it was too late. He was dead on arrival.

It was nine a.m. and the funeral was already scheduled for one p.m. only four hours from now. According to

Venezuelan law, burial services must be held within twenty-four hours after death. Services were scheduled to be performed in the office.

It broke my heart to look at Angelina sitting next to the open casket. She was absolutely devastated and appeared to be in a state of shock. I wanted to express my condolences, but could not find the words. Unable to say anything, I just pressed her hand. I had the impression she hardly recognized me.

Lu followed me closely. She was frustrated by her limited knowledge of the Spanish language and was close to tears. I knew she was taking it very hard, because Señor Casas had become a father figure for both of us and she liked him very much. We had lost a very dear friend.

The next hour was a shocking display of religious and funeral services neither one of us had ever witnessed before. During funeral services I had attended in the past, a priest had always found a few good words about the deceased, and words of comfort for family and friends. These services had the appearance of a speed contest. It was all over, before I even realized what was going on.

A priest, followed by two little altar boys, entered the office. He mumbled a few words to Angelina, turned and sprinkled holy water on the casket while saying a few words in latin, and he was gone. In a country where everything is measured in terms of mañana, this funeral had the appearance of an assembly line.

The priest was closely followed by a crew from the funeral institute, who came to take the casket to the cemetery. The funeral procession turned into a grand prix through the streets of Caracas. Within five blocks from the start I had lost sight of the other cars. Since this was the first funeral I had ever attended in this city, I had only a vague idea where the cemetery was. When we finally arrived and found the grave site, all the others were already assembled. If we had expected any ceremony or grave site services, we were in for another surprise. When I looked around I could not find Angelina, and when I asked someone I was told it was not customary for the widow to attend.

I was glad she was not there to watch the show. It seemed

to me that we had only come to witness the lowering of the casket. Was it not for the fact that we had just lost a very dear friend, I might have found this entire show extremely funny.

Before this spectacle was allowed to continue, the financial part had to be settled. A spokesman for the gravediggers wanted to know who was in charge. Angelina's brother, who was the closest relative present, stepped forward. In front of all mourners he had to pull out his wallet and pay the men in cash. The casket was now lowered, and after a short prayer we all went home.

"I can't believe he is gone," said Lu.

"Neither can I," I answered, and then added, "What a way to start the new year."

The two dutchmen bought out Angelina, who wanted to return to her native Spain. As far as the company was concerned, it was never the same again. The guiding hand of Señor Casas was missing, and when the two partners started disagreeing on almost everything, things went downhill. When they also began cheating and arguing about my commissions, I started looking for greener pastures.

Exquisite Form de Venezuela was one of a number of companies taking advantage of the governments push for a national industry. Not only was it easy to obtain low interest government loans for industrial development, but the application of import tariffs made it easy to compete against foreign made products. Exquisite Form was such a fast growing and progressive company.

The company was located in Caracas and manufactured the Exquisite Form and Maidenform line of brassieres.

A friend of mine introduced me one day to Gene Bell, the general manager of the company, who made me an offer I could hardly refuse. Never in my wildest dreams had I seen myself peddling brassieres in the jungles of South America, but the same could be said for many things I had done in my life. The company had a few ladies selling their products in Caracas, however travelling the interior of the country was a different story. Only men would do it.

For a few months I worked in Caracas, and Lu was quite happy to have me at home all the time. One day Gene Bell called me into his office.

"You have been doing real well with us," he said. "How would you like to go to Maracaibo?"

"What's the deal?" I asked, and Gene started painting a picture of great potential for that market. The offer was tempting. He offered me to represent the company in the states of Zulia and Falcon. Since it involved moving to Maracaibo, I had to talk to Lu about it, and Gene Bell was willing to wait a few days for a final answer.

"Think about it, I would like to have you there," he said.

Lu and I had a hard decision to make. We loved our little apartment, and we hated to give up our friends, but the offer was financially tempting. Besides, we were young and ready to accept a challenge.

The following day I told Gene Bell I was willing to give it a try, as we started preparations for our big move to Maracaibo, the second biggest city in Venezuela.

Maracaibo, the New Frontier

Selling our furniture was not difficult at all. There was such a demand for our studio apartments that the interested party would pay almost any price to get it. Most of the apartments being vacated in our building were immediately snatched up by well to do older men, using it as headquarters for their extra matrimonial activities. There was no question that our buyer had the same intentions.

With our furniture sold and everything ready to go, all that remained to be done was to squeeze our personal and household belongings into good old Henry J. There was not a square inch of unused space left, when the time for departure came.

It was truly with mixed emotions, when we looked back at Edificio Monteverde (name of building) for the last time. We had experienced the first happy days of married life here, but we were also looking forward to a new beginning in Maracaibo.

Lu was a nervous wreck, because the car was so overloaded. I was probably just as nervous, except I was not going to admit it.

The first phase of our 600 mile trip did not present any serious difficulties. With the exception of a dangerous stretch of mountain road, it was an all paved road to Barquisimeto, our first stop. It was almost midnight when we reached the town. I was so tired, I could hardly keep my eyes open. The last few hours of driving in the dark were quite strenuous, because one had to be alert for donkeys and other wild animals on the road.

Our trip continued in the early morning hours, in spite of the fact that we had arrived late. Under normal conditions we needed at least ten hours to reach Maracaibo, but nothing was normal on a trip like this. Lu was almost sick in anticipation of the next phase of our trip. She had heard all the horror stories about the road ahead of us.

After another hour of driving we had reached the town of Carora. This was the end of the line as far as paved roads were concerned. The next few hours would be miles and miles of potholes, dust and heat, until we reached the town of Motatan.

Lu got her first taste of what it meant to travel the interior of the country, and some idea of what I had to endure while I was on the road. With the overloaded car, I tried to drive as careful as I possibly could, but soon I realized that at this speed we would never make it. After another hour of heat and dust I threw caution to the wind and stepped on the gas. My theory was that with enough speed I would just fly over the potholes.

There must have been some flaw in my theory, because after a while things began to rattle. At first I accused Lu of not properly packing her pots and pans, but a few miles later she protested.

"Those are not my pots and pans," she said. "It's your car that's making all the noise."

After a few more miles I was convinced that she was right. When I got out of the car, I discovered that my exhaust pipe was dragging over the ground. In order to reach my toolbox I would have to remove at least one half of our belongings from the trunk of the car. I was afraid we would never get it back again. We finally solved our problem with the help of a piece of wire and continued our trip.

Our repair job was short lived. After less than ten minutes the banging continued. Again we stopped for a quick repair job, but with the same result. By this time I had enough.

"To hell with it," I said. "We will go as far as we can. If it falls off, let it go."

There was not much left of the pipe when we arrived in Motatan. The car sounded more like a truck, but we had reached the end of the dirt road. We stopped at a dusty old roadside stand for a refreshing drink of orange juice. Nobody felt like eating there. Our clothing was sticking to our body. At this moment Maracaibo looked like the promised land. A nice shower, clean food, and a clean bed to sleep in was all we could think of.

With the broken exhaust pipe the car was so noisy that we

hardly talked as we covered the final miles to the ferry terminal in Palmarejo. It was dark when we arrived there. The ferry left every hour and was capable of carrying about fifty cars. Fortunately we got on the next ferry and arrived in Maracaibo at ten p.m.

For the next two weeks the Hotel Bustamante became our home. It was not a luxurious place, but it was owned by a German couple, and it was clean and served good food. That's all we could ask for. I was anxious to meet my predecessor, but had a hard time finding him. When I finally met him, I could understand why I had been unable to find him. I had neglected to check out the local bars. He was not much help in getting me started, and I had a suspicion he had not seen any customers lately. No wonder Gene Bell wanted to replace him.

In the weeks and months ahead I would get a better understanding of why people would come to the point of giving up. The heat in this part of the country was brutal. Maracaibo, in spite of the heat, still offered some comfort. Travelling between the little towns of the state was an ordeal. There was no comfort, just heat, sweat and dirt.

Maracaibo, capital of the state of Zulia, and second largest city of Venezuela had a population of over 420,000. There were no tall buildings, no subways, no railroad stations. It was mostly a small town growing out of shape. The city itself had a few department stores, but most of the stores were still of the hole in the wall variety. Not far from the city was an old indian village called Santa Rosa del Agua, and it was a village like this which had given the country it's name. A year after the Spaniards had established their first permanent settlement near Cumana, an expedition had entered the Lago de Maracaibo. When they saw all the indian huts built on poles above the water, they called it Venezuela (little Venice). Santa Rosa is one of the remnants of these indian villages.

About eighty miles southwest from Maracaibo was the little town of Machiques. The town was situated against the foothills of the high rising Andes, and there was no road leading out on the other side. Machiques was the end of civilization. Its jungle covered hills to the west belonged to the Motilones.

I had only one customer in this small town, but once a month I had to visit the place.

One day Lu came along for the ride, and also to see what the end of the world looked like. A few miles to the west we could see the last outpost of civilization, a little missionary station established by the Catholic Church to make contact with the elusive Motilones. They succeeded about five years later.

When we returned to Maracaibo, we came upon a snake, draped all across the highway. Thinking she had been killed by a car, I drove right next to her and stepped out. I had just enough time to jump back into the car, when I noticed she was not dead at all.

At this moment two natives came along and dispatched her with a mighty swing of the machete. They said it would make a beautiful purse, but I did not want a snake in my car, dead or alive.

This side of the lake was so much cleaner and the scenery more impressive. The other side of the lake was covered with oil wells, on shore and in the water. The little towns surrounding the lake were dusty and dirty, and during the rainy season turned into one big mud hole. The worst part was that most of my business was located on this, the eastern side of the lake. Fortunately I was able to return home on most days, provided I left very early in the morning to catch the ferry.

The rainy season got me into trouble with the law again. I had just passed through the little town of Lagunillas and was on my way to Mene Grande, when I was passed by a taxi. As soon as he had moved ahead of me he stopped, blocking the road and forcing me also to stop. The driver got out of the car and approached me, cursing loudly all the way.

"What's your problem?" I asked him. I did not have the faintest idea of what I could have done to him. After another barrage of four letter words, I was beginning to get the message.

According to him I had passed him in town, and while passing I had splashed mud all over him. I did not recall that I had ever seen him or his car before, but I did not want to make a big issue out of it.

So I simply said, "I am sorry Señor, but I did not see you. If I really did what you say, I apologize."

I did not have to wait long to discover the real reason behind his act. He had seen a musiu and recognized an easy source of income. Money is what he wanted, and he was not even bashful. Fifty Bolivares would calm his pain and suffering he said. By this time I had enough of his big mouth.

"Get out of my way," I said.

Another barrage of foul language was the answer.

To show him I was not bluffing, I stepped on the gas pedal and the car jumped forward. He jumped out of the way, and I could still see him in my rear mirror as he stood on the road, wildly swinging his arms.

His accusation was absurd, because during the rainy season all cars in this part of the country were covered with mud. It was nothing unusual.

I had reached the town of Mene Grande and was talking with a customer, when a policeman walked in, followed by the taxi driver.

"Is this your car out there?" the policeman wanted to know.

"Si, Señor," I answered.

"This Señor is accusing you of splashing mud all over him and his car," the policeman continued.

"Sure," I said, "I have heard the story."

"Are you willing to compensate this Señor for the damage?" the policeman asked.

By this time I figured that enough time had been wasted, so I offered to pay three Bolivares, which was about the price of a car wash and the price of washing a shirt.

The two retired to the back of the store for a short conference. I was certain that they would split the loot, if successful. When they returned the policeman informed me that the taxi driver had reduced his price to thirty Bolivares.

"No deal," I said, "three Bolivares is my last offer."

For a moment the policeman was stunned and uncertain of his next move. When he recovered, he informed me that I was under arrest.

My customer had watched the proceedings with great

interest. I told him I would return shortly and followed the policeman and the taxi driver to the station. Before we entered, the usual negotiating about dropping the charges against payment of a certain amount of money was made. The price had now been reduced to twenty Bolivares, but I refused. It was not the twenty Bolivares any more, it was now a matter of giving in to extortion.

At this stage the policeman had no options left. He led me inside the station and made his report to a sergeant on duty.

El commandante in charge was not present at the time and the sergeant asked the taxi driver and me to wait for his arrival.

"When would that be?" I asked politely.

"Quien sabe Señor," was the answer. Who knows? Two hours passed, and no commandante showed up.

"You are wasting a lot of time," I said to the taxi driver sitting next to me. He just looked at me.

"My offer is still good," I continued, "three Bolivares."

After a long silence he came to a decision.

"Give me the three Bolivares," he said. I handed him the three Bolivares and he informed the sergeant that he was leaving.

After he had left, I got up and informed the sergeant that I was also going to leave.

"Wait a minute," he said. "You have to wait for the commandante."

"What for?" I asked, "the man has dropped his charges against me."

"It does not matter Señor, you have broken the law," he insisted.

"What law did I break?" I asked. He was not sure. "That is for the commandante to decide," he said.

He continued to play with his gun, which made me extremely nervous. If he accidentally killed himself, they would probably blame me for it. The other possibility was of course that I would get hit by a stray bullet. He could always explain that by saying I had tried to escape, or had attempted to attack him. I simply had to find a way to bring this episode to a conclusion. It was time for me to bring up some of my connections. The problem was that I did not have any good connections yet in this area, and Caracas was too far away. This guy would never allow me to make a long distance phone call. Besides the transmission was so bad that most of the time it was hard to understand. I had to try something new.

"Would you do me a favor?" I asked. "Call the governor's office," I continued before he had even time to ask me.

He looked at me with suspicion. I was sure he would not make this phone call.

"Why should I call the governor?" he asked.

"Because I know him real well, and he is a very fair and honest man," I said.

"You tell him of the charges against me, and we will let him decide what's right."

He wanted no part of this. There was no need for this he insisted. We could settle this on the local level, without involving the honorable governor. In fact, he would even be willing to take the responsibility to let me go without waiting for the commandante.

I protested lamely that I did not want him to neglect his duties, but I did not want to push my luck too far. He was almost grateful when I finally left.

My customer was also relieved when I returned.

"There is a lot of this going on," he said. "They are all bandidos, all the way to the top." The Americans from the oil companies supplied most of the victims, mainly because they did not speak the language and most of them paid, considering it a necessary living expense.

"Well, I have paid my dues for the sake of convenience," I said, "but there comes a time when you are just fed up with it."

"I know what you mean," he answered, "we are paying for protection all the time, but we have to live here." He was a musiu like I was. Like most businessmen in this area, he was from Lebanon.

I had to think of Caracas, where the extortion business started at an early age. Every time we would go to the movies or see a show, we would be approached by young boys or teenagers, offering to watch the car for a small fee. God help the poor guy who thought he could do without this additional expense. The price of protection would be trivial compared to the expense of fixing the damage to the car if no protection had been hired.

The rainy season also spelled disaster for our first car, good old Henry J.

I was on my return trip somewhere between the towns of Lagunillas and Cabimas. The roads in this area were maintained by the oil companies with some kind of a crude oil by-product. Add water to this surface, and it becomes as slippery as an ice rink. I was more gliding than driving, at no more than twenty miles per hour. Not only was it slippery, but the visibility was almost zero in this heavy downpour. Out of this gray mass I see a big truck coming straight at me. It is doubtful the driver ever saw me, because he continued right in the middle of the road. I had no choice but get down on the right shoulder.

At the precise moment the truck was passing on my left, my car started sliding and pointed it's nose under the big truck. Hoping to get some traction, I stepped on the gas pedal and the car jumped forward, missing the tail end of the truck by only a few inches. The rest happened so fast that it is hard to describe.

The car started spinning at a speed which felt like hundred miles an hour. Then, as if shot from a catapult the car flew across a ditch, broke through the heavy underbrush and landed in the middle of the jungle. I was lucky there were no big trees.

When I recovered from the scare, I was glad to discover that I was not hurt. The engine was silent. The only sound was that of the rain beating down on the metal roof of the car. I decided to wait for the rain to end before looking for my way out. When I turned the key in the ignition, the engine started without hesitation. That was a good sign. After another twenty minutes the rain subsided, and I went out to look for the road and possibly for someone to help.

Within a short time a big truck from an oil company stopped to see if they could be of any assistance.

"Can you pull me out?" I asked.

The two guys looked around for my car. I pointed at the jungle.

"In there," I said.

Fortunately they carried all the equipment, and without mayor problems my Henry J was put back on the road. With the exemption of a few scratches and some minor dents, no damage was visible.

They had barely disappeared around the next curve, when it became apparent that more damage had been done to my car. A grinding noise came from the gearbox when I shifted into first. To make matters worse, the whole body of the car seemed to rest on the rear wheels. I had to make a decision. Since Henry J. was not a horse, I could not shoot him to get him out of his misery. Neither did I want to abandon my car on this side of the lake.

I decided to drive as far as I could, provided the car would move at all.

The shifting into first gear was accompanied by a nerve wrecking noise, but it worked. Although the rear end of the car rested on the wheels, the car started moving. Unable to shift into higher gear I crept along at a snail's pace. Smoke was coming from the rear wheels, and the smell of burned rubber filled the air. What would have taken thirty minutes under normal conditions turned into a three hour affair, but eventually I reached the ferry terminal at Palmarejo.

The crossing on the ferry became a welcome rest period for me, until I was confronted with a new challenge. All roads leading to our home in Maracaibo involved climbing a hill. I was forced to circle half the city to avoid those hills, but against all odds I finally parked the car in front of our apartment. I was exhausted, but happy to be home.

Lu was glad that I had not suffered any harm.

"The car would be easier to fix," she said.

It was however not as easy as we thought. The parts needed were not available in Maracaibo, and it could take weeks before they would arrive. I needed the car and could not wait for the parts. A new car was the only answer.

A local mechanic offered to buy the wreck, and the last we saw of our first proud possession was good old "Henry J," hanging on a tow truck and disappearing down the Avenida 24 de Julio.

Our next car was a Dodge coupe, a beautiful car with only 5,000 miles on the odometer. It just so happened that one of my customers in Maracaibo had purchased a new car, and was ready to sell this one. The price was right, and I was able to take possession immediately, thus solving my serious transportation problem. Although this new car was considerably more luxurious and also more expensive, our "Henry J" had served us well. He was our first proud possession on a long list of automobiles we have owned since. He will always be affectionately remembered as a part of our early beginnings in Caracas.

Another event in our lives took place at about the same time. One of the fashion stores in Maracaibo was owned by a Hungarian couple. The Horvaths had fled from communist Hungary, and now called this part of the world their home. It was through the Horvaths that Mimi entered into our lives.

Mimi was a two year old wire hair fox terrier, a real beauty and a bundle of dynamite. She stole our hearts the minute we laid eyes on her. The Horvath's had made the difficult decision to give her up, because both of them worked at the store, and the poor dog was left alone at home all day long. They were very happy, when Lu and I agreed to give her a home.

For Lu it was a welcome addition to her daily life. While I had my job to keep me busy, Lu was beginning to get bored. The brutal heat made it very uncomfortable to do anything during the day. I left home very early in the morning on most days and returned late at night. At times the lines at the ferry were so long that I came home after midnight. We had only three weekends for ourselves, because on one weekend every month I was flying to Caracas for a meeting at headquarters. So little Mimi was a welcome addition to our family.

The first night was rough on all of us. We had taken her into the bedroom, hoping she would not feel so lonely. One of us would constantly try to comfort her, but she was pacing the floor and wailing softly. Neither one of us slept during that first night. The following night was a little better, and after another night Mimi was at home. She could be a little darling, and most of the time she was, but the little sweetheart turned into a raging street fighter when she met her four legged friends. Her love for fighting went so far, that one day she jumped out of the moving car to get her teeth into an innocent little mutt who was minding his own business.

As far as my business was concerned, it could not have been any better. My company gave me all the support I requested. Advertising on radio and in newspapers helped to boost my sales. They even sent a few models from Caracas, to stage fashion shows in a few selected locations. This was something never seen before in this region and the response was tremendous.

Within six months I had increased sales by 600 percent. One of the disadvantages of this success was that another sales representative was sent in to take over half of my accounts.

Although I agreed that there was a great potential in this market, I resented the fact that I had to give up half of my accounts. I had worked hard under extremely difficult conditions, and since most of my income was from commissions, I didn't think it was fair. For the moment I went along with the decision, but during our next meeting in Caracas I let the boss know how I felt about it.

My new partner was a Spaniard by the name of Rodriguez. We developed a good working relationship and became good friends.

Rodriguez was a poet and a comedian. I can still see him standing in front of Lu and reciting love poems to her. When I took him across the lake, to introduce him to some accounts on the other side, he got seasick on the ferry. At first I thought he was giving another one of his comedy performances, until I realized he was really sick. It was a stormy day, seldom seen on the Lago de Maracaibo, but Rodriguez was apparently not the only person on the ferry feeling the effects.

As far as mechanical know-how was concerned, Rodriguez had about as much knowledge as a cave man. One night, after a meeting at the plush Hotel del Lago in Maracaibo, his car would not start.

"Get in," I said, "I'll give you a push." After pushing him three turns around the landscaped isle in front of the hotel, his car had not started. I signaled for him to stop.

"What speed are you in?" I asked with suspicion.

I should have known from the empty look on his face.

"I am in neutral," he answered."

"You fool," I said laughing, "If you don't put it in gear, I can push you around this isle all night."

On another occasion he drove all the way from the airport to downtown with his emergency brakes applied. I was driving behind him and saw the smoke coming out from under his car. It got so bad that all traffic behind him was engulfed in a cloud of black smoke. When I had a chance, I pulled up next to him and waved and leaned on my horn. Rodriguez was apparently listening to some hot latin music, because I could see him singing and his fingers playing drums on the dashboard. The only response I got was that he waved back at me. He finally stopped, when the stench of burning rubber penetrated his car.

Rodriguez would never make it as a mechanic, but he brought the right attitude to this job. He was a fine salesman who could communicate with his customers. If anything went wrong and we had a complaint, Rodriguez handled it with ease. He was one of those rare persons that nobody could get mad at. Even all our Lebanese customers on the other side of the lake, who got on my nerves with their constant whining and complaining, did not disturb Rodriguez. We both knew that it was part of an act, but I never really got used to it, while Rodriguez just ignored it. Sometimes I wished I had his sunny outlook on life.

One week of every month I had to travel to the neighboring state of Falcon. It was a week I would have rather spent some place else.

Although bordering the state of Zulia, there was no decent road connection. I was forced to fly to the town of Coro, and travel by taxi from there. My second stop would be on the Peninsula de Paraguana, with more oil towns like Punto Fijo, Las Piedras and El Cardon. From there I would travel to the higher elevations of Churuguara and Maparari. Especially during the rainy season, with the clouds hanging low, it could be very uncomfortable there.

However, the highlight of this trip was my last stop in the town of Dabajuro. The place was located halfway between Coro and Maracaibo, in the middle of nowhere. The only good thing about this place was the knowledge that tomorrow I would be home. I had only one account in this place, but I had to stay overnight. Dabajuro had only one flight a day.

They called it hotel, but the place I slept in was probably the lowest class hotel I ever set foot in. There was no running water, The room was about the size of a dressing cabin in a public bathhouse. The walls were only six foot high partitions, made from some kind of particle board. In each corner was a sturdy post, with a hammock strung across the room. Up front was an open dining room with a dirt floor. The dogs wandered in and out from the dusty street, hoping for a handout. One dog I saw was so grateful for a little bite that he went over to the next table and lifted his leg.

This was always the night of my trip where I skipped dinner. Instead I was going out for a night of great entertainment.

At the end of the block was the plaza, and facing the plaza was the most important building in town. The building was a combination of city hall, radio station and movie theater. It even had a bell tower. For this radio station the people did not need a receiver, because the loudspeaker was built into the tower and the transmission was blasted all over town all day long. In addition to the only record in their library, the station broadcast commercials and public announcements. At seven p.m. the station played "Gloria Al Bravo Pueblo," the national anthem, and the town was ready for the movies.

My presence at the movies had about the same effect as the arrival of dignitaries and stars at the Oscar award ceremony. Everybody wanted to get a glimpse of the stranger in town. When I entered, I discovered that this movie theater was only a big courtyard, surrounded by four eight foot high walls. As the yard began to fill I made another startling discovery. This must have been the origin of drive-in movies. People came from everywhere, many of them on bicycles. They parked their bicycle inside against the wall, grabbed a folding chair, and planted it as close as possible to the screen. Apparently this was considered the best seat in the house.

I sat all by myself in the rear, like someone with an infectious disease.

The movie was one of those low budget Mexican movies, with mucho amor and lots of action. I had no eyes for the movie. Instead I was watching one of the most interesting shows I had ever seen, the people. Every scene in the movie was followed by loud and spicy comments from the audience. There was never any lack of suggestions for the hero, on what to do with the girl. If the movie itself was not x rated, the comments from the crowd certainly should have been. Never again did I see an audience so involved with the action on the screen, and I had a ball watching them. After the show the town fell silent.

When I returned to the hotel, I found an unexpected visitor waiting for me. Not exactly the kind of visitor I was crazy about.

A sharp hissing sound from the corner of my little room caught my attention. In the dim light I recognized a snake, coiled and ready to attack. I slammed the door as fast as I had opened it and went looking for the owner of the hotel.

He was not too pleased that I got him out of bed, especially for a minor disturbance like a snake.

"She is harmless," he said. "She lives around the house."

I was not ready to give up.

"Listen Señor," I answered. "I paid for a room without a snake, so if she is your pet, you take her out of my room."

I was not willing to go back and tangle with the beast myself.

Mumbling and grumbling he followed me to my room, grabbed the snake and carried her outside.

"She won't trouble you again Señor," he said as he left.

I was always amazed how these people could handle snakes, because I never lost my fear of them and still have a healthy respect for any snake.

The heat and the mosquitoes kept me awake for a long time. Next to me I could hear someone snore, but the sound of crickets drowned out almost everything else. The fact that my hammock was hanging at least two feet above the ground made me feel a little more relaxed. I was glad not to have any furniture in my room. Who knows what else would be hiding under it.

Early in the morning I was awakened by loud music. The radio station was back in business, playing that damn record over and over again and advertising "Colgate, la crema dental ideal."

I felt like a bum from skidrow, when I made my official call on Señor Henrique, my only customer in town. His shirt was just as dirty as mine and he didn't smell any better than I did. After we had covered the family, women, and politics, we settled down for business.

Señor Henrique sold everything, from hardware to milk powder and ladies' underwear, and it was obvious that he had not studied the latest in store display technique. Everything was hanging from the ceiling or nailed to the wall, and a brassiere was prominently displayed next to a roll of barbed wire. He must have been successful, because I always walked out with a good size order.

It was siesta time when I left, and I would have loved to take a little nap, but I didn't dare. My biggest concern was that I might not wake up in time, miss my flight, and be forced to stay another day. I was always an hour early at the airport, just in case.

In less than an hour I was back in Maracaibo, where Lu was waiting for me at the airport. After a refreshing shower and a shave, I felt like a human being again. A home cooked dinner with Lu was the crowning event of the evening.

The eastern side of the lake was not much better than the territory of the Estado Falcon, but from most locations I was able to return at night and sleep at home. The only exemption was Santa Barbara and San Carlos, located south west of the lake. It was on the same side as Maracaibo, but a deep inaccessible jungle and several rivers made passage on this side impossible.

Once I made the trip by airplane. While there was nothing wrong with the plane trip, the rest of the trip was a complete disaster. The most popular mode of transportation was a station wagon, where passengers just paid for one seat. It was called "por puesto." Each wagon would travel a specific route in a city or between towns and villages.

With my business completed in Santa Barbara, I was able to catch a wagon shortly before dark. My plan was to go to a little town of La Ceiba and stay there overnight. From there I was going to work my way back on the east side of the lake. At my request, the driver dropped me at a crossroads in the middle of the jungle. According to him, a car should stop here at least once an hour. For more than 6 hours I sat on my sample case, while the mosquitoes had a field day eating me alive. It was past midnight, when I finally caught a ride. After this miserable experience I returned to driving my own car again.

Lu came along once on a trip to San Carlos and Santa Barbara. She needed a break from boredom, but she got more than what she bargained for. If Maracaibo was hot, this place was even hotter. Covered by the high mountains of Los Andes, and surrounded by hot, steaming jungles, this place never seemed to drop below 100° F. The dinky little hotel offered no comfort of any kind. Air conditioning had not yet reached this part of the country. If nothing else, Lu got a good understanding of what my life was like, when I was on the road.

Maracaibo was an interesting experience for us, but neither one of us was very happy here. We missed going to a concert, or other cultural events we had enjoyed in Caracas. The extreme heat made life even more unpleasant. Most of our free weekends were spent with our friends Elba and Bruce. She was a Venezuelan girl, who had worked for our company as a consultant. Bruce was an Australian engineer, who worked for a local branch of General Electric. The two had met at a local hotel, fell madly in love, and got married a few months later. Their house was located on Avenida El Milagro, with the backyard facing the lake. Here we enjoyed most of our weekends.

Otherwise our whole life turned around the company. There were always people coming and going, and if we did not entertain at home, we would attend parties at the Hotel del Lago.

My problem was that I would attend a party at night, and still get up early in the morning for a visit to the other side of the lake. The pace was brutal, and so it came as no surprise that things came to a clash at our next meeting in Caracas.

Gene Bell informed me that he was seriously thinking of adding another man to our territory. I left no doubt as to what he could do with his job, if he went ahead with his plan. I was getting tired of working my butt off, and having my income cut every six months.

For two months I didn't hear any more about his plan, and was beginning to believe he had changed his mind. However, one day he called me to let me know of his decision to go ahead with his plan.

"Fine," I said, "I quit."

There was a long silence on the other end.

"You are not serious." he said.

"Very serious," I responded.

If he didn't think I was serious, he would soon find out otherwise. A week after our conversation he had my resignation in writing. I felt betrayed by the company. For years they had allowed their representative to lead a life of leisure, barely venturing out into the market place. Most of his time had been spent in his air conditioned hotel room, or in local bars. Now the company was demanding more and more. My sales had increased by 800 percent in one year, but they wanted more. Instead of receiving words of praise, or a letter of recognition, I received statistics about the state's population.

One time after receiving such a statistic, I sat down and wrote a sarcastic letter to the main office, where it originated. I was deeply concerned about the accuracy of their numbers, I said in my letter, and I wanted to find out if all the indians had been accounted for. There was no response.

Under these circumstances it was no wonder that I was disillusioned by now. Gene Bell tried to repair the damage to our relationship, but it was too late. In a last minute effort he offered me a territory in Caracas, if that was what I wanted. I accepted, and Lu did not need any encouragement to return to Caracas. She was more than ready .

Now it was only a matter of turning over the business to my successor, sell the furniture and we were ready to leave.

Our return trip was considerably more comfortable than

the trip from Caracas a year ago. Much work had been done on the country's highway system. With a new connection opened, the trip was now shorter and mostly on paved roads. Only a few miles of dirt road through a jungle remained, and by leaving Maracaibo early in the morning we were able to reach Caracas by late night.

After a night in a hotel, it was time again to look for a place to live. The building boom in the capital continued, and it was now a little easier to find an apartment. We got especially lucky, when we found a little two story building with only six apartments. Location was it's most attractive asset. It was located near our old residence in Colinas de Bello Monte, but this building was high in the hills, overlooking the entire city. Set against the hillside, ours was the only apartment building in the street. Below us were only single family homes, above us the virgin hills. The air was clean and the tranquillity was relaxing. Even our Mimi enjoyed the new neighborhood and never refused to go for a walk. Around the next hill, at only a few minutes walking distance, was the open air concert bowl.

There was only one disadvantage to living in the higher elevations. The city was unable to keep pace with the ever increasing demand for water. When the rainy season was over, and after only a few weeks into the dry season, the water pressure began to decrease. People in the higher elevations were the first ones to suffer.

A person who has never stood under a shower, with shampoo in his hair and running out of water, can hardly understand how precious this liquid really is. We are so used to open a faucet and have running water that we take it for granted. In Caracas we gained a new respect for this priceless element.

There were people however, who were looking forward to this season, like a ski lift operator is waiting for the first snow to fall. This shortage had created a new source of income for some public employees. The city of Caracas provided tanker trucks for the purpose of supplying water to neighborhoods such as ours. According to city officials the service was free of charge, yet for some reason the trucks never made it to the people who did not pay. Our building with six paying families was classified as a preferred customer and received first class service. We did our best to preserve our top rating with the water crew. As a precaution we learned to live with the shortage. Bathtubs, wash machines and extra containers were filled at all times. It was the only way to survive until the rains came again.

Meanwhile I had taken over my new assignment in Caracas, but I was not happy. Ever since we returned I was playing with the idea of changing jobs.

One morning, while I was having a cafecito at a favorite cafe in downtown Caracas, an old friend walked in. My friendship with Juergen Luchting went back to my early days in Carupano. At the time we met he was a sales representative, travelling for a German export company. He was my age, his home town was Hamburg, and we always had a lot to talk about. We had kept in contact and had seen each other on different occasions after I returned from Carupano.

Juergen had given up his job with the export business, and was now working for a new national paint company, called Pinturas Montana. In glowing terms he told me about his job and the company.

"Why don't you come to work for us?" he asked.

Well, I was more than ready for a change and willing to listen.

Pinturas Montana was one of the rising stars among the new national industries. Established only a few years ago by the Neumann brothers, who had left a paint factory behind, when they escaped from their native Czechoslovakia. One of them was a chemist, the other a brilliant accountant. With loans and help from the government they had built a modern paint factory which was going to be one of the biggest in all of Latin America.

All this sounded good to me. I had always been interested in colors and decorating, and I had certainly done a lot of painting during my stay in the merchant navy. If the company was good, I could see a job with a future for myself.

Juergen was happy that I was willing to give it a try. He arranged a meeting with his boss, and after an extended talk we had come to an agreement. The only thing left to do, was to give notice to my current employer.

Gene Bell was not happy at all, but I don't think he was too surprised. I guess he knew that after Maracaibo our relationship had been on shaky ground.

As far as I was concerned, I could see something more solid in my new job in the paint business, something with a future. And the future would prove me right. Years later I would realize that this casual meeting in a downtown Caracas cafe would have a lasting effect on my life.

It was a pleasure working for this new company. Although I discovered that there was a lot to learn, I studied every book and every technical paper I could get my hands on.

Juergen was more interested in industrial coatings, used in the manufacture of cabinets and office furniture, and he devoted most of his time to this line. I got a lot of support from him, but made good progress on my own. After only a few months I began to specialize in industrial maintenance and was soon ready to take over this department for the greater Caracas area.

The job was extremely interesting, because each customer was unique, and presented a different problem to solve. It was a challenge which kept me constantly searching for new answers to their questions. Communication within the company was excellent, and so was the technical support from our laboratory. My customers included several large hotels, breweries and large manufacturing companies, as well as the electric power companies, oil companies and several government agencies. Next to technical problems to be answered, there was the issue of keeping some important people loyal and happy. Not so much in the private sector, but in the lucrative government business there was a constant challenge from competitors trying to get what we had.

Strangely enough, the people in charge would suddenly find some fault with our products. This would normally be an indication that the competition had offered higher pay-offs, or more lavish gifts. A special gift, or a re-negotiated "commission" would then be required to improve the quality of our products.

With the exception of specific jobs at more remote locations, all my work was in or around Caracas. Lu was of course happy to have me at home, and I could preserve my health and my stomach, by eating at home. Another advantage was that I had more leisure time. For the first time in my life did I have the time to do the things I always wanted to do. I wanted to make up for lost opportunities in my past. Besides reading all the technical manuals of my new trade, I signed up for courses in architectural interiors and accounting.

Lu was almost jealous of my books, and even Mimi felt neglected by her master. She got caught chewing up one of my books. But maybe it was not jealousy. Maybe she just had a craving for fancy foods, like women have when they are pregnant.

Yes, our Mimi was expecting. A few weeks later she became the proud mama of two little puppies, an event which also brought new duties and responsibilities for us.

When the time came, Mimi retired to the comfort and safety of her little bed. Her pains seemed to be increasing, and when her soft crying turned into bone chilling screams, Lu could not stand it any longer. She fled the scene, leaving me alone with the suffering Mimi.

Her dark eyes looked at me in absolute helplessness.

I tried to encourage her by petting her gently and talking to her in a soft voice. A complete change came over her, when the first puppy was born. Just as if she had done this many times before, she turned and started cleaning the first born. Only moments later the second puppy was born. This one came easy.

Mimi was all business now. She had her hands full with the new family members, and let me know, that my services were not required any longer. Within a few days those naked little rats turned into cute little bundles of fur. But they could also become little monsters who turned our household into turmoil, and stretched our nerves to the breaking point.

Our day started between three and four in the morning, when the high pitched screams of the youngsters threatened to awaken the neighborhood. One of us was constantly on duty as a baby sitter. We were not only concerned about our neighbors, but also about our furniture. Everything at floor level would be chewed up by these little rascals. Shoes, furniture, nothing was safe. If they were not chewing on our belongings, they would give mama a bad time by hanging on her tail or biting her ears. When things got out of hand, mama would gently squeeze the offender around the neck, in order to re-establish respect. Most of these family fights ended, when the little ones fled under a low bookshelf where mama could not follow.

In spite of all the attention required, we had a lot of fun with our tribe. No matter what they did and what they destroyed, we could never remain angry for more than a minute. One look into those cute sparkling eyes would melt any heart. It had been clear to us from the beginning that we would be unable to keep them. The time for parting had now arrived.

We probably acted like parents, when the time has come for their children to leave the house. Lu was going to make sure our babies would find a good home, and when the first qualified buyer finally came, she stood at the curb and cried when he left with our puppy. The scene was repeated a week later, when the last one left home. Mimi kept searching for a few days, but then gave up and returned to playing the number one roll in our family.

Lu had taken up dressmaking, a job she was very talented at. A talent she probably inherited from her grandmother. She also worked part time for a German family, which operated a store and a little chocolate factory. It was no wonder that she felt more useful and was a lot happier than she ever was in Maracaibo.

We both had adapted well to our new country. Our biggest dream now was to have a home of our own. At this moment we didn't have enough money for a down payment on a house, but we did the next best thing we could afford. We purchased a building site.

On the outskirts of Caracas, halfway between Petare and Guarenas, was the newly formed club Mampote. Located among the green hills, it's main attraction was a clubhouse, pool and tennis courts. The membership was very international, a point very much to our liking. This club was still in the early stages and offered some choice residential lots.

We made our down payment on a beautiful piece of land which measured about one half of an acre. The balance was to be paid off within a few years, at which time we hoped to be in a position to start building our dream house.

We spent many weekends, enjoying the activities in the clubhouse and especially around the pool. Never did we miss to go up to our lot, and look down on the clubhouse with it's green lawns and tropical colors of bougainvillea, hibiscus and others, always planning and dreaming of the day our home would be finished.

Prelude to the Next Revolution

Over the years, opposition to the Perez Jimenez dictatorship had intensified. The poor people of the interior despised the regime for ignoring their problems and concentrating all its attention on Caracas. Student agitation became a growing menace, and in 1957 the church came out openly against the government. An election was called for December, but when the government began to realize they might loose, several leaders of the opposition party were arrested. The election was changed to a simple referendum to approve or disapprove Perez Jimenez as president.

In December the referendum was held, and only hours later it was reported that 85% of the vote cast was in favor of the president, obviously a farce. As we celebrated the last hours of 1957, and the arrival of the new year, we had no idea what the year 1958 had in store for us.

Retiring in the early morning hours, we were shaken out of bed by the sound of several jets streaking across the sky above the city. It was shortly after 8 a.m.

"Can't these idiots from the Air Force wait until a more civilized hour for a New Years parade?" I said to Lu.

I had barely said it, when we heard the unmistakable sound of anti aircraft guns. Jumping out of bed and running to the window, I saw the puffy clouds of bursting shells in the air. There was no doubt, the gunfire came from the compound around the presidential palace of Miraflores.

By this time the jets had reached the far eastern end of Caracas, turned around in a tight circle and came roaring back.

"Holy smoke," I said, "this is no New Years parade, this is serious."

The jets swooped down again at the palace, their cannons blazing and the anti aircraft battery returning the fire. There was the sound of bombs exploding. In a matter of minutes it was all over, as abruptly as it had started.

"Revolution," was all I could think of. I turned on the radio, expecting to hear an announcement by a new president or by a revolutionary council, but nothing happened. The revolution had not reached the airwaves yet, and programming was proceeding as usual.

We kept the radio turned on all morning, but not a word about any uprising.

There had been rumors on the street about a possible revolt, although we had heard all this so many times before.

In the afternoon, feeling the need for some fresh air, we decided to drive down to Mampote. My suspicion was confirmed, when we reached the city limits at Petare. Army troops had set up roadblocks and forced all people out of their cars. It was too late for me to turn around, but this time I had nothing to worry about. What a difference a little piece of paper made.

I remembered the day I almost got caught in a similar situation on the other side of the city. Then, like today, I had nothing to do with the revolution. The difference was, that seven years ago I could not identify myself. Only the cool response of a friend saved me on that day.

Today I sat calmly in my car, waiting for my turn to be inspected, and telling Lu not to worry. The soldiers looked tense and nervous when they approached our car. Normally very casual and jovial, on this day they were all business. On any other day I might have tried to strike up a conversation, but today I didn't have the guts to ask what was going on. I was certain I would not get an answer today.

Out of the car everybody, open the hood, open the trunk, and then they almost took my seats out of the car.

Mimi, who was with us for the ride, started growling. Somebody was tinkering with her car, and she did not like it at all. It was easier to take a bone from her than touch our car. I had to restrain her before she got a hold of the guy who was taking our seat out.

After showing our identification we were allowed to continue. We drove down to Mampote, but we were both anxious to return home. I was afraid this situation could blow at any moment, and I did not want to get caught out on the road. The bad part was that we had to go through the same procedure again in order to return home. It was a great relief, when we got there without further incident.

The city was quiet, but it was an eerie quiet, like the calm before a storm. Rumors were flying all over town the next morning. There was talk about the Air Force having rebelled, but nobody knew for sure. It was however obvious that something was brewing. One sign of what happened on New Years day, was there for everybody to see. Although not visible on the presidential palace, the Ministry of Defense on the other side of the avenue, showed clearly the impact of the jets attack. The outside walls had the appearance of a swiss cheese, full of holes.

I found out later that planes from the air base in Maracay had carried out the attack on the presidential palace. This was supposed to be a signal to Army and Navy conspirators that the revolution had begun. However, timing was bad and Army units loyal to the government marched on Maracay and put down the rebellion. Several high ranking officers were either arrested or fled the country. It was only a temporary setback for the rebels. The days of the dictator seemed to be numbered, as students and citizens began clashing with police and loyal Army troops in the streets.

My government contacts seemed to be more humble now. Was it a sign of impending doom, or the realization that a profitable career was coming to an end?

Within a few days the newspapers increased their attacks on the largest opposition and their exiled leaders. Another clear indication of trouble ahead. The mood in the country was explosive. Business began to slow down, with many businessmen adopting a wait and see attitude, and at the same time forgetting to pay outstanding bills. Most of my private customers were convinced that president Perez Jimenez was on his way out.

Finally, at the end of January, the opposition called for a general strike. The strike was supposed to take effect at noon on January 21. At the office we didn't know what to make of it and went about our business as usual.

I had an appointment with a customer in the barrio of El Valle, and when I left his office the clock showed five minutes before noon. With the two hour siesta I would go home whenever I could, and on this day I was especially anxious to get home. Somehow I had the feeling that something was going to happen.

When I approached my car, it was surrounded by a bunch of shady looking characters. One of them was sitting on my hood.

Without hesitation I stepped toward the group, trying bravely not to show any fear.

"Como estan Señores?" I asked as cheerful as I could. (How are you gentlemen?)

"Muy bien Señor," answered one of them, while the others just stared at me. The guy sitting on the hood made no effort to move. He was still sitting there when I opened the car and entered.

"Can I give you a lift?" I asked bluntly, at the same time starting the engine.

He didn't want to back off too fast in front of his buddies, but he got my message and started moving.

"The worms are crawling out of the woodwork," I thought.

I had barely left the scene, when the trouble started. Well aware that I was not exactly in a first class neighborhood, I sought the shortest way out of the area.

Groups of mostly men assembled on street corners and in the plaza. It was twelve o'clock. The sound of automobile horns and church bells filled the air.

Without incident I reached the freeway. Travelling at 80 miles an hour I was home within minutes. At least I was home and could now wait and see how the situation would develop.

Only minutes later our neighbor Doctor Pieck came home and rang our doorbell.

"Did you know that you have a flat tire?" he asked.

No, I did not, and I thanked him for telling me. After lunch I went down to look at my car. I was in for quite a surprise, when I discovered not one, but all four tires flat. At first I thought somebody had let the air out, but a closer inspection revealed nails.

I don't know how I got home, because I counted a total

of eleven nails distributed in four tires. Someone had deliberately thrown nails on the road with the intention of disrupting traffic. The question now was, how do you fix four tires with only one spare.

Meanwhile the sound of gunfire could be heard from the city. The radio again made no mention of the disturbance, a sign that the government was still in control.

I waited until two p.m. and called the office. Juergen was one of the few people who had returned from lunch.

"Stay home," he said. "We are closing down for the day."

I told him about my predicament and he agreed to pick me up in the morning, provided that things would calm down.

Darkness had barely descended on the city, when the revolt started heating up. Gunfire could now be heard from many different parts of Caracas, mostly small arms and automatic weapons. A few fires could also be seen. The sound of cars and trucks racing down the freeway, and again shooting. At times the gunfire came awful close, but in general our neighborhood remained calm during the night. It was three a.m. when we heard a big blast, answered by automatic weapons, after that things began to settle down.

At daybreak the city was calm again. Juergen stopped at our house, and we loaded my four tires into his car. When we arrived at the station nobody was there, but I was optimistic that somebody would show up. We agreed that I would remain at the station while Juergen would go to the office. I would call him when I had my tires fixed.

The manager of the station arrived, and only minutes later at least one of his men reported for work. He had just finished the first tire, when the sound of heavy gunfire came from across the freeway. We did not pay much attention to it, but when the impact of some bullets ripped through the metal canopy over our head, my man dropped his tools. He jumped on his old motorcycle and disappeared into the nearby hills.

The manager, after expressing a barrage of carambas and other choice words, locked the doors and split.

"Lo siento mucho Señor," he said. (I am sorry.)

There I stood with my tires, and with bullets whistling overhead. Since the manager had locked the station, I had no access to a phone. All I could do was take cover behind the station and pray that Juergen would return.

The streets were almost deserted now, but my prayer was answered fifteen minutes later when Juergen returned.

"I just talked to our downtown office," he said, "there is trouble all over."

"I got trouble right here," I answered. "Just get me out of here."

We loaded the tires into his car again and headed for home.

During the day the street fighting intensified. Hundreds were killed and wounded and thousands were arrested. In La Guaira, the Navy under admiral Wolfgang Larazabal revolted and was joined by several Army units. Heavy fighting raged throughout the night. Finally, a group of Army officers, fearing for their own safety and wishing to stop the bloodshed, forced the dictator to resign. In the early morning hours of January 23, a speeding motorcade took him to the airport of La Carlota, where he boarded a plane taking him and his entourage to the Dominican Republic.

With Perez Jimenez gone, the fighting was not over. Under the leadership of Admiral Larazabal, a junta composed of five officers from all branches of the Armed Forces,attempted to take over the government. The Junta Patriotica, a union of the political opposition parties, ordered the rebellion to continue until civilian representation was assured. Promptly the provisional government was reorganized to include two civilians.

Fighting was now subsiding. Only a few pockets of resistance remained. One of them was the headquarters of the hated Seguridad National, the secret police. Many of their members had been hunted down on the streets and lynched by the mob. A great number of them was holding out at their headquarters behind the Bosque Los Caobos.

From our bedroom window we could follow the action as it developed. At first the Air Force was ordered into action. The result was a few bombs dropped on the surrounding residential area, missing the intended target.

When they still refused to surrender, the Army moved in the tanks and began shelling the building at short range. The survivors finally surrendered.

Officially this was the end of the revolution, but a lot of chaos remained. The fury of the mob had been unleashed and they had smelled blood. Looting became now the order of the day. With police and other law enforcement agencies dismantled, the Army was hard pressed to maintain law and order. The mob almost seemed to be better organized than the new government. Many business establishments in the downtown El Silencio area boarded up and did not even bother to replace broken glass.

For us musius it was extremely dangerous to get caught in the middle of these disturbances. The lower classes did not like the foreigners and blamed them for all their ills. Some people got caught by the mob, their cars overturned and put to the torch. A lot of burned out cars could be seen in the streets of Caracas.

I almost became a victim of the mob a few days later, when I thought that life was slowly turning back to some kind of normalcy.

After visiting a customer, I was returning to the office and was driving through the old section of the city. I was only two blocks away from the Avenida Bolivar, near the old Santa Teresa church, when trouble broke out just ahead of me. Shots rang out, but I had no idea where it was coming from. I was following a city bus which offered good protection, but the bus came to an abrupt stop, the driver jumped out and started running. He was followed by the only three passengers on the bus.

By using the bus as a shield, I was so close behind him that I was trapped for a moment. I was not about to abandon my car like the bus driver had done. Besides, I didn't know where to run.

After backing up, I came out from behind the bus and was able to see for the first time what was going on. At the end of the block was an overturned car on fire, and coming right at me a screaming mob of about twenty men. There was no way to turn around in the narrow street, besides by this time there were a few cars behind me and no chance to back up. I was determined to step on the gas and go for broke, when from behind came an Army truck loaded with troops.

The truck came to a stop, the troops dismounted and came running up the street.

An officer came over and screamed "Get out of here, get out of here." I almost ran over one of his men, when I stepped on the gas and the car jumped forward.

There was barely enough room to get past the burning car, but I made it through. The body of a dead man was laying face down on the pavement. When I reached the Avenida Bolivar, there was more trouble and more burning cars. Black smoke and the smell of burning rubber filled the air. When I saw another horde of gun and machete swinging rioters approach, I pointed the car in a straight line toward the Avenida. The car jumped the curb, smashed through a hedge and plowed up a bed of flowers. Seconds later I had reached the Avenida Bolivar and with it the freeway to the eastern part of town.

What if the troops had not arrived, or what if the car had stalled? I asked myself. That dead man on the street could have been me. I could not get the picture of the dead man out of my head. Who was he? The way he was dressed, he looked like a businessman.

I was so shaken by this encounter that I went straight home.

When I came to the office the next morning, the entire crew was laughing about Pedro, one of our drivers. Only the boss was not laughing. It seemed that Pedro's delivery route had taken him through one of the finer sections of town. One of the elegant villas, belonging to a former high government official, was just in the process of being looted, when Pedro drove past.

"Well, why not get my share," thought Pedro. "Everybody else is doing it."

In fact he was better prepared than anybody else. He had a truck.

The boss might have never found out about this, if this event would not have been recorded on a photograph and spread across the page of a local newspaper. The picture clearly showed Pedro, with the help of two other guys, loading a piano onto a truck. On the side of the truck it said "PINTURAS MONTANA."

"This is not the kind of publicity I want," said the boss. Pedro just smiled and declined to answer, when asked what he did with the piano.

The old political leaders were released from jail or returned from exile, and the job of rebuilding the country began. A new government structure had to be established. Economically the country was in bad shape because of corruption and mismanagement. Millions had been wasted on frivolous toys and buildings for the military, and of course millions had been taken out of the country by the dictator and his fellow generals. Unemployment became a serious problem and the new government started handing out money to the poor. Word of this spread like wildfire to other parts of the country, setting off a stampede to the capital. The influx of people from the interior and the lack of housing was so great that the hills around the city turned into shanty towns again. Even the signs put up by the government, proclaiming the building of ranchos illegal, were used as building material. The Army attempted in vain to prevent the spread of these shanty towns. Only brutal force could have prevented it, but the Army was also afraid of starting new riots.

Admiral Larrazabal had emerged as the hero of the revolution and was now the head of the junta. He was loved by the mob, but the church and business leaders were suspicious of his leftist connections.

Frustrated with the constant hit and run riots in the city, I tried to stay away from downtown as much as I could. It was however not always possible, and a few more times I had to endure the smell of tear gas and the watering eyes connected with it. At the office we tried hard to get back to normal, and I almost believed it was business as usual when I faced my first government customer after the revolution.

I entered the office of the newly installed purchasing agent with nervous anticipation. We spent a few minutes like two dogs sniffing each other. I congratulated him to his new position, while he asked me questions about my past relationship with the agency. The word kick-back or bribe was never mentioned. When I expressed the hope that we would be able to continue our good relationship, he countered with a real bombshell.

"That depends on what is in it for me," were his exact words. For a split second I was taken by complete surprise. He is testing me I thought.

At this time after the revolution the papers were filled with stories about corruption and bribes of former government officials. The witch hunt was on. I was convinced the guy was testing me, but I was not going to fall into his trap. On the other hand, I was not willing to loose a good account either. Diplomacy was called for.

"I don't know what you mean," I said with an expression of pure innocence.

"Come on amigo, let's talk man to man," he replied, following with his personal interpretation of public morals.

His theory was very simple and straight forward. The other guys before him had taken advantage of their opportunities and had filled their pockets. Now his moment had arrived, and it was time to fill his pockets and look out for himself and the family. "God knows how much time I have," he said.

I was still not convinced that he was not testing me, so I told him I would talk it over with the big boss.

"I understand," he said and added, "let me know as soon as possible." At the same time he pointed to a sample my competitor had left. He did not have to say any more. I got the message.

The "big boss" threw the hot potato right back to me by saying, "What do you think?"

"I think the guy is serious, but I am not one hundred percent sure," I replied. "What worries me is that I have to go out there again and stick my neck out."

We both knew that we had done it before and that we would do it again. I had known all along that the boss could not possibly know any better than I could, if this guy could be trusted.

With his blessings and encouragement I went back the following day, and after a little more careful conversation I let him know that we were ready to play the game. I was cautious enough to let him do most of the talking.

My instinct turned out to be correct. The man was working for himself, and for us it was business as usual."

During the summer of 1958 it was moving time again. In the eastern suburb of El Horizonte we rented the upper floor apartment in a private house. It was a gorgeous location at the end of a street. A large terrace surrounded the whole upper floor. Our view was over fields of flowers, belonging to a catholic convent and stretching all the way up to the foot of mount Avila.

The house was owned by Alexander and Maria Frolow, a Russian couple who had come to this country under the displaced persons program after World War II. Alexander had been a soldier in the Russian army. During WWII he fell into the hands of the Germans, and when the war was over he decided not to return to the Soviet Union. Two lovely children made up the rest of the family. The oldest, a girl by the name of Gala was eleven years old and her brother Igor was seven.

Across the street lived an old friend of mine. He was now happily married and his wife was expecting their first baby.

I had met Carel Brosz in not so happy times, when we were both inmates of Carcel Modelo in 1951. We could now sit down and talk and laugh about the "Good old times," but it was not a laughing matter back in 1951, when we both faced a questionable future. Carel was now working as an engineer for a large manufacturing company in Caracas. Our lives had certainly changed since 1951. We had come a long way since the day we scrubbed the floors of Carcel Modelo under the whip of the infamous El Jefe. Within a few months our good friends the Thomsens purchased a home next to the Brosz family, and Sunday morning cocktail at the Thomsens home became a tradition. Hannes Thomsen would mix the drinks, while I was in charge of supplying crushed ice. The specialty of the house was planters punch, and Hannes made the best. His agent in Jamaica supplied him with the best rum I have ever tasted. If it was not for the unstable political situation and the constant unrest in the city, it would have been a happy time for us. El Horizonte was far enough from the turbulent city, but I still had to face reality every day.

For a weekend of relaxation we had discovered a new location. Instead of driving down to the hot and crowded beaches, we would now escape to the more relaxing atmosphere of the mountains.

About forty miles from Caracas was the little village of Tovar. At 5,800 feet its air was fresh and one could drink clean, cool water right from the many natural springs. The village was over hundred years old, but had only recently been re-discovered by civilization. Three years ago the village could only be reached by climbing over mountains and crossing jungles. Now for the first time it could be reached by automobile, although the last seven miles was a dirt road through the jungle. Getting trapped during the rainy season could mean disaster.

What made this village so different from any other village in Venezuela, was its population and its architecture. The ancestors of these people had come from the south western part of Germany. A visitor might think to be somewhere in the Black Forest, when he first sees the buildings with their elaborate wood carvings. Most of the population was extremely shy, which was no surprise after the long time of isolation. The families had intermarried for several generations, and most of their off-springs looked very much alike, with blond hair and blue eyes. Their language was a curious mixture of southern German dialect and Spanish. It was said that the original settlers had been brought over with the intend to establish european agriculture in this country. Things had not worked out as planned, mainly because these farmers had found a different climate and a different environment from what they had known at home. With changing times and changing politics, the country had forgotten them in this isolated and remote valley for over a hundred years. The remaining families had learned to grow coffee instead of barley and oats, and had just barely survived to the present day.

Since its re-discovery and with better access, Tovar had become a favorite weekend retreat, especially for the Germans of Caracas. Some had even managed to purchase land to build vacation cabins, and some of those could be rented. We had been up there with Juergen and his family and had enjoyed lighting the fireplace, when it got cool enough at night. Our friend Rudy Klampferer also had a cabin on a lot overlooking the whole valley.

When the Thomsens had a visitor from Germany, we rented two of the cabins for a weekend of fun and relaxation. The visitor was the son of one of the directors of the Horn Line. At age nineteen, the kid wanted to learn all he could about this country, and Hannes Thomsen was determined to show him as much as he could.

While visiting Rudy Klampferer on Saturday afternoon, he had a brilliant idea. He was going to get some horses for Sunday morning, and we could go for a ride into the mountains. The kid, who had never sat on a horse in his life, got all exited. He saw himself as a big cowboy riding into the sunset. The only person who did not want to join was Hannes Thomsen. He was more concerned about his delicate posterior.

"I am from the North Sea coast," said Hannes, "I grew up on the water, not on the farm."

We met the next morning at the place where Rudy had made the arrangement for the horses. Horses of course were not available, only mules, but I had not expected anything else.

We let the kid have the most placid of the bunch, a mule called Pancho. The trouble was that he could not convince Pancho to take even the first step. Anxious to get going, I traded mules with the kid, only to find out that Pancho was not ready to listen to me either. I didn't seem to have any better luck with this stubborn creature.

Finally I decided to show him who was in charge here. After a good beating, Pancho agreed that I was in charge and took off like a rocket, followed slowly by the other two. I am sure the kid was glad he was not sitting on this one any longer. I did not even try to stop Pancho until I had reached the center of the village main street. There he stood and waited for my companions to catch up with us.

As they approached, a jeep came from the other side, but Pancho made no effort to let him pass. He stood there in the middle of the dusty road like a monument. The jeep came to a stop, with only a foot separating us. Again I tried to get Pancho to move, but he had other plans.

The guy in the jeep started to get impatient, but Pancho could not be bothered. Finally the driver leaned hard on the horn, Pancho went sky high while I went in the other direction. Everybody was laughing.

I was not hurt, but my pride was hurting. Pancho stood there looking down on me as if he had nothing to do with all this. He was stretching his luck to the breaking point. By unloading me in the dust of main street he had embarrassed me once, now he refused to move after I had mounted him again. With my temper reaching the boiling point, I gave him a tremendous slap on his behind, while at the same time digging my heels deep into his flank. That helped. Pancho decided it was time to move again and just as he did the first time, he took off like lightning. This time I was better prepared for it.

For the next two hours the battle of wills was raging. There was not much togetherness with my companions. I was either far ahead or far behind. Every fifteen minutes Pancho would stop for another round of endurance testing, to see who would give up first. Today I know where the expression "stubborn as a mule" had it's origin.

When we saw dark clouds coming up on the horizon, we decided it was time to return to the village. We never made it before the gates of heaven opened up. This was nothing unusual during the rainy season, and we just sought temporary shelter until the worst was over.

After we continued, at about a mile from the village, we ran into a group of native men and women who came from the village. Some of the women carried a load on their head, while the men carried their usual machetes. Unfortunately we met on the trail where we had jungle on both sides, and in the middle a big pool of water and mud from the recent rain. We had brought our animals to a halt and waited patiently for the natives to pass.

At first two of the women came toward us on that narrow strip of ground next to the mud hole.

Suddenly disaster struck. Nobody knows what spooked the animal, but the mule with our German visitor jumped forward, going straight at those poor women. One was pushed into the jungle to the right, the other went flying face down into the mud hole. It was a scene for the funny books. She was face down in the mud, her skirt had lifted above her waist and all we could see was a shiny posterior with no panties to obstruct our view.

Our kid and his mule had disappeared, leaving Rudy and myself to face the wrath of the offended.

Under normal circumstances we should have waited at the scene of the tragedy, apologized and offered to pay for possible damages. However, this was far from normal. Neither one of us was ready to stand there and argue with a bunch of irate men who were now swinging machetes in our face and calling us dirty names. Even Pancho must have smelled the trouble we were in, because for the first time this day he responded instantly when I kicked him.

Mud was flying in all directions as we splashed through the mud hole to safety. It was the only thing we could do, because those men were in no mood for a civilized conversation. I was grateful to good old Pancho for not letting me down when I needed him. There is nothing worse than a get-away car that won't start when it counts. In this case it was a get-away mule.

Our troubles were far from over. We had just returned our animals when the gang showed up, accompanied by the local law. After a heated debate on the street, the party moved on to the jefatura, where we spent the rest of the day. Only Rudy's connections with the Jefe Civil saved us from spending the night in jail. A payment of a few Bolivares finally calmed down the hot tempered natives and made them disappear into the hills.

It was dark when we returned to our cabin and the worried women in our party, hungry and ready for a good strong drink. I am sure our visitor must have had something to talk about, when he returned to Germany. He could now tell the story about his South American adventure.

On our return trip to the city the seven miles of dirt road presented quite a challenge. The rain had left a sea of mud, and in certain spots we had to climb into the mess and help pushing. After escaping the last mud hole, the original color of the car could hardly be recognized. A fitting ending to a weekend of rest and relaxation.

Shortly after our trip, Juergen was the next of our friends to start construction of his own cabin. A local carpenter built it under difficult conditions on the other side of the valley on a slope covered with dense jungle. All building materials had to be lowered to the job site on a makeshift elevator. When it was finished, it was an idyllic setting in the middle of deep green jungle, and with a beautiful view of the picturesque village on the other side. In order to have year round access to his new property, Juergen bought a jeep with four wheel drive.

Politically the country was adrift. There were signs of serious discord among the members of the junta, as the country prepared for free elections in December. The business community and the upper class was worried about admiral Larrazabal, who was leaning too far to the left. As the election campaign heated up, so did the violence in the streets. Most of the violence was concentrated in the downtown sector around the Plaza Bolivar and the shopping center of El Silencio, which was the favorite spot for the mob. They were of course more interested in looting the stores than in any political demonstration. By this time almost every store was boarded up and also secured with iron bars.

I tried to avoid this neighborhood like the plague, but it was not always possible. The main avenue went through a tunnel under El Silencio, where the freeway to the east began.

Elections were held on December 7th, 1958, but if anybody had hoped for peace and stability, they would be disappointed. The mob was not satisfied with the outcome, because their hero admiral Larrazabal had lost. The leader of Accion Democratica, Romulo Betancourt, had won 49% of the vote against 35% for Larrazabal.

The mob went into the streets again and bloody riots followed. It was almost revolution all over again, but the Army supported the newly elected president. Order was restored after a few days of fighting. When it was over, burned out buses and automobiles littered the streets again. Admiral Larrazabal returned to active duty in the Navy and was later given the job of Ambassador to Chile, to get him out of the country.

As we entered 1959, the political instability was beginning to take it's toll on the foreign community. Many foreigners were fed up with the unrest and left the country, while many others were preparing to leave. They were concerned about their safety and the well being of their families. It might have been an easy decision for some, but it was not an easy decision for the many fugitives from Communist countries. Where could we go? I was determined to stick it out, although I was seriously beginning to doubt that anything would change soon. What made me even more worried was the thought that a real leftist government might take over, like Fidel Castro who had just come to power in Cuba.

Somebody almost succeeded in eliminating our newly elected president, by blowing up the car he was riding in. A car loaded with explosives had been parked on the curbside of the Avenida leading to the military club. As the presidents motorcade passed, the explosives were detonated by remote control. A high ranking officer next to him was killed by the blast. Miraculously the president sustained only burns on his hands and face. It was politics as usual, nothing had changed.

This was also the year where our greatest dream became the casualty of the times. The dream to build a home of our own.

Development in Mampote had almost come to a standstill since the revolution. Now the company declared bankruptcy, costing us about 20,000 Bolivares (about $6,000) of our hard earned money. It was a hard blow to our plans for the future, and for the first time Lu and I started talking about the possibility of leaving the country.

Both of us had enjoyed living here, although it had not always been easy, especially for me. It had been an uphill struggle, but it was getting better every year until the revolution. I had never forgotten where I came from, and I had appreciated the possibilities I had found in this country. Now our world was disintegrating and with it our dreams for a secure tomorrow. We wanted to escape the political turmoil of Europe and the destruction and misery of war, now I was afraid we had only traded it for the political turmoil of Latin America.

It was the uncertainty for the future which in the end helped us make the decision. The only big question was, where do we go from here?

Friends of ours were in the process of returning to their native Chile and urged us to come along. It was my feeling however, that we would only trade one trouble spot for another, and history would prove me right. Many of our friends returned to Europe, while others had applied for visas to the United States.

As far as I was concerned, I had invested too much time and effort to escape from Europe. It was not the place I wanted to return to.

The Frolows were also talking about joining other Russian friends who had immigrated to the United States, and we came more and more to the conclusion that the United States was the land for us.

The decision was reached at the end of 1959, and in December we filed our application at the American embassy in Caracas. Immigration to the U.S. was still on a quota system, and since we still carried a German passport we had to register under the German quota. At this time the likelihood of quick approval was favorable.

Now the waiting began, and until our application was definitely approved I did not want anybody to know. Juergen was the only person who knew of our plan to leave the country.

It was shortly after our conversation, when Juergen received some disturbing news that would change his life and the life of his family. For a long time he had a little mole-like growth on his ear lobe. Lately it had started getting bigger, causing him to see a doctor to have it removed. Now the result was in. It was cancer. He was scheduled for treatment in Munich-Germany and was now preparing to leave within a few days. Juergen had no idea how long he would be out of the country. As a favor he had asked me to accompany him to his cabin in Tovar. On Friday night we drove up to the cabin for a final inspection and to pick up a few things he needed. We sat outside the cabin until late after midnight. The sky was clear and sparkling with millions of stars. It was so quiet up here that we could understand almost every spoken word on the other side of the valley. We talked about the past, about Carupano where we met, and about our job, family and friends. We talked about everything, except the one thing that was always in the back of our mind. His illness, the cancer. How serious was it?

Finally, after a long silence Juergen started talking about it. He was worried, not so much for himself, but for his Ingeborg and his two little boys. He knew that his cancer was a deadly one, and that his chances were not very good.

I tried to be upbeat, but deep inside I felt so sorry for him. At age thirty one he had everything to live for. A good wife, two beautiful little boys and a promising job.

We tried to get a few hours of rest, but sleep would not come easy that night. All I could think of was how cruel life could be, and how fast it could change. The next morning we loaded a few belongings into the jeep. Juergen went down to lock the cabin and take a final look, while I waited on the road above. On our return trip to Caracas we didn't speak for a long time.

Juergen broke the long silence first, when he said. "Damn it, I have to lick this one, that's all there is to it. We are just beginning to live, I am not going to give up now."

"You are right," I replied. "Besides, maybe this doctor made a mistake, maybe it's not as bad." I was hoping I was right, at least this time.

Two days later Juergen left for Germany. He had asked me and Lu to come along to the Maiquetia airport. He was concerned about the stress his family had been under since the disclosure of his illness, and thought it would be less emotional if we came along.

The children were too small to understand what was happening, why their daddy had to go away in such a hurry. We grown-ups tried hard to keep a smile on our face, even though the uncertainty was hanging over us like a storm cloud. It was a relief for all of us, when it was time for Juergen to board his plane. When he returned three weeks later, the diagnosis was not optimistic at all. The doctors in Munich had operated, but found the cancer had already spread to his lymph nodes. They gave him a year, perhaps two at best.

I admired the courage he showed in the face of adversity. His only concern now was his family, and he was going to provide whatever he could for as long as he was around.

Our own life was now beginning to get hectic. The Frolows, who had started immigration proceedings to the U.S. some time ago, had now received their visa. Alexander was real proud when he showed it to me. Their house was going on the market for sale, and with it of course our beautiful apartment.

Our salvation was a friend with a brilliant idea, which would also be the solution to their problem. They lived in a large house in the suburb of Los Dos Caminos. The lady of the house had been dreaming of a European vacation for a long time. There was family in Germany, and there was always a yearning to see the old country again. With a business, a husband and two children at home, she had never been able to convert her dream into reality. If Lu would take care of the family, she could leave in the knowledge that everything was under control. At the same time it would also solve a number of our problems.

With our house up for sale, and probably no more than a few months left in the country, we would have a hard time to find a rental for such a short period. We also had to sell our furniture before our day of departure. This would enable us to sell our belongings now, and live in our friends house for the time remaining.

It was the perfect solution and perfect timing for everybody involved. We gladly accepted the offer, and our friend made preparations for her trip to the old country.

Next came the hardest part of our preparations. A home had to be found for our little Mimi. As much as we would have liked to take her to our new country, we had decided against it. It was a painful decision, but we knew it was the right one. A fox terrier is a very temperamental little animal, and our little Mimi certainly was a bundle of energy. To put her on an airplane into possible quarantine was not fair. It would be a tremendous stress on all of us, especially since our first residence in the new country would undoubtedly be a hotel.

On a Sunday morning we went for a drive to the city of Valencia, about 100 miles from Caracas. Friends of the Brosz family had expressed interest in adopting Mimi, and we wanted to meet and get to know each other.

A Spanish couple in their forties, with two little children, greeted us when we arrived. Mimi was an instant hit with the kids and she seemed to enjoy the attention given to her. When we left that afternoon, we were sure we could not find a better home for her. This family was ready to move into a brand new home within the next two weeks, and Mimi would have a nice big yard to roam in. Before we left, it was agreed that the family would come to us in Caracas in two weeks and pick her up.

Little Mimi was as rambunctious as ever, jumping from the back seat to the front and back again, unaware of the negotiations which had taken place and how they would effect her life. Lu and I sat quietly during our return trip, each one of us thinking what life would be like without our little companion.

When the time came, and the whole family arrived on the specified Sunday, Mimi greeted them with a howl of joy while our own mood hit bottom. Before they left for home, Lu served coffee and cake which was attacked with a healthy appetite. Lu could not eat at all, and I had the feeling something was choking me. We knew the dreaded moment was here. It was good-bye forever. Within a few minutes Mimi would be out of our life.

Her love for a ride in an automobile made the final moment easier for us. All a person had to do was open a car door and she would jump in. For the first ten miles she would be so exited that she forgot time and the people around her.

Before the car disappeared behind the next corner, we could see her jumping up and down, while her new owners waved good-bye. Lu and I stood at the curbside fighting the tears and hoping we had done the right thing.

The house seemed empty now, something was missing. Within days after this event we sold our last furniture and moved in with our friends.

The excitement of our move as well as our new

surroundings helped us over the initial impact of our loss.

Another great help in filling the gap was Meggie, a good natured bundle of fur which was supposed to be a sheep dog. My guess was that she had never seen a sheep in her life, although she was herself as soft and as tame as a little lamb. Meggie came with the territory, she was part of our new family. She got a lot of love and attention from us, because she was filling a missing link in our life.

Meggie was a lover, not a fighter at all. She would never have qualified for police work. No matter who entered her territory, Meggie wanted to play, not to fight anybody or protect anything. After only a short time in the house, she made a liar out of me and made me loose face and respect in the neighborhood.

There was a big mango tree in the backyard, attracting a lot of kids from the neighborhood. It was not so much that I wanted to deny them a few mangoes. There were plenty of mangoes on that tree. The trouble was that they would damage the fence and break whole branches from the tree. So when I heard the noise of breaking branches again one day, I went out there holding good old Meggie on her collar.

The kids were terrified. Two of them jumped off the tree, climbed the fence and left half of their pants hanging there in the process. One kid was too slow and got trapped on the tree.

"This dog is going to tear you apart if I let him go," I said. "Don't you ever come back here."

"Please Señor," the kid on the tree pleaded with me, "Hold the dog and I will never do it again, I promise."

"Muy bien," I said, "I won't let him loose this time."

The poor kid climbed down and had barely touched the ground, when Meggie tore loose and raced over to the terrified kid.

He must have thought the end was near, when Meggie jumped at him that he fell to the ground. All she wanted to do was play with him. Violence was not in her blood. She must have sensed his terror, because she stood there kind of undecided and then started licking his face. The other two kids, watching from a safe distance on the outside, started laughing. Whatever respect there was left, evaporated when Meggie even refused to return to me. She just stood there and looked at me with that "come and get me" expression, I knew so well.

The kid took advantage of the opportunity and disappeared over the fence, where he joined his buddies in laughing at me and my dog.

Meggie, with her tail hanging down, looked at me and at the kids, wondering why nobody wanted to play with her.

At the end of April the Frolows had sold their house in El Horizonte and were getting ready for the big move to the United States. Alexander had been busy studying the English language and was anxious to try it out on me. I had trouble understanding it, because it all sounded so Russian to me. To this day we are laughing about the way he pronounced the word "Tomorrow." I thought he was talking about a Russian person by the name of Tommorov, and not until he said the Spanish word mañana, did I know what he was talking about.

The destination of the Frolow's was the state of Connecticut, where they had friends from the old country. It was unfortunate to see all our many friends go off in different directions, and I was now glad that we had also initiated our own travel plans.

I could not help but wonder how much Alexander and I had in common. We were both the children of oppressive political systems. We had fought a war on opposite sides, and both of us had lost. Neither one of us could go home, still struggling to find a new place where we could live in peace and freedom. How was it possible that we had been enemies at one time? I thought about Popiolo, a Russian Jew, and Wladimir, who had helped me to get over the first rough spots in Carupano. I had realized a long time ago that the Russian people were just as much a victim of their system, as many Germans had been of the Nazis.

We promised to stay in touch, and I am glad to say we have to this day. The Frolows still live in Connecticut, enjoying their American born grandchildren.

Planning the Big Move

When we filed our application for entry to the United States, we had not decided on any specific location. Now the time had come to make that decision. We had talked about it, read books and travel brochures, and studied maps. Since we had no friends or relatives anywhere, everything was under consideration.

Our first priority of course was a job, and here it was that I had established my first valuable contact. I met an executive from a paint company in Cleveland, who promised me a job if I wanted it. He asked me to call him as soon as my visa was granted. The promise of a job was the first step toward settling the burning question of "where do we go?" It made me feel more secure. Now there was a goal. I didn't know very much about Cleveland, only that there was a lot of industry in the area. This meant jobs, but I also knew that the winters were very cold, a fact I was not very pleased about. Although Lu and I were born in a cold winter country, we had discovered that we could do very well without it.

"How about California or Florida" I asked myself.

"You are not planning a vacation," I answered, "a job is the most important thing."

So it came down to Cleveland as our first new home in the U.S.A.

At the end of April we received notice that our visa was approved, and I thought it was only fair to tell the boss about our impending departure. The company had been good to me and I wanted an orderly transfer of my duties. Since Lu had made a commitment to take care of the house and family of our friends, we were in no extreme hurry to leave the country, and the boss was grateful when I promised to remain on the job through the month of July.

By early June we had found a man to take over. He had no previous experience in the paint business, but neither did

I when Juergen offered the job to me.

As I started introducing my replacement to the people I was dealing with, he got a detailed report on the variety of their problems and the products which could solve them. When it came to the government agencies it was not so much a question of products and problems to solve, but a matter of whom to know and how much to pay.

Naturally everybody wanted to know my reason for leaving, but I was careful not to hurt anybody's feelings. As far as Venezuela was concerned I still liked the country and its people. What I didn't like was politics and the unrest in the streets. That was not my battle to fight.

During all my years in Venezuela I had never known the pleasure of a vacation. In the early days, life was a matter of survival and vacation was a luxury for the rich. As our financial situation began to improve, I could never find the time to get away from the job. We both would have loved to visit our families in Germany, but it required too much time. The jet age was in it's infancy and the era of inexpensive charter flights had not arrived. Furthermore it was still impossible for us to visit my family in East Germany. The border between the two German states remained sealed as tight as ever.

When we began planning our trip to the north, we wanted to take advantage of this opportunity and include our long deserved little vacation. After a long study of available options we decided to take it easy, and sail north on a ship of the Grace Line. For the first time in our lives we wanted to travel in style.

Our last few weeks in Venezuela went almost too fast. Suddenly there were so many details to take care of, so many friends to say "Adios," and so many places we wanted to see, perhaps for the last time. There was of course Laguna Caribe, site of my humble beginnings.

What a change had taken place down here. Once a quiet little lagoon and a deserted beach that had attracted only some hardy beachcombers, was now a fancy marina filled with expensive yachts. A multi story hotel and clubhouse on the same spot I sat 10 years ago on an old piece of driftwood. It was all pretty now, but it had no resemblance

Laguna Caribe 1951

to the place I remembered. But then I thought about my own life, and how it had changed in those years.

"Some time it is all like a dream," I said to Lu, "it feels as if it was fifty years ago and I wish I could see it one more time the way it was." As we sat down on the beach, a gang of kids came running along, kicking sand in our faces in the process.

Again I drifted off into the past, remembering the days when I had the whole beach to myself. All of a sudden that time looked like the good old times to me, forgotten was the uncertainty of being an illegal alien with no papers and no money in his pockets. Forgotten was the feeling of not knowing what tomorrow would bring. But there was also a feeling of pride, when I thought of being one of only a

Urbanización Caribe, Vista aerea, VENEZUELA

Laguna Caribe 1960

handful of people who had laid the groundwork and started it all. This place was too close to the big city to be left undeveloped. The country had still many places like this, waiting to be discovered and developed.

Another spot that held many memories for us was Pepe's place. It was still there, but the city of Caracas was creeping closer and closer to Baruta. It was just a matter of time when this charming little village would change it's face forever.

A casual encounter in the hallway of the company's office building should have a profound impact on our future. One morning on my way to our lab, I bumped into our public relations manager.

"What's this I heard you are leaving us?" he asked.

"That's right," I said, "this is my last month."

He pulled me into his office, and over a cup of coffee I told him about my travel plans.

I knew that he was born in Uruguay, but I never knew that he had graduated from the University of California in Berkeley.

Sipping our coffee, he was reliving the good old times in Berkeley and the San Francisco Bay Area. He spoke in such glowing terms that I could almost see the sailboats on the bay and the green hills surrounding it.

His eyes had a distant look when he said, "If I should ever move to the States, that would be the place I wanted to live."

These words kept ringing in my ears all day long. By the time I got home I had almost changed my mind about our travel plans, and when I told Lu about my conversation at the office, she supplied the final support I needed.

"Lets face it," I said, "all I have in Cleveland is the promise of a job. Why shouldn't I be able to find a job in California?" Looking at it from this point of view, California was much more appealing to us, especially the climate. Neither one of us was crazy about living in a cold winter climate again.

The map of California was pulled out and studied all night, and before we went to bed we had reached our final decision. It was going to be the golden state of California.

Our decision came just in time. Within a few days we would have to make the payment to the Grace Line. Now it was only a matter of booking passage on another vessel with destination San Francisco. This however was not as easy as we had first thought, and after extensive searching we had to settle on air travel.

"We will take our vacation when we get there," I told Lu.

One of my last visits to my customers was to a manufacturing plant, which was located in an old industrial section of town. The plant was surrounded by some of the worst slums in town, and before my partner and I returned to our car, I wanted to snap a few pictures for my collection. During the last few weeks I had always carried my camera for this purpose.

I tried to be as discreet as I possibly could, but when I took a shot of an old lady doing her laundry in a rusty old drum, she did not like the attention she was getting. Rocks started flying, and we had to retreat in a hurry before the neighborhood crowd was going to scalp us.

"Now you know what a war correspondent has to go through in a combat zone," said my partner.

"We should be grateful that nobody carried a gun," I responded.

Only a few days later and with only two days remaining on the job, I attended my last street battle and received my last dose of tear gas. On this day Juergen had accompanied me to visit a mutual business friend, and on our return we had to drive through the center of town. One of the buildings of the Silencio Center housed the offices of the Ministerio de Hacienda, the equivalent of the Internal Revenue Service. Here I had to pick up a tax declaration, which was required for our exit visa.

We parked our car and approached the building, when I noticed the crowd milling around the center. There was something odd about it, and suddenly it dawned on me what it was. The mob was assembling for another riot. We could almost feel the explosive atmosphere. All it would take now was the spark to set it off.

I didn't feel very comfortable, but we were too close to the building now to call it quits. I needed the paper and tomorrow might not be any better.

We had barely entered the building when we heard the first shots being fired. The sound of gunfire could also be heard at the upper floors, where the staff tried bravely to maintain the appearance of normalcy. Riding the elevator down again to the street level we could smell tear gas entering the elevator shaft, and when the door opened we faced a heavy cloud of it. The National Guard was already gaining control of the situation, but the tear gas was so intense that we took refuge in a clothing store where the manager let us in. Here we soaked our handkerchief in water to cool our burning eyes. When we returned to our car, which fortunately was not damaged, we looked at each other and laughed.

"What are you crying about," said Juergen, "you are leaving in a few days, you should be happy."

Poor Juergen, in spite of all adversity he had kept his sense of humor. He was now himself making preparation to return to his native Germany, but what was for us a new beginning, was for him a preparation for possible disaster.

While we were looking to the future with new hope, all Juergen wanted to do was bring his family to safety and prepare for hard times ahead. He had kept up his health insurance in Germany, and with more cancer treatments scheduled there, it was the only sensible move to make. There was still family in Germany. His wife Ingeborg could go back to work if necessary and the children would have good schools to attend. I knew how hard it was for him to return to the country he had left for a better life in the new world, but Juergen did not think of himself. The family was his only concern now.

My last day at the office was a somber affair. I had enjoyed working for this company and it's people. Over the years I had developed a close relationship with many, and now the time had come to leave all this behind. Ever since I had made the decision to leave this country again, I had my doubts about it. When I was at the office in the company of my colleagues or at home in the company of friends, I felt I might have reacted to hasty. Things would calm down again and the revolution and its aftermath would be forgotten like a bad dream. But every time I was out on the street, facing reality and getting tear gassed one more time, I was so glad in the knowledge that all this would be over soon. When I felt sadness on this particular day, I only had to think about the previous day in downtown Caracas, and I knew that my choice was right. It was time to go.

During our siesta time we had a last little get-together at our favorite restaurant next door, and after a last adios and mucha suerte (good luck) I was on my way home.

Driving up the Avenida Urdaneta, temptation took over when I spotted a policeman standing at the next crossing.

The sign clearly said "no u-turn," and I was wondering what he would do if I did one right in front of him. I wanted to see his face, when he stopped me, asked for my drivers license and found no bribe in it.

All this went through my head in a split second, and the next thing was that I found myself doing a u-turn right under his nose.

As expected he blew his whistle and came strutting over when I came to a stop at the curb. He was all authority, his face was serious and his voice was firm. I had made an illegal u-turn he informed me, and he would like to see my drivers license.

I handed him my license.

He looked at the license, and after he was absolutely certain there was nothing in there, he looked at me with a question mark on his face.

"Is there anything wrong with my license," I asked as innocent as I could.

I knew, I had a beginner on my hands. He was new at this.

"You know we can settle this," he said almost in a whisper.

"I don't understand," I responded, wondering how far he would go. I had no intention to spend any more money on bribes in this country. I had paid my dues. If he was going to give me a ticket, so what. In a few days we would be leaving the country.

For the next five minutes this game continued. He tried desperately to give me a clue as to what was required to settle this case, without ever mentioning the word money. All his insinuations fell on deaf ears, as I continued to play the innocent dummy.

Maybe he felt sorry for me, because suddenly he handed me my license and said, "I'll let you go this time, but don't do it again."

It was funny. All the other guys had said the same thing to me with only one exception. They had taken my money first. I was almost embarrassed now, because all of a sudden I felt as if I had cheated him out of part of his hard earned income.

Adios Venezuela

All good-byes had been said. Packing our suitcase was the only thing left to do. Two big crates, loaded with household goods and personal belongings stood ready for shipment. Since luggage on an airplane was limited, and excess weight very expensive, we had no choice but to ship by boat. The furniture had been sold before we moved from El Horizonte. Our car was sold, and would be picked up the next day.

In the early morning hours of August 4, 1960, we drove through the streets of Caracas for the last time. Juergen had insisted in driving us to the airport. There was the usual traffic chaos, but at least no riots or demonstrations. Cruising down the autopista to the coast, we had one last look at the port of La Guaira where it all began ten years ago. Where seven years ago I held Lu in my arms after a long separation. There were a lot of memories down there. La Guaira faded into the background as we turned left to the airport of Maiquetia. A Pan American super constellation was getting ready for take off. The hectic activity at the airport did not allow us to get sentimental. Paperwork had to be taken care of, luggage to be checked in. By the time everything was done, only a few minutes remained before check in time.

A somber mood descended over our little group. We all wanted to get it over with, but couldn't find the right words to say.

"I wish I could go with you," said Juergen, breaking the long silence.

"I wish you could," I replied. "We will miss you all."

There were no more words for what we all felt at this moment. We all tried to smile bravely, but it was a forced smile while our eyes were getting shiny. A last embrace and Juergen walked briskly out of the building. It was time to board.

The big Pan Am super constellation picked up speed as it raced down the runway. A short moment later we were airborne.

There was no joy when I looked down on the deep blue waters of the Caribbean, only sadness. Everything had seemed so promising, why couldn't this beautiful country find its peace? I still loved this land, that's what made it so difficult to part.

Lu must have had the same feelings, because she just sat next to me and pressed my hand without saying a word.

Our first stop was Baranquilla-Columbia. From there our flight continued to El Salvador, and Guatemala. It was almost midnight when we arrived at Los Angeles International Airport.

Poor Lu was suffering through it all. Shortly before leaving Caracas she had taken some medication for a minor ailment. Too late she discovered that the cure was worse than the disease. She was allergic to the medication. By the time we arrived in San Francisco she looked as if she had the measles.

At two o clock in the morning our plane touched down at San Francisco International. A cold wind was blowing heavy layers of fog over the nearby coastal mountains. Was this the sunny California we had heard and read about? Here it was the month of August, the temperature was in the low fifties, and we were not dressed for the occasion. I looked over to the airport terminal to reassure myself that we had landed at the right airport, but there was no doubt.

''Welcome to San Francisco,'' the sign said.

The Golden Gate

I remembered the words of my dear colleague in Caracas. "There is only one place I would like to live in the United States, the San Francisco Bay Area."

I thought about those words when I looked at the famous Golden Gate bridge for the first time. What a sight it would have been, if we could have sailed into San Francisco Bay under this imposing structure. It would have been so much more fitting instead of landing on a fog shrouded airport in the middle of the night. What a marvelous picture it was to look at the beautiful city from the vista point on the other side of the bridge. There she was under a brilliant blue sky. In the distance to the left was Treasure Island and the bay bridge. The sparkling blue waters of the bay were dotted with hundreds of sails, while a big tanker came steaming in from the Pacific.

We stood in awe under the towering, giant redwoods of the Muir Woods, many of them over a thousand years old. Their crowns reached up to the sky like the spires of a great cathedral. One can not help but feel small and insignificant in the presence of these masterpieces of nature.

Someone once said, "the first impression is the best impression." If that was true, we certainly liked what we saw on our first outing.

Epilogue

Our troubles with Venezuela were not over yet. The two crates containing most of our household goods could not be found anywhere, and was it not for the intervention of our good friend Hannes Thomsen I'm sure we would have never seen them again. Thanks to his excellent connections in shipping circles, he was able to locate them in a padlocked warehouse in La Guaira, and using all of his influence he was able to get them released. After six months of anxious waiting we finally received the crates which contained most of our belongings.

I had found a job in the paint industry and was content with my new life. It was at the home of my boss where we celebrated our first American Thanksgiving. We had a lot to be thankful for. Our life was revolving in normal channels now. The people I worked with, as well as our new neighbors, did everything to make us feel welcome. We never had the feeling of being strangers. Many people we met pointed with pride to the fact that they or their parents came to this country just like we did. An immigrant from somewhere.

In 1961 Lu went home to Germany for the first time in eight years, and also for the first time she met my parents in East Germany. She had barely returned to West Germany, when the Communists started building the infamous wall. Too many of their citizens had fled to the West for freedom and a better life. Although building the wall was an admission of failure, the Communists had no choice if they wanted to stop the stampede westward.

I had planned to visit my family the following year if I could, but this development put a damper on my plans for years to come. The iron curtain was now closed tighter than ever.

In 1963 our biggest dream became reality. We moved into

the first home of our own, and the site of our dream was the beautiful little city of Walnut Creek.

Nestled between the Mount Diablo to the east and the rolling East Bay hills to the west, the town was truly a paradise in a nutshell like the sign on main street said.

I had to join the army of commuters every morning and night, but living out here made it all worth it.

In 1963 we also received word that Juergen had lost his battle with cancer. We were deeply saddened by the news, even though we had expected it for some time. A very dear friend had been taken from us in the prime of his life at the age of thirty four.

The following year we got the distressing message that my dad had died of a heart attack.

All these years I had been looking forward to the moment when I could see him again. Now that moment was gone forever. So many things I wanted to tell him about. Now this conversation would never take place. I could not even attend his funeral.

I thought a lot about dad and his life, and I could not help but feel angry about the country and the system he grew up in. He had never done anything to help or promote the Nazis before the war. He had never joined or supported the Communist Party after the war, and yet he was paying the price. He was still paying when he died, and he had nothing to show for a life of hard work and suffering. I know he was proud that at least one of his sons had made it to freedom and a better life, a life he had never known for himself.

On June 7, 1966, Lu and I stood in the courtroom of the federal building in San Francisco. The occasion was the swearing in ceremony, which made us a new citizen of the United States. It was an emotional moment, when we repeated the pledge of allegiance in the presence of people from all corners of the globe. A long journey had come to an end, a journey which started twenty years ago at the Iron Curtain and ended here at the Golden Gate. It had not always been easy, but this moment made it all worth it. This was our home now, our country.

In August of 1968 I returned to Germany for the first time in 18 years. I was surprised and impressed with what I saw in West Germany. The city of Hamburg, in my memory a giant pile of rubble, was now reborn from the ashes and presented a picture of a clean and modern city. People were well dressed and enjoyed the fruits of their hard work.

We spent a few happy days with Lu's family in Kiel, before entering East Germany. Before the start of our trip we had been told that we would not be allowed to visit my home town. A ten kilometer strip along the entire East German border had been declared off limits to any person not living there, including East Germans. This was supposed to make it more difficult for would-be escapist to get close to the border.

We had received our visas only under the condition that we meet in a city 40 miles inland. Even there we could not stay in the same hotel. While my family was lucky to get rooms in a hotel designated for local people, Lu and I had to go to the only hotel in town for foreign travelers.

Driving a rented car we approached the border at the same location where I had made my perilous escape twenty-two years ago. It all seemed so peaceful now, yet the picture began to change in a hurry. As we moved toward the first checkpoint, we could clearly see the fences and watchtowers stretching along the border as far as one could see. A wide strip of land had been cleared of every tree, shrub and building and was now covered with land mines instead. There were armed men everywhere.

We parked our car in a designated area and presented our passport and visa to an East German official. The whole border control was now in East German hands. Our American passport was treated with respect but suspicion. With suspicion, because he could see that I was born in Germany, and worse yet, my birthplace was the nearest town. Evidently this called for special treatment.

I was ordered to drive my car into a building and onto a grease ramp, where it was painstakingly searched. Everything was taken apart, including our suitcases. Not only was it forbidden to be in the possession of western newspapers, books and magazines, but also things we had wrapped in old newspapers had to be taken out. Again and again I had to bite my tongue and control my anger, realizing we were at their mercy. After more than an hour had passed, we were considered sanitized enough to continue our trip.

The reason for our delay became obvious in a hurry. As we approached my home town after only a few minutes drive, a uniformed border guard on a motorcycle swung in behind us. He made no attempt to hide the fact that he was following us, but neither he nor anybody else was going to stop me from taking one look at the house of my parents.

There was very little traffic, a sharp contrast to the hustle and bustle on West German streets. Here the only sign of life was in the long lines in front of the few stores, where housewives stood for hours, hoping to get inside before the short supply of goods ran out.

Rounding the next corner, my old neighborhood emerged like a dream from the past. I pulled over to the curb and came to a stop. There was the house of my childhood, so close that I could almost reach out and touch it. Eighteen years had passed since I last saw it. I had witnessed eighteen years of enormous building and progress all over the world, yet here it looked as if time had stood still. Everything looked the same, just a little older and more deteriorated. There was no sign of new buildings anywhere, not even the sight of fresh paint on the old buildings.

I was harshly aroused from memory lane when our ''body guard'' drove up next to me.

''No stopping, no stopping,'' he screamed at me. Judging by the way he carried on, one might have thought I had stopped in front of a top secret missile site and got caught in the act of taking pictures.

Oh, how I would have loved to say a few choice words to this guy, but again I bit my tongue. I knew it would not do us any good, and that I was treading on thin ice here.

Taking one last look I continued our trip, followed by our ''body guard'' until we reached checkpoint number two.

After again checking our papers, and checking the time it had taken us to get there from the border, we were allowed to continue . Our shadow remained at the checkpoint.

By the time we arrived at our destination, we had been stopped two more times for pass control. All within a period of one hour and less than forty miles. The roads were swarming with police.

When Lu returned for the first time in 1961, the Communists had erected the wall. As it turned out, our timing had been wrong again. This time the Russians and their East German allies had marched into Czechoslovakia, another Communist neighbor. The Czechs had the audacity to ask for more freedom, and now their partners had marched in to bring them back into line.

Our joyous reunion was only overshadowed by the inconvenience of our separate accommodations. Fortunately the weather was good, so we could spend our time in the park. There was nothing else to do. The streets looked drab and deserted, the shops empty. How I wished I could pack them all in my car and take them to the western side. These people could only dream about the things we took for granted. The West was so close and still so far. We were brothers and yet the passport in my pocket made all the difference in the world.

I have never felt more grateful in my life for that little piece of paper in my pocket.

We stayed only for three days. Although we enjoyed our reunion and had a lot to talk about, it was not like visiting home. Instead of walking through old familiar neighborhoods and visit old friends and relatives, we were walking through a strange town which held no memories for any of us. When the time came to say good-bye, I felt like I was abandoning my family on a desert island. All we could do now, was to go home to California and send a package once in a while, to make their days a little brighter.

After we had crossed the border again I stopped the car and looked back. There was a sigh of relief from both of us, and turning to Lu I said, "I have the feeling I have escaped one more time."

San Francisco Bay never looked better to me when our Pan American 747 jet came in for a landing. I could have knelt down and kissed the ground. If this trip had accomplished nothing else, it had again confirmed my solid belief that my escape in 1946 had been the right move. It was certainly worth the risk I had taken.

I just hope the Communists may one day recognize the futility and bankruptcy of their system and make the changes necessary for the benefit of their own people and the world.

We are getting married! November 14, 1953, Caracas, Venezuela.

In Maracaibo, Venezuela, 1955.

In Walnut Creek, California, 1988.